The Specter of Races

New World Studies

J. Michael Dash, *Editor*

Frank Moya Pons and
Sandra Pouchet Paquet,
Associate Editors

The Specter of Races

Latin American Anthropology and Literature between the Wars

Anke Birkenmaier

University of Virginia Press
Charlottesville and London

University of Virginia Press

Printed in the United States of America on acid-free paper

First published 2016

9 8 7 6 5 4 3 2 1

Library of Congress Cataloging-in-Publication Data

Names: Birkenmaier, Anke, author.
Title: The specter of races : Latin American anthropology and literature between the wars / Anke Birkenmaier.
Description: Charlottesville : University of Virginia Press, 2016. | Series: New world studies | Includes bibliographical references and index.
Identifiers: LCCN 2015045230 | ISBN 9780813938783 (cloth : acid-free paper) | ISBN 9780813938790 (pbk. : acid-free paper) | ISBN 9780813938806 (ebook)
Subjects: LCSH: Latin American literature—History and criticism. | Literature and anthropology—Latin America. | Race awareness in literature.
Classification: LCC PQ7081.A1 B56 2016 | DDC 860.9/868073—dc23
LC record available at http://lccn.loc.gov/2015045230

Cover art: Emiliano di Cavalcanti, *Mulata,* 1938. Oil on canvas, 93 × 74 cm.
(© Elisabeth di Cavalcanti. Museu de Arte Brasileira da FAAP, São Paulo, Brazil)

Contents

Acknowledgments vii

Introduction: The Americanist Years 1

1 Fernando Ortiz and the Meanings of *raza* 19

2 Paul Rivet's Museum Matrix and the "Drama of Inadaptation" 47

3 Jacques Roumain, Haiti, and the Margins of Latin America 75

4 Gilberto Freyre and the Science of Culture 111

Epilogue 143

Notes 147

Bibliography 179

Index 199

Acknowledgments

THIS PROJECT took shape over a number of years, and many institutions and people have assisted me generously with aspects of my research and thought process.

In Havana, I want to thank Araceli García Carranza and Ileana Ortega at the Biblioteca Nacional José Martí, who guided my search through Fernando Ortiz's archive, as well as José Doll Pérez. At the Instituto de Literatura y Linguística, Cira Romero made the impossible possible and introduced me to the Cuban scholars Sergio Valdés Bernal and Patricia Motorola and to José A. Matos Arévalos, from the Fernando Ortiz Foundation. In Paris, I was fortunate to have office space at Reid Hall, with the wonderful Mihaela Bacou. In Paris, too, I consulted the Paul Rivet Archive at the Muséum d'Histoire Naturelle and at the Bibliothèque du Musée de l'Homme, which at that point had closed already, and where I was assisted by Adrien Mattatia. I'm particularly grateful to Christine Laurière, now at the CNRS, for her expertise and generous orientation in all matters concerning Paul Rivet. At the Laboratoire d'Anthropologie Sociale I am grateful for having been able to consult the Fonds Alfred Métraux and even to have had a brief conversation with Claude Lévi-Strauss. In Mexico at the Colegio de México, Clara E. Lida and Andrés Lira shared their knowledge on anthropology, literature, and European exiles in Mexico, and Adolfo Castañón took time to talk about Roger Caillois. Sibylle Fischer introduced me to Jean Casimir, who opened doors for me in Port-au-Prince in 2008; in Haiti I also thank Rachelle Doucet, Suze Mathieu, and Rachelle Beauvoir-Dominique and the staff of the Bibliothèque Haitienne des Frères de l'instruction chrétienne and at the Petit Seminaire of the Collège Saint-Martial for letting me consult their collection. My Brazilianist colleagues at Indiana University, Darlene Sadlier and Luciana Namorato, gave me important feedback and recommended additional bibliographic works. Finally, the Schomburg Center for Research in Black Culture in New York offered all the resources that I had not been able to find in Haiti, Cuba, or Brazil, and it has been a privilege to work there.

My research travels were made possible by three generous field research grants from the Institute of Latin American Studies at Columbia University, under the directorship of Thomas Trebat and then Pablo Piccato. Much of the writing and rewriting was done during junior faculty leaves from Columbia University and from Indiana University.

I'm grateful for conversations with colleagues at Columbia University, in particular Vincent Debaene, Maja Horn, Alfred MacAdam, Gustavo Pérez Firmat, Pablo Piccato, and Alessandra Russo, and at Indiana University with Deborah Cohn, Melissa Dinverno, Patrick Dove, Lessie Joe Frazier, Ilana Gershon, Edgar Illas, Eden Medina, Alejandro Mejías-López, Kate Myers, John Nieto-Philips, Estela Vieira, and Steve Wagschal. Also at Indiana University, I received assistance from my undergraduate research assistant, Rachel Colegrove, and from graduate assistants Olivia Holloway Salzano, who took care of translations from Portuguese into English, and Krista Weirich.

My friends Rubén Gallo, Jacqueline Loss, Viviane Mahieux, and Rafael Rojas listened and commented on versions of this project; Viviane in particular was a great friend in all walks of life and a patient reader of a number of chapter drafts. Parts of the project were presented at the Caribbean Studies Group of New York University, Brown University, the Université d'Etat d'Haïti in Port-au-Prince, and the Annual Meeting of the American Comparative Literature Association in Providence, at a seminar hosted by Charlotte Rogers.

I am deeply appreciative also of the comments that I received on the entire manuscript from Emily Maguire of Northwestern University, and from two anonymous readers. They all have contributed to making this book much better, even though its flaws are, of course, still mine. I also thank my editors at the University of Virginia Press, Cathie Brettschneider and Eric Brandt, for their expertise and decisiveness, as well as Ellen Satrom and Mark Mones.

Finally, my parents in Germany and my partner, Roman, have been like rocks in my life, and I thank them for having stayed with me, all the way.

The Specter of Races

Introduction

The Americanist Years

The Brazilian artist Jonathas de Andrade's 2013 installation at the Guggenheim Museum, *Posters for the Museum of the Man of the Northeast* (*Cartazes para o Museu do Homem do Nordeste*), is a jumble of allusions to the past. Founded by Brazil's perhaps most recognized anthropologist, Gilberto Freyre, the Museum of the Man of the Northeast opened its doors in 1979 in Recife, during the military dictatorship. Yet, de Andrade's installation is less interested in the politics of the museum itself than in shifting the focus away from the racial construction of Brazilian society that had been central to Freyre and other early anthropologists, to questions of masculinity.[1] De Andrade's seventy-seven posters of randomly selected men living in Recife, serving as alternative advertisements for the museum, amplify at once the nineteenth-century tradition of physiognomist portraits and what Jossianna Arroyo has termed the "masculine ethic" of early Latin American anthropologists like Freyre and Fernando Ortiz, exaggerating Freyre's conspicuous identification of Brazil's northeastern culture with Brazilian "Man." He uses the photographic, objectifying perspective of the anthropologist but then invites visitors to randomly arrange the posters. A projector with slides of diary entries again compares anthropological method and artistic manipulation by letting the visitor view documents of de Andrade's process of chronicling his interviews with men willing to pose for his photographs. De Andrade's installation turns the exhibition craze that anthropology became from the 1930s on into a metaperformance, having museum visitors act as participants in the process of fabricating racial- or gender-inflected cultural identity. In doing so, he also turns the museum into an open source archive, where this time around, all the materials collected by the artist-anthropologist get exposed to public view, effectively deauthorizing the artist's work and opening it up to play.

Fig. 1. Jonathas de Andrade, *Cartazes para o Museu do Homem do Nordeste,* 2013. Installation: seventy-seven c-prints, mounted on acrylic panels, ten inkjet prints, and six photocopies on acetate with overhead projector. Dimensions variable. Photo: Joerg Lohse. (Image courtesy Alexander and Bonin, New York)

De Andrade's installation piece speaks to the enduring attraction of earlier anthropological paradigms of race and culture in a time when it falls increasingly to artists to reflect in publicly visible ways on the visual and discursive regimes of regional identity formations. In gesturing back to Freyre's controversial ideas about Brazil as a multiethnic society without racism, de Andrade's revisiting of the Brazilian Museum of the Man of the Northeast brings to mind the enduring question of what role anthropologists and artists have played in challenging ideas about race and gender in Brazil and other Latin American societies.

This book studies Latin American anthropology as a powerful discourse that for better or worse has given shape to many contemporary ideas about Latin American culture and race, in ways that I attempt to reconstruct and analyze here. Surprisingly, the historical rise in the 1930s and 1940s of Latin American anthropology as a field of knowledge has been relatively little studied. While there are famous anthropologist-writers such as Gilberto Freyre and the Cuban Fernando Ortiz, whose works have received a lot of attention from critics and historians of Latin America, there is great reason to study how their works developed in dialogue with other currently lesser-known anthropologists such as the French Americanist Paul Rivet and the Haitian Jacques Roumain, better known today as a novelist and poet. (Each one of those four anthropologists is the focus of one chapter in this book and will be introduced in greater detail below.) Not much has been said, for example, about their move to establish new methods in the study of Latin American culture—the museums founded in the 1920s through the 1940s; the new journals, critical editions, and archaeological excavations; and the international conferences and lecture series through which discussions circulated. We know that Ortiz's and Freyre's views on race and culture were, just like any other fiction of unity, fraught with problems, but we know much less about the larger discussions on race and culture at the time, taking place on the shifting grounds of an "anthropology" that was relatively young as a scientific discipline, especially in Latin America. Their "anthropology" was admittedly different from how the discipline is understood today. The U.S.-based American Anthropological Association (AAA), for example, defines *anthropology* broadly as the study of humans in the past and present, with a view to solving human problems and training anthropologists in one of four fields, either biological, sociocultural, archaeological, or linguistic. In the interwar period that I consider fundamental for the anthropology movement in Latin America, cultural anthropology was just beginning to be accepted as a field of inquiry in the United States and elsewhere, and many anthropologists combined expertise in all four branches. Anthropologists like Ortiz, Freyre, Rivet, and Roumain also often relied on archival study and extensive readings of colonial chronicles, testimonies, novels, and other documents more so than on the field research and individual community studies that were to become the dominant approach in cultural anthropology later on. Their combination of skills has been institutionally separated out today in most cases. Most important, perhaps, the way they study "race" often seems influenced still by biological definitions that are reductive in the way they focus on the origins of individual ethnic groups and on the effects (or lack thereof) of racial mixing. Yet, as one studies the diverse -isms of the time, it becomes clear that between "evolutionism" and "diffusionism," cultural relativism and scientific racism, some of the questions these anthropologists asked haven't changed that much today—how cultures evolved in relation to each other and how cultural contact under conditions of slavery or imperial domination impacted societies in the long term. One question they confronted was indeed how best to account for human biological differences in skin color or shape as responses to natural and social conditioning, all the while debunking deterministic notions of race. Another concern was the role of a shared language or shared languages in the formation of communities and their ways of remembering. Standing at the beginning of a discipline, these anthropologists asked fundamental questions, using a multipronged arsenal of analytical methods that, even if not always up to contemporary scientific standards, profited from the lack of disciplinary divisions that existed at the time.

LATIN AMERICAN anthropologists were placed at a special vantage point from which to discuss the relation between race and culture. Even though postemancipation Latin American nations had drafted constitutions granting equal rights to indigenous, racially mixed, and European-descendant people, Creole elites remained predominantly white, whereas the lowest classes consisted largely of black and indigenous populations, with mixed race groups occupying an ambivalent place. While during the Spanish colonization the Spanish statutes of "limpieza de sangre" ironically had allowed for a considerable degree of social mobility (Bernand), this was no longer the case from the nineteenth century on. Latin American intellectuals and scientists became influenced by social Darwinist or positivist European writers such as Arthur de Gobineau, Madison Grant, and Herbert Spencer (Helg 62–63). The Argentine intellectuals Domingo Faustino Sarmiento and Carlos Octavio Bunge based their theories of national culture on racialist distinctions between "superior" pure-bred and "inferior" mixed or "colored" human races.[2] Many came to believe that the "whitening" of countries like Brazil, Cuba, and Argentina by way of inviting a massive European immigration would help societies to advance socially and economically.[3] Toward the end of the nineteenth century this belief gave rise to eugenics, a social movement focused on hereditary laws and human "breeding."[4] At the same time, the mixed-race *mulata* acquired an erotic lure as a signifier of precisely that cultural otherness that places like Cuba and Brazil seemed to offer (Kutzinski). The focus on race and anthropometric analysis carried over well into the twentieth century, with a number of eugenicist organizations and conferences being founded in Latin America and the United States to address notions of "racial hygiene." Nineteenth-century anthropologists were often complicit with the eugenics movement. As Edward Said and others have argued, British, French, and German anthropology was used well into the twentieth century to account for supposedly irrefutable biological indicators of cultural inferiority or superiority, functioning as an imperial science that made the colonized racial "other" manageable for colonial officials.[5]

The move of Latin American social scientists away from race to a less deterministic culture concept happened gradually over the first few decades of the twentieth century. It can be read in part as a response to the crises of the two World Wars, which translated in Latin America into enthusiasm for a "New World" that seemed full of promise and in stark contrast to the destruction that had been wreaked upon the "old world" during World War I and the conflicts that ensued. Encouraged by Oswald Spengler's philosophy of decline and by the rising field of sociology and anthropology in Europe and the United States, many began to look at the New World with new eyes.[6] The 1920s through the 1940s were for many middle- and upper-class Latin Americans a period of expansion in terms of cultural and scientific horizons, of reflection at multiple levels on the values of an international world system and on the limitations of isolationist approaches to culture. This expansion of horizons also meant for Latin American scientists that they wanted to be on a par with others in the United States or in Europe, where a new anthropological culture concept was beginning to replace studies of physical differences between human races. As a result, culture became in the 1920s an anthropological spectacle, represented through museum exhibits, concerts, lecture series, academic conferences, and novels by those scientists and writers who were eager to integrate their countries into larger international circuits of knowledge. Still, even in 1946, Ortiz himself was aware of the uncanny continued existence of race studies and racism on an international scale. In his book *El engaño de las razas* (1946), he wrote: "Certainly, one can speak of the 'racial specter' in more than one sense. Races are unreal like specters, but they inspire very strong emotions. That is why racism is so fearsome."[7] It became his strategy to simply deny the word *race* a place as a scientific concept, hoping that to eliminate the word from the dictionary would eliminate the problem of racism. Antiracism became a rallying point for many Latin Americanist anthropologists and intellectuals, mobilizing a new interest in syncretic religious practices, popular music, dance, folklore, and other everyday practices.

Following Rivet, I have found it useful to think of the interwar period as the "Americanist years" because the entire western hemisphere, North and South America, arguably became during that time a laboratory for antiracist theories about cultural sameness and difference. During this period the work of French "Americanists" and Latin American anthropologists overlapped in many aspects, in their shared interest in the long-term history of the Americas, from the first settlements through colonial history until the present, but also in the comparative ethnography of individual culture areas, something that the Boas school of anthropology, for example, deemphasized. There was also a considerable degree of idealism that became attached to the idea of a "Latin America" where the indigenous and Afro-American past was mobilized to craft new, uniquely "American" histories of individual nations. The question of what united Latin American nations beyond their common language and colonial heritage was more urgently posed than ever, and it came to comprehend in some contexts the Americas at large. As the Mexican philosopher Leopoldo Zea wrote in 1945: "It is now and not before that the American man, inserted in the situation called America, has posed himself the question whether there exists an American culture, and if so what that culture might be."[8] There was a shared sense among U.S. and Latin American anthropologists about the necessity to work together. The term *Americanist years* circumscribes then a triangulated network of contacts among Latin American, U.S. American, and French Americanist anthropologists, who rallied around the cause of antiracism, attempting to devise an applied cultural anthropology that would represent to the public at large a culture without racism.

In Spanish America, this new kind of anthropologically informed Americanism was motivated by a changing relation with the former imperial power Spain. In the aftermath of the independence movements, Spain had managed to hold onto a certain cultural presence in the new nations by insisting on its legacy of language and religion in the former colonies. It also profited from Spanish American writers and essayists, who in response to positivist race theories began to talk about a "Hispanic race" as a way to refer not so much to biological races, but to the aesthetic and cultural contributions of Hispanic traditions to Spanish American societies. In the twentieth century, however, anthropologists and historians began to resist the Spanish emphasis on language and philology. While some Spanish American writers such as the Dominican Pedro Henríquez Ureña and the Mexican Alfonso Reyes still went to study in Madrid under the Spanish philologist Ramón Menéndez Pidal, Spain, having remained on the sidelines of World War I, had a brief decade or so of renewed cultural prestige in the 1920s but, with the Spanish Civil War and the onset of Franco's dictatorship, definitively lost its clout in Spanish America. The major Spanish philologists and writers dispersed, with many of them spending long years in exile. Ortiz, a member of the new generation of Latin Americanist anthropologists, had repeatedly criticized Spanish philological or other pretensions at exercising control over Spanish Americans and turned in the 1930s entirely toward cultural anthropology and away from Hispanic philology.

For the sake of clarity I will distinguish among three interconnected scientific and intellectual networks of the interwar period that proved crucial for the development of Americanism. First, there is a group of Latin American anthropologist-writers (Freyre, Ortiz, Roumain) who were known as authors and public intellectuals but whose connections and collaborations as anthropologists were less well known. They constituted an elite network of their own, exploiting international connections in the United States and Europe; spending extended periods abroad; and occupying important academic, editorial, or other positions in their countries. They had shared interests with diaspora networks of black intellectuals, writers, and artists living in the Caribbean and the United States, who were negotiating through performances and through their literature new racial and transnational identities.[9] However, Freyre, Ortiz, and Roumain moved in academic and intellectual worlds that were distinct, separated by privilege and by the way in which they were able to publicly represent their views through nationally or internationally funded institutions, museums, book series, journals, and individual publications.

Second, perhaps the most tightly knit network, and the least known by Latin Americanists today, was that of Paul Rivet's French Société des Américanistes. This comprised the *Journal de la Société des Américanistes* (*JSA*) and regularly scheduled international conferences bringing together, from the 1910s on, scholars from across the Americas and Europe. I dedicate a chapter to Rivet's work and contacts in Latin America, because Rivet is a prime example of how a progressive, antiracist anthropology was built into a cross-Atlantic alliance including local and foreign Latin Americanists. Rivet's approach was diffusionist; that is, Rivet studied Latin American cultures comparatively, positing cultural centers from which cultures had extended through trade, conquest, or exploration to other areas. A medical doctor by training, Rivet built a sophisticated matrix of institutions in Paris that were to study discrete world areas: the Institut d'ethnologie (at the Sorbonne); the Bureau d'ethnologie, where objects were cataloged and classified; a book series; the journal; the society; and the flashy Musée de l'Homme (Museum of Mankind), which opened its doors under his directorship at the Palais de Chaillot in 1937. Part of Rivet's network were a number of Latin American intellectuals and scientists who studied with him in Paris, among them Roumain. As a committed socialist, Rivet embraced a policy of internationalist outreach from early on, and he traveled and made contacts in many Latin American countries and in the United States with similarly committed anthropologists, among them Franz Boas. I will also mention in this book another crucial member of Rivet's network, the Swiss anthropologist Alfred Métraux, a student of the Swedish anthropologist Erland Nordenskjöld, who spent several years in Tucumán, Argentina, to build an anthropological museum, institute, and journal there following Rivet's matrix. Métraux in turn made close connections with a number of Argentine intellectuals and studied the indigenous Chaco populations in the north of Argentina. He later traveled to Haiti, where he met Roumain and began to study Haitian vodou, publishing his classic *Voodoo in Haiti* in 1959. After his stay in Haiti, Métraux went to live in Washington, D.C., working for the *Handbook of South American Indians* until the end of World War II.

A third network referenced here at several moments is Franz Boas's U.S. American anthropological network. Even though Boas himself took only a fleeting interest in anything to the south of the United States, his four-branch approach to anthropology as a science covering physical anthropology, linguistics, archaeology, and cultural anthropology was perhaps taken more seriously in its interdisciplinary ambition in Latin America than it was in the United States.[10] Boas not only trained a number of Latin American anthropologists, among them Freyre and the Mexican Manuel Gamio, but exerted, through his writings, his antiracist activism, and the generation of anthropologists he trained, a continuous influence. More than anyone else perhaps, Boas dedicated himself to combating racial prejudice, introducing ideas crucial to the modern anthropological culture concept, such as historicity, plurality, behavioral determinism, integration, and relativism (Stocking, *Race, Culture, and Evolution* 230). His studies, published in 1911, of the changes in the bodies of immigrant children in New York were revolutionary in using anthropometrical methods to challenge the belief in the United States in stable racial types and thus countering concerns in the United States about the racial "deterioration" of its population with the latest immigration waves.[11] Boas's student Melville Herskovits became one of the first anthropologists to study Haitian rural life, doing field study in Mirebalais and publishing his seminal book *Life in a Haitian Valley* (1937), where he made a passionate argument not only for paying attention to the complex organization of Haitian peasant society but for the importance of analyzing society with a historical perspective in mind, paying attention to the process of acculturation Haitian peasants had undergone. Throughout the 1940s and later, Herskovits was in contact with Latin American anthropologists, sending students to Haiti and Cuba and also having the Mexican anthropologist Gonzalo Aguirre Beltrán study with him at Northwestern University. Ruth Benedict, another student of Boas, also made a great impact in Latin America through her study *Patterns of Culture* (1934; *El hombre y la cultura,* 1939), where she employed a comparative method to argue that all cultures developed individual styles or patterns that characterized them uniquely, like great artworks, and were a result of largely unconscious behavioral attitudes evolving over time.

The conversation between Latin American and U.S. American anthropologists came to center most notably on the concept of acculturation, the term coined by Herskovits to describe the ways in which African slaves had adjusted to but also impacted U.S. American culture. Ortiz, in his *Contrapunteo cubano del tabaco y el azúcar* (1940; *Cuban Counterpoint: Tobacco and Sugar,* 1995), famously referred to Herskovits's concept of acculturation but insisted that a new term, *transculturation,* was needed to better describe the two-way process of cultural change that he had studied in Cuban culture. He also had his book prefaced by the functionalist anthropologist Bronislaw Malinowski, who had popularized the synchronic study of communities and a focus on kinship relations more so than on historical change. The French- and U.S.-based networks were thus referenced in an often eclectic and idiosyncratic manner by the Latin American network of anthropologists that I study.

The personal bonds with French and other European anthropologists, on the other hand, became stronger as the 1930s went on, and more and more scientists and intellectuals, including Rivet himself, had to escape Germany or France, or Civil War Spain, seeking exile in the Americas. A number of today lesser-known European scholars and writers, like José Gaos, Paul Kirchhoff, and Roger Caillois, came in this way to Latin America and there became interested in the regional cultures they encountered.[12] All the major figures that I study (Ortiz, Freyre, Roumain, Rivet) were temporary or permanent exiles, a certainly difficult and isolating condition, but one that also instigated new reflections on one's own culture and that of "others" and on cultural contact. On an institutional level, the Spanish philologist Federico de Onís, at the Instituto de las Españas at Columbia University, worked with Ortiz and his Sociedad Hispano-Cubana in Havana, and in Mexico with Alfonso Reyes's newly founded Colegio de España, to organize lecture trips and prolonged stays for exiled intellectuals and writers from Spain. As the historians Jonathan

Bethell and Ian Roxborough summarize, the migrations and exiles caused by the political crisis of World War II ironically were "the inter-American system's finest hour," allowing Latin American countries to newly envision themselves as inclusive and open toward all races and classes (31).

Rethinking Latin Americanism

The Latin Americanist that came of age in the interwar period took up two open questions: how cultural contact had affected individual societies over long periods of time, on the one hand, and, on the other, in what way the history of language and the history of culture were related. With respect to cultural contact, Ortiz's concept of transculturation introduced a crucial shift away from *mestizaje,* the ideology of racial mixing and integration that had broadly characterized the discourse of Latin America in the first half of the twentieth century.[13] In contrast to the vague idea that racial mixing could be taken to stand metaphorically for all sorts of cultural mixing, Ortiz spelled out the process of loss and then the acquisition and accumulation of new traits that in his view characterized Afro-Cuban and broadly Latin American culture. Similarly in Brazil, Freyre's book *Casa-grande & senzala* (1933; *The Masters and the Slaves,* 1946) proposed that the process of creating a new Brazilian culture had relied on *plasticidade,* the ability to adjust to new circumstances that characterized Portuguese colonizers and African slaves alike.[14] On the basis of Freyre's book, the concept of "racial democracy" became an ideology popular in the 1930s and 1940s, promoting the somewhat problematic notion that Brazil did not suffer from racism. Both concepts, Ortiz's transculturation and Freyre's *plasticidade,* were, however, meant to provoke a broader discussion on cultural change. Their provocative theses were supported by the today lesser-known studies of Rivet in his book *Los orígenes del hombre americano* (1943; The origins of American mankind), where Rivet argues that from earliest times on, the Americas had seen migrations from Asia, Australia, and Melanesia, testifying to a most diverse racial and cultural group of American indigenous populations. Roumain in his studies also focused on cultural contact, studying Haitian culture as an amalgam of social and political influences from Africa and from neighboring Caribbean islands. This discussion on cultural change became central to Latin Americanist literary critics and anthropologists after the war, as we know, with transculturation becoming a fundamental concept for the field of Latin American literary and cultural studies, in studies by Angel Rama, Mary Louise Pratt, and Néstor García Canclini, to name just a few.[15]

The question of language and of monolingual or multilingual cultural traditions was taken up in several ways in the Caribbean and in indigenous-dominant areas. In the Caribbean, Ortiz insisted on Cuban Spanish as the only language spoken on the island, writing two dictionaries of African-derived expressions and words in Cuban Spanish. His aim was to contradict the normative Spanish and erroneous, to boot, etymologies, imposed by the Spanish *Diccionario de la Real Academia Española,* and to have Cuban regionalisms accepted as such. To this effect he invited Spanish philologists and writers for lectures in Cuba, maintaining cordial cultural relations with Spain, all the while insisting on having linguistic sore points corrected in the *Diccionario.* In Haiti, in turn, the dominance of French as the only literary language written became more and more problematic during the 1930s, with different groups of anthropologists voicing contradictory ideas about how to incorporate Creole oral storytelling and religious practice into their writing. Roumain defended a universalist position on Haitian French and against Creole as a language of its own. Rivet similarly chose to study local languages in the Andes, compiling a bibliography of written documents in the Aymara and Quechua languages, yet he did not pay much heed to the spoken present-day language use of indigenous groups. All the while, philological methods of collecting and editing long-lost documents became a major part of the work of Latin American anthropologists. The use of non-European languages or non-European elements of language became a battleground underlying arguments among anthropologists and writers.

While transculturation and the question of language were thus at the center of an emerging field of Latin Americanist anthropology, the interdisciplinary scope of these studies was not "undisciplined" or hybrid, in the sense that some cultural studies scholars have given to it. Román de la Campa, for example, in his book on postwar Latin American cultural criticism entitled *Latin Americanism* (1999), considers Ortiz's theory of transculturation a model for the kind of cultural and postcolonial studies that he hopes will unseat the all too exclusive focus on the literary as a matrix of Latin America. In Abril Trigo's view, too, Latin American cultural studies have moved away from distinguishing strictly between literary and scientific or other "texts" and analyze instead the ideologies that sustain them: "The main objects of inquiry of Latin American cultural studies are the symbolic production and living experiences of social reality in Latin America. In a word, what can be read as a cultural text, what carries a sociohistorical symbolic meaning and is intertwined with various discursive formations, could become a legitimate object of inquiry, from art and literature, to sports and media, to social lifestyles, beliefs, and feelings" (in: Del Sarto, Ríos, and Trigo 3). Cultural studies has therefore been described by some as strategically challenging the integrity of disciplinary boundaries, with cultural studies scholars in the United States often housed in language departments reaching out into the visual arts, popular music, and anthropology (Del Sarto, Ríos, and Trigo 8–9; Szurmuk and McKee Irwin 31). The anthropologists and writers presented here, however, even though they chose the most diverse objects of analysis, such as economic commodities, indigenous names, religious rituals, metal production, and plantation houses, in fact stayed quite close to scientific discourses of anthropology or philology, without having any principled disciplinary challenge in mind.[16] On the contrary, many of them (Roumain, Rivet, Métraux, Boas) were eager to establish one field, namely cultural anthropology, as a recognized discipline.[17]

A History of "Science" and "Culture" in Latin America

As Roberto González Echevarría has argued in his *Myth and Archive,* different historical periods in Latin America have been dominated by different scientific or learned discourses. For González Echevarría, these discourses were, during the first centuries of colonial domination, the legal discourse, then, in the nineteenth century, that of the natural sciences, and finally, in the twentieth century, the discourse of anthropology. Even before anthropology came into view as a hegemonic scientific discourse, however, by the beginning of the twentieth century, much local anthropological and philological knowledge had been produced to which intellectuals like Ortiz, Roumain, or Freyre could look when seeking to intervene in debates on Latin American culture. Already early Spanish chroniclers of the sixteenth century had taken a keen interest in and described their knowledge of indigenous populations in "anthropological" detail, including Fray Ramón Pané's early-sixteenth-century *Relación acerca de las antiguedades de los indios* (*An account of the antiquities of the Indians,* 1999), dedicated to the *taínos* of Hispaniola (today's Dominican Republic and Haiti), and Bernardino de Sahagún's *Historia general de las cosas de la Nueva España* (1540–85; *A History of Ancient Mexico,* 1932), dedicated to Mexico. Similarly, later accounts of mestizo chroniclers, such as the Inca Garcilaso's *Comentarios Reales de los Incas* (1609; *Royal Commentaries of the Indians,* 1609) and Felipe Guaman Poma de Ayala's *Nueva coronica y buen gobierno* (1616; *The First New Chronicle and Good Government,* 2009), described the agricultural traditions, the educational system, and the religion of the Andean indigenous populations of the time before the Spanish conquest with great empathy.[18]

With independence, as newly formed nations stood in need of rethinking a history that had been dominated by Spanish and Portuguese colonialism, efforts to encourage the scientific exploration of South America were made, and new museums of natural history were founded, exhibitions organized, maps drawn, in Argentina and Brazil and elsewhere, and congresses organized (Andermann).[19] Latin America's pre-Hispanic history was rediscovered by natural scientists like Alexander von Humboldt and a host of travelers, who in the wake of independence visited with often fantastic theories about similarities they observed between the Mayan and the Egyptian cultures, for example.[20] These travel accounts, as well as realist novels and picture books, gave visibility to ancient ruins and exotic fauna and flora, as well as to uniquely Latin American landscapes and populations; they would loom large in later, more systematic studies by Latin American anthropologists and literary essayists.[21]

While natural scientists mapped the newly independent nations, efforts were made to educate the populations of the new republics. New institutes of higher education were founded, university reforms implemented, and laws on public instruction created (Saldaña 151–62). Philology, the study of historical texts and written records, became yet another discourse used to project a science of uniqueness for the new nations, allowing them to fully realize themselves. Bello wrote his *Gramática de la lengua castellana destinada al uso de los Americanos* (1847; Grammar of the Castilian language for the use of Americans) as a prescriptive manual for independent Americans, basically in accordance with the norms of European Spanish yet clearly meant to prevent the linguistic fragmentation of Spanish America and insisting on the legitimacy of so-called Americanisms and regionally specific pronunciation.[22] A plethora of dictionaries of regionalisms emerged, too, published by lexicographers all over the continent, among them the Colombian linguist and philologist Rufino José Cuervo, as well as Rodolfo Lenz, a naturalized Chilean of German descent, and, in the Caribbean, the Cuban lexicographer Estéban Pichardo and the Puerto Rican Cayetano Coll y Toste.[23]

Philologists and linguists importantly shaped nineteenth-century Latin American ideas of nationhood and culture as they were looking to determine the "objective" laws that regulated language in its historical evolution.[24] The German romantic philosopher Johann Gottfried von Herder had first suggested a link between what he called the "spirit of a people" and the use of one shared language, arguing that language and education were the essential elements uniting nations. The idea caught on all over Europe, including Spain, and in Latin America.[25] Spanish American nations became set on the idea that a "monoglossic regime" of one national language only, in this case Spanish, had to be preserved at all costs (del Valle and Gabriel-Stheeman).

In Brazil, without universities until the twentieth century and having reached independence at the hands of the Portuguese monarch in 1822, the drive toward science as a form of warranting national unity took different routes, but its goals were similar (Moritz Schwarcz). More broadly even than in other Latin American countries, positivism became a pervasive philosophy guiding the drive toward empirical sciences taught at the professional schools attended by aspiring Brazilians. Yet here too, toward the end of the nineteenth century Simón Romero bemoaned what he called the "scientific anarchy" in his country, asking with Herder for the study of Brazil's *Völkerpsychologie* through the study of poetry. In his view, literary analysis had to complement the study of the people: positivist ideas were not enough.

By the end of the nineteenth century, as poets and intellectuals began to react against the uncritical importing of positivist scientific theories from abroad and worried about the domineering presence of the United States, the parallel trajectories of the natural sciences and philology as nation-founding sciences became fraught with tension.[26] José Enrique Rodó in his essay *Ariel* (1900) associated culture with spiritual Latin values and with an "auratic concept" that was tied to the authentic experience of art. Similarly, the Ateneo group writers in Mexico City, an association of writers and philologists, projected the humanities as sciences of the nation, seeking in Spain a cultural homeland less ferociously modern and pragmatic than the United States, with several Ateneo members studying philology in Madrid at Ramón Menéndez Pidal's Centro de Estudios Históricos.[27] For Julio Ramos, what was at stake was a broad change in the way literature functioned as a central vehicle of expression, on the one hand seeking to become autonomous, part of the purely aesthetic realm of the *modernista* poets, and on the other hand moving progressively into mass consumer industry, with writers becoming professionalized as chroniclers and correspondents (219–50). The contrast between humanistic and scientific approaches to culture became apparent in the work of the *modernista* poet Rubén Darío, who emphasized his spiritual connection to Catholic Spain and its Golden Age literature and nodded to the idea of a "Hispanic race" even though he would have been opposed to the biological determinism that was implicit in the term for many U.S. Americans. As Alejandro Mejías-López has written, this was a battle of ideas whereby *race* came to mean very different things for Spanish Americans and U.S. Americans (40–48).

The relationship between writers and artists, on the one hand, who were little inclined to accept purely empirical anthropological research, and, on the other, anthropologists like Ortiz, Rivet, Freyre, and Roumain, who were themselves driven by a desire to offset purely taxonomic approaches to race by more empathetic, organic studies of cultural phenomena that seemed uniquely Latin American, had to be fraught with tension because of the way in which Latin American science had often been appropriated for nationalist or colonial purposes. The Latin Americans, Ortiz, Freyre, and Roumain, all responded by seeking out precisely those literary or artistic strategies that seemed to contradict earlier empirical approaches, using metaphors and, as Freyre called it, an almost Proustian "introspective method," imagining as much as researching Latin American societies in a given moment.

What's in a Place

It might seem problematic to speak of "Latin American" anthropology and literature when the focus of individual chapters is more narrowly on the Caribbean and Brazil, with short inroads into Colombia, Argentina, and Mexico. Indeed, this book focuses on individual scientist-writers and their intellectual networks, existing in often marginal locations such as Havana, Port-au-Prince, Tucumán, Bogotá, and Recife. Yet, while these sites of encounters are not representative of all Latin American cultures, they do stand in for those almost arbitrary sites that against the backdrop of the shifting political alliances of the interwar period became safe havens and places of encounter for local scientists and intellectuals, visitors, and exiles, where new ideas could take shape.

The Caribbean and the Brazilian Northeast, however, are not entirely random locations in this study. They are the areas most marked by the sugar plantation economy, relying on the importation of large numbers of African slaves, where indigenous populations did not figure prominently. It was precisely because indigenous cultures played only a small role that the Caribbean and the Brazilian Northeast became sites where anthropologists turned to studying cultural contact, since the community studies of traditional indigenous groups that were done by Robert Redfield in Mexico and by Claude Lévi-Strauss in the Brazilian Amazon area were not possible. As Greg Beckett puts it, with reference to Michel-Rolph

Trouillot and Sidney Mintz: "Caribbean societies were populated by others whose difference was known to be due to a specific history. Caribbean societies were not only 'anciently colonial' but 'inherently colonial,' since their basic characteristics 'cannot be accounted for or even described without reference to colonialism'" (174).[28] Anthropologists and intellectuals had to address questions of race, culture, and cultural contact in an entirely different way than in regions with large surviving indigenous populations such as the Andes or Mexico. This book then, in studying mainly Caribbean and Brazilian anthropologists, while not being a study of the Caribbean, intends to be a study of Latin America as seen from the Caribbean, counting the Northeast of Brazil as a part of its extended economy and colonial cultural sphere.

Along with individual anthropologists, their works and networks, I also spend considerable time discussing the institutions, dictionaries, book series, and journals they founded to promote their ideas on anthropology as a science of culture incorporating philology. However, I do not discuss in greater detail the Argentinian school of philology founded by Amado Alonso or the Mexican school of anthropology; these two schools came out of well-defined national projects and continue to exist today, unlike the more ephemeral institutes and initiatives that I look at in this book. They both also have merited books of their own that have informed my approach.[29]

Each one of the four following chapters depicts one anthropologist and his network of contacts. It is characteristic that these contacts were not formed primarily by professor-student relationships, as in the Boas model. Rather, the four anthropologists studied formed often tenuous alliances with each other or with writers or artists who would momentarily enter their orbit. They coalesced around key concepts, such as race (but, more important, antiracism), culture, language, and transculturation, and they employed often heterodox stylistic means to convey their message, not unlike what Jonathas de Andrade has done in his poster installation for a new anthropological museum. Chapter 1 centers on Fernando Ortiz and his shift from studying Afro-Cubans as racial "others" to philological discussions of race and culture. He then developed transculturation as a new cultural paradigm, allowing him to project Cuba as a modern nation but also to project himself as an anthropologist in dialogue with specifically U.S. American cultural anthropologists. As I show, Ortiz's transition from his early positivist work, notably *Los negros brujos* (1906), to his *Cuban Counterpoint* (1940) could not have happened without his polemic rejection of philology and decisive turn toward anthropology as a science supple enough to incorporate literary analysis, history, and folklore. Chapter 2 is about Paul Rivet, who established anthropology and a new museum matrix in Paris that became influential in several Latin American countries. I analyze Rivet's diffusionism and emphasis on comparing the material cultures of individual culture areas in relation to Franz Boas before him and Claude Lévi-Strauss after him. Two specific scenarios help us to understand Rivet's influence and the criticism he received in Latin America, one being the unsuccessful attempt of his student Métraux in early 1930s Argentina to initiate a discussion of the "drama of inadaptation" of the Chaco indigenous people, the other being Rivet's own exile in Colombia and Mexico and his controversy with *indigenista* intellectuals in Colombia. Chapter 3 is about Jacques Roumain, the founder of the Haitian Communist Party in the 1930s and the author of a regionalist novel, *Gouverneurs de la rosée* (1944; *Masters of the Dew,* 1946). His studies in anthropology with Rivet in Paris and in New York led him to create the Haitian Institut d'ethnologie and Musée d'Ethnologie in Port-au-Prince, which attracted important scientists and artists from the Caribbean and beyond. I read Roumain's literary work in dialogue with his anthropological and philological works and in the light of his engagement with Haiti's integration into the larger Caribbean. I also note his argument for leading Haitians more decisively toward a modern secular society and his implicit critique of Haitian vodou, comparing him to Jean Price-Mars and other Haitian anthropologists at the time. Gilberto Freyre, the focus of chapter 4, established with his work *The Masters and the Slaves* an entirely new kind of cultural history of Brazil, which valued the day-to-day contact among Portuguese colonizers, African slaves, and indigenous servants. I analyze the discourse of race and culture in Brazil, looking at Freyre's own scientific method and dialogue with the U.S. American anthropologist Franz Boas, on the one hand, and, on the other, with his much more social science–oriented colleague Arthur Ramos. I also compare Freyre's views on Brazilian culture and race to those of some of his Brazilian artist contemporaries. The epilogue, finally, offers new perspectives on postwar Latin American literary and area studies.

These four anthropologists have important points in common—a humanist, antiracist stance; an emphasis on long-term history; a concern with issues of language; and the moving back and forth between literary interpretive and scientific descriptive registers. At the same time, their ideas on the meanings of culture and race differed greatly, as each one of them tried to situate Latin American culture between the social sciences and the humanities. All of them were haunted by the specter of race, which they dismissed and yet to which they kept returning.

Latin Americanist anthropology between the wars was situated in this way at the threshold between nineteenth-century taxonomic approaches to Latin America by philologists, natural scientists, and early physical anthropologists and the more strictly scientific separating out of spheres of Latin Americanism that accompanied the Cold War era.[30] It was perhaps that in-between position of anthropologists, as they sought to think in creative ways about cultures they came to consider their own yet wanted to explain to an incipient international audience, that produced exceptional reflections on culture and cultural contact, language and race. Yet if there is a lesson to be learned from de Andrade's recent art installation, it is perhaps that anthropologists like Freyre, Ortiz, Rivet, and Roumain told stories about local or regional cultures that somehow became part of a collective imaginary that, right or wrong, is in need of being revisited. One might want to critically revise Freyre's ideas about racial democracy or Ortiz's perhaps not so original concept of transculturation. Yet, what seems to be more necessary than ever is to engage with the history of ideas on race and culture in Latin America, not to either vindicate or reject it, but to know what has been tried and what must be tried harder.

A Word on Terminology

Terms that have racist connotations in English today, referring to skin color or apparently fixed traits, such as "black," "negro," and "mulatto," will be used only in translations of quotes in order to indicate the original word usage of the author. Similarly, authors at the time used terms such as "primitive culture" or "exotic culture" more liberally than would be acceptable today. I use quotation marks when referring to the language of individual authors.

Even the spelling of certain terms has changed today. While Haitian "voodoo" was at the time regarded as a superstitious, "primitive" practice that featured in Hollywood movies as well as in popular and serious science books, today the more common and less offensive spelling is "vodou." This is what I use, unless referring to original titles or quotes. On the other hand, Haiti's national language Creole is today often spelled Kreyòl, following new orthographic conventions. However, since both continue to be recognized as legitimate spellings, I have chosen in this case to stay with "Creole," as it was spelled consistently at the time that I study.

1 Fernando Ortiz and the Meanings of *raza*

THE HOLIDAY celebration that marks Spain's status as the first modern world empire is October 12, Columbus Day. It is called Día de la raza in most Latin American countries and among U.S. American Latinos, celebrating Christopher Columbus's "discovery" of the Americas in 1492. It is not clear what kind of *raza* Latinos and Latin Americans refer to, but somehow the term has become a point of identification for people from all over Spanish America.[1] The political party "La Raza," founded in the 1970s in California to represent Latinos' rights as a community, chose the name referring back to the Mexican essayist José Vasconcelos's idea that the mixture of races in Latin America represented the "cosmic race" of the future.[2] In Mexico, as Claudio Lomnitz notes, "la raza" refers to the in-group, the family or group of friends to which one belongs, rather than to an ethnic group.[3] To be sure, politicians have become aware of the problematic notion of a "race" that originates in the European conquest, colonization, and destruction of indigenous American peoples, and many countries have changed the official name to other less compromising ones. Venezuela has celebrated October 12 since 2002 as Día de la resistencia indígena. In Chile, the official name, since 2000, is Día del encuentro de dos mundos. In Costa Rica it has been known as Día de las culturas since 1994. Some countries have opted for simply calling October 12 "Fiesta nacional" (El Salvador, Ecuador, Colombia) or, in Cuba, Día del Descubrimiento de América. Uruguay is the only country to have maintained from early on a name with pan-American resonances: Día de las Américas (1915).[4]

From its creation in the early twentieth century on, Spanish American intellectuals like Manuel Gálvez, Ernesto Quesada, Pedro Henríquez Ureña, and José Vasconcelos greeted in the new national holiday the idea of one unified Spanish American culture, in enthusiastic public speeches pronounced sometimes in solidarity with Spanish intellectuals of the so-called 98-generation.[5] Their understanding of *raza* was strictly nonscientific and, as Henríquez Ureña emphasized, uniquely "Hispanic":

> The word *raza* has acquired among us, despite its striking inaccuracy, a currency, which the celebrations of the 12th of October help to charge with sentiment and emotion. El Día de la Raza could of course also be called the Day of Hispanic Culture, because this is what it really represents; but it would be useless to propose such a substitution because the word *culture,* with the meaning it carries today within the technical language of sociology and history, does not awaken in the listener the same affective resonance that habit lends to the word *raza.*[6]

For Henríquez Ureña, *raza* had to do with tradition, whereas *cultura* was only a scientific term for the same. That local and affective flavor of tradition, however, was Hispanic to him, because Spanish was the language spoken by everyone. This conviction also led him to reject the possibility of African or indigenous influences on the Spanish spoken in America. In his linguistic essays, indeed, Henríquez Ureña argued, as Juan Valdez has noted, that neither the indigenous languages nor African influences had ever penetrated Spanish enough to leave a lasting imprint and that the Spanish language was what had most shaped Spanish American cultures (Valdez 95–131).

Many Latin American writers used *race* and *culture* interchangeably in the early twentieth century when speaking of Latin America's identity as a region, especially in contrast to Europe. As Laura Gotkowitz has argued, culture and race typically coexisted as concepts in the period of the 1920s through the 1960s, framed by the ideas of "mestizaje and indigenism" (1–39). This trend had been inaugurated before by a debate, called by Rafael Rojas the "cultural war between postcolonial elites in Latin America," on the decline of the "Latin race" in the face of the rise of Anglo-Saxons ("Moral" 28–29). Works like Faustino Bulnes's *El porvenir de las naciones latinoamericanas* (The future of Latin American nations), Carlos Octavio Bunge's *Nuestra América* (Our America), José Enrique Rodó's *Ariel,* and Cesar Zumeta's *El continente enfermo* (The sick continent), coinciding with the Spanish-American War of 1898, often conflated European theories about the inferiority of "mixed" biological races with the more general understanding of *race* as another term for *culture* that includes the history, language, and literature of a people.

José Martí's famous assertion in his essay "Nuestra América" (1891; Our America) that there were no races was unique in differentiating between biological races as "library-shelf races" and "natural man" and became foundational in Cuba:[7] "There is no racial hatred, because there are no races. Sickly, lamp-lit minds string together and rewarm the library-shelf races that the honest traveler and the cordial observer seek in vain in the justice of nature, where the universal identity of man leaps forth in victorious love and turbulent appetite. The soul, equal and eternal, emanates from bodies that are diverse in form and color" (295–96). As Lillian Guerra has suggested, however, Martí's views on race were still quite traditional and even paternalistic in the sense that Martí depicted blacks, indigenous populations, and also peasants as ignorant and childlike, insisting that they were in need of education in order to unite with their country's elite to become one and govern themselves without violence (Guerra 31–32). That is, for Martí, racial divides were associated with cultural divides, and while he emphasized the unity of the human spirit, he still made value judgments about individual ethnic groups. In Cuba as well as in Mexico there was then a divide between scientific theories of race that underscored the inferiority of mixed-race nations and the culturalist claim that Latin American nations had to find their own "authentic" self, which for some lay in their Hispanic linguistic or religious heritage and for others in education and interaction with nature.

Given this commonly known and accepted vagueness of the term, it was unusual that Ortiz would protest adamantly against the introduction of the Día de la raza in Cuba in 1922 and even more so that he would return to the topic time and again in the decades to follow, leading him finally to produce his book *El engaño de las razas* (1946; The deception of the races). As I will show, Ortiz's turn against scientific theories of race was a result of his obsession with questions of philology, on the one hand, and, on the other, his dialogue with international anthropologists such as Franz Boas, Bronislaw Malinowski, and Melville Herskovits, who were turning away from biological race definitions toward cultural anthropology as the new field of scientific knowledge able to refute what they had come to view as scientific racism.

Ortiz Philologist: The Argument against Pan-Hispanism

With a doctorate from the University of Madrid, where he had studied anthropometry and anthropology under Francisco Giner de los Ríos, Ortiz's early career was strongly impacted by theories of criminal law focusing on the relationship between heredity and crime. Ortiz spent time in Genoa studying with the Italian founder of positivist criminology, Cesar

Lombroso, who wrote a prologue for his first book publication in 1906, *Los negros brujos* (The black sorcerers). By then, Ortiz had returned permanently to Cuba and would soon begin to practice and teach law at the University of Havana. *Los negros brujos* studied the religious practices and witchcraft of blacks in Cuba, whom Ortiz here called for the first time "Afro-Cubans," considering them superstitious. Most critics have seen this book as a problematic first phase in the work of Fernando Ortiz, even more so since Ortiz never distanced himself from it but, on the contrary, had it reprinted. Luis Duno Gottberg notes, for example, that the revised edition of *Los negros brujos* in 1917 still contained passages on the "atavic" conduct of the Afro-Cuban population and their influence on crime (126), whereby Ortiz would have moved away relatively late from anthropometrics and the positivist tradition that used empirical science to further projects of "social regeneration" in Spain or in Cuba (119).

Looking closely, however, one could argue that Ortiz's turn away from notions of racial determinism did not consist at first of a critique of his former mentors, but rather of his reaction against a linguistic ambiguity, the all too vague identification of the idea of a Hispanic race in Latin America with the Spanish language and with Catholicism. Ortiz had come into contact with the ideas of Ramón Menéndez Pidal, Miguel de Unamuno, and other progressive intellectuals through his Spanish mentor Giner de los Ríos. In the aftermath of Spain's loss of its last colonies in 1898, the notion of a Hispanic race came to represent for Menéndez Pidal the popular spirit of a people that continued to thrive even when others spoke of degeneration in biological terms (in: del Valle, "Menéndez Pidal" 110–11). His own editions of Spanish *romances* (ballads) and other popular literature sought to restore the continuity of Spanish oral and written literary expression from its beginnings until the present. In the 1920s Ortiz would start a similar initiative through the foundation of the Sociedad del Folklore Cubano and its journal, aiming to encourage a sense of the popular oral culture of Cuba. He opposed, however, the cultural politics that went along with the emphasis on the continuity of the Spanish language in Spanish America and the contamination of humanistic exchanges with economic purposes. He lashed out especially against Rafael Altamira, a professor at the University of Oviedo who in 1909 toured five Spanish American countries, including Cuba, to deliver lectures about the Americanist commitment of Spanish humanist scholars.[8] In several articles, published in the Cuban press and then collected in a volume titled *La reconquista de América. Reflexiones sobre el panhispanismo* (1910; The reconquest of America: Reflections on pan-Hispanism), Ortiz took Altamira's visit as the occasion not only to distance himself from his former mentor Sales y Ferré and other Spanish intellectuals of the period but also to condemn the idea of Spanish "Americanism" itself. What worried him most was the concept of a common race as a justification for the Spanish "collaboration" in the study of the Americas. Ortiz, referring to a letter sent out by the University of Oviedo to announce Altamira's visit, insisted that the notion of a "Hispanic race" and of pan-Hispanism in general was derived from European nationalist currents like the pan-German or the pan-Slavic movement that were based in turn on the racist works of Gobineau, Lapouge, Ammon, and others. Refusing to bow to their authority, he argued that in Spain there had never existed pure races in the sense given to the term by these writers, given the contact with Jewish and Muslim cultures. Instead of making "dubious anthropological" use of the term, he favored using *raza* only in reference to "civilization" or to a "community of language" (*La reconquista de América* 25). But even with respect to the linguistic unity of pan-Hispanism, Ortiz criticized the pan-Hispanist ideology for its inconsistency, citing as an example the *Revista Unión Ibero-Americana*'s cover page, which included Lusophone Brazil but not Francophone Haiti (he neglected to mention Creole as a language spoken in Haiti). For Ortiz, what was really at stake with pan-Hispanism was Spain's attempt to obtain economic and political power in its former colonies (*La reconquista de América* 53). Ortiz objected to Spanish governmental institutions such as the Union Ibero-Americana that were trying to exploit humanistic arguments about the continuity of the Hispanic race in America in order to regain political influence and economic markets.

But while one might be tempted to call Ortiz's strategy simply that of a positivist anthropologist, unable to tolerate ambiguity with respect to a term like *race* that for anthropologists had a clearly defined meaning, he soon turned in the 1920s into what one might call a philologist with anthropological leanings. He began to study Cuban folklore—publishing articles first in the *Revista Bimestre Cubana,* the journal of the Sociedad Económica de Amigos del País, whose secretary Ortiz became from 1910 on, and later in the journal *Archivos del Folklore Cubano.*[9] In founding the Sociedad del Folklore Cubano in 1923, Ortiz worked together closely with the Cuban diplomat José María Chacón y Calvo and with a heterogeneous group of friends who defined their objective mostly as collecting stories, legends, ballads, proverbs, and other popular expressions, activities the group called "popular philology":[10]

> The Society of Cuban Folklore has as its objective to copy, classify, and compare the traditional elements of our popular life. Therefore the materials belonging to this society are the collecting and the study of stories, didactic tales, legends preserved in the oral tradition of our people; the ballads, the *décimas,* the chants, the boleros, and other typical manifestations of our poetry and our popular music; the idioms, the typical turns, the tongue twisters, the Cubanisms, and so many other forms of popular philology; the proverbs, riddles, and other models of expression that are characteristic of the particular genius of peoples; the popular knowledge preserved by tradition and referring to the different branches of science (geography, botanics, medicine, agriculture); the phantastic and supernatural beliefs.[11]

Archivos del Folklore, published in five volumes between 1924 and 1930, featured sections on language, notable among them a column by Juan Marinello titled "Un guacalito de cubanismos," the Brazilian philologist Antenor Nascentes's "Glosario de afronegrismos," and articles by Ortiz on the word *folklore* and by Francisco Galbis on *congrí.*[12]

Ortiz's two dictionaries, the *Catauro de cubanismos* (1923) and the *Glosario de afro-negrismos* (1924), were by-products of this work and of other articles on Afro-Cuban language published in *Revista Bimestre Cubana.* As Ortiz stated in the preface to the *Glosario,* this linguistic activity was fully part of his "comprehensive approach" to the study of African influences in Cuba and Spain (xiii). As an impromptu lexicographer, Ortiz was ambitious, pursuing a doubly scientific and polemical purpose motivated by the omissions and errors of the fourteenth edition of the *Diccionario de la Lengua Castellana* (Dictionary of the Castilian language) of the Real Academia Española. Already in 1921 the Cuban philologist Constantino Suárez had published a *Vocabulario cubano* meant to complement the Spanish *Diccionario,* to which Ortiz's own *Catauro* was a further complement. As Sergio Valdés Bernal ("Por qué Catauro?") and Gustavo Pérez Firmat have noted, Ortiz's work on the *Catauro* was not very systematic. Ortiz had published it quickly in an edition of only one hundred copies, assembling the entries he had published in the *Revista Bimestre Cubana* without even the time to sort them, hoping for an augmented reedition in alphabetical order by a Spanish publisher. He wrote to Chacón y Calvo to this effect, apparently without a result.[13] In any case, Ortiz made sure that copies of the *Catauro* reached relevant philologists in Spain, such as Bonilla, Menéndez Pidal, and Rodríguez Marín. This first dictionary was quickly followed by the *Glosario,* and Ortiz again asked his friend Chacón y Calvo for addresses of academics of the Real Academia Española (RAE) or of "any other linguist" to whom he could send his volume.[14] Still, while Ortiz employed the methods of a lexicographer with great ease, the purpose of these dictionaries gives us pause. Pérez Firmat calls them Ortiz's "philological fictions," texts written to establish Cuba's independence from the West down to the last etymology. For Pérez Firmat, many entries "not only complete or correct the information in the Royal Academy Dictionary but also expose, indeed toy with and undermine, the conventions of the dictionary form" (203). Even though his main interlocutors were philologists, Ortiz indeed did not fully subscribe to their methods, mocking etymological methods in numerous instances through witticisms and other rhetorical strategies. On the other hand, Ortiz clearly was trying to make himself known in the Spanish academic world, repeatedly inquiring in his correspondence with Chacón y Calvo in 1924 and 1925 how his dictionaries had been received in Spain and being exceedingly pleased about any reaction at all. On May 20, 1924, Ortiz wrote triumphantly to Chacón y Calvo: "I am delighted to know that you will contribute to the academic reclaiming of fried plantains. They deserve it! I have ordered from here that copies of more than four hundred pages of proofs that have been already printed of my next book, the *Glosario,* be sent to Menéndez Pidal, responding to a most lovely letter in which he announces to me his intention to take advantage, in the fifteenth edition of the Dictionary of the Royal Academy, of the juice that I am going to get out of the Cubanisms of the little *Catauro.*"[15] Ramón Menéndez Pidal indeed politely called Ortiz's *Glosario* "an extremely rich compendium of materials studied using a wide range of information and with very suggestive points of view" (in: García Carranza, Suárez Suárez, and Quesada Morales 28). Some changes in the fifteenth edition of the *Diccionario* were made by Ortiz as responses to his critics. In his letter of July 8, 1925, he commented on the fifteenth edition of the *Diccionario:* "I haven't read it yet, but I have already noticed an improvement in the Cubanisms, even though many are missing and some have errors. Time and patience, and we will do a project for him for the sixteenth edition."[16]

Ortiz's polemic dialogue with the Real Academia is noticeable in many entries of the *Catauro* and the *Glosario,* despite the fact that Ortiz made sure to include deferential gestures to philological luminaries at strategic places. The *Glosario* was dedicated to Adolfo Bonilla y San Martín, a student of the Spanish philologist Marcelino Menéndez y Pelayo, who had visited Cuba in 1924, and it also included a prologue from Juan M. Dihigo, a professor of philology and linguistics at the University of

Havana—ironically, Dihigo had been responsible for inviting Altamira to visit Cuba in 1909. By including two philological authorities from Spain and Cuba at the head of the book, Ortiz emphasized his respect for philology as a field in Spain and in Cuba. In his prologue, in turn, Dihigo described Ortiz as an anthropologist expanding into linguistics but also as a linguist with anthropological interests: "With surprising activity, you have decided that your scientific investigations not be reduced to what anthropology in its ethnic expression may offer, but you went beyond and have successfully scrutinized the sphere of language within the race you have been analyzing with singular care; and your desire has not only been to tell only what the languages of those peoples mean, but to go deeper."[17] Dihigo recognized Ortiz's philological ambitions, all the while clearly trying to limit the scope of his philological activity to the "languages of those peoples." Ortiz chose to ignore this division between Afro-Cuban languages and Spanish, however. In his own introduction, he again emphasized his seemingly humble attitude toward philology, explaining that his "glosario" was conceived not so much as a list of Africanisms, but as a "gloss" of each one of them, that is, an additional commentary on an already existing philological entry, where semantic analysis, "hypothetical propositions," and etymologies were combined in a relatively free and often long-ranging format (*Glosario de afronegrismos* xiv). In practice, however, he commented not on what were commonly understood as Africanism, but on words whose origin was erroneously attributed to Latin, when more than one possibility existed. Sometimes Ortiz pointed here to the African origins of a term, but often he simply critiqued errors by either Hispanists or Africanists.

Ortiz exposed omissions of the Real Academia even on the most basic content level, suggesting that they were due to the ideological bias of the Real Academia. For example, he pointed out that neither *centroamericano, latinoamericano,* nor *iberoamericano* figured in the Real Academia's dictionary, whereas *hispanoamericano, América latina,* and *América española* did appear (*Catauro de cubanismos* 73–75). In the *Glosario de afronegrismos* Ortiz intentionally chose terms that spoke not only to linguistic particularities but to historically significant names or objects. The *mambís,* for example, were the legendary heroes of the Cuban struggle for independence. Ortiz explained the African provenience of the word, citing hypotheses by historians such as the Cuban Antonio Bachiller y Morales and the Puerto Rican Coll y Toste about its indigenous, Dominican, or Cuban origin, and then added:

> For our part, we have found the Word *mambí* with various meanings in the languages of Africa. *Mamby* is a chief's title in one region of Senegambia, *Mambí* is a region of the French Congo, close to *Mayumba*, a word that in Cuba refers to a kind of witch practice. *Mambí* in the Congo language means "bad man," "abominable," "injurious," "pernicious," "repulsive," "mean," "dirty," "cruel," "hurtful," "vicious," "wicked," etc. The last one of these three words seems the easier one to adopt as origin for the runaway *mambís*, or Dominican rebels. The Congo slaves called the rebels in their language *Mambí*, using the most derogatory term and translating thus the hate of their lords toward them, and the injurious words with which they called them. We don't advance this opinion as certain; but we believe that the queer word comes from Africa and then was turned into a glorious title for our heroic freedom fighters.[18]

This was as much an intervention in a debate among philologists, where Ortiz suggested that dictionaries of African languages had not been consulted yet, as it was one about the "anthropological" analysis of the Mambís and their ethnic origin, the last sentence mocking those who had turned Mambís into national heroes at the cost of obliterating their national and racial origin.

It was Ortiz's most frequent line of attack against the Real Academia's faulty etymologies that in his view the academy omitted possible African roots of words. On the other hand, Ortiz's own Africanist speculations were also sometimes considered excessive by reviewers who recognized, however, that they were usually well informed and at least plausible. Ortiz's friend Chacón y Calvo wrote, for example, that Ortiz's work was of great importance to folklore studies, noting about its philological credentials that more properly linguistic studies of "black African dialects" were necessary but that Ortiz had documented his entries well: "And philologically, even though the real value of a vocabulary of afronegrisms cannot be appreciated without the scientific study of Negroafrican dialects, the lexicological notecards that Dr. O. ordered in this recent glossary of Afronegrisms will always be a precious element of consultation, since every word is illustrated with an authority or with a concrete indication and popular source out of which it comes."[19] Similarly, the anonymous author of another review published in the *Journal of the Royal African Society* noted the diligent research and remarkable quantity of entries, even though it also corrected several errors (A. W.). One example of an excessive etymology contrived by Ortiz would be the term *bobo*, for which Ortiz claimed a possible onomatopoetic but still African origin. Ortiz cited the Real Academia's etymology "¿del latín balbus, balbuciente?" and then commented:

> This academic hypothesis is very likely, even though one should not ignore that this expression radically belongs to the group of onomatopoeic universals, by its phoneme *bab*. Among the Negroes of Sierra Leno the one who is "born deaf" is called bobo (Thomas 16). The same happens with the Malinkés (Un Miss. Ob. Cit. P.110), which can be explained by way of an onomatopeyon, like the one of balbucency, like the Latin *balbus*. For the same reason the "deaf" is called in Congo *ebaba* (Bentley, 264), *ribubu* in Angola (Cannecattim, p. 11), *bebi* for the Hausas, *obu* for the Ibos, *mumo* for the Fulas, *mumuo* for the Mandingas, and *bobo* for the Bambara. Should the *bobo* of the black slaves have had an influence on Castilian? In order to determine this, one would have to study the history of the word, and the period and area of its appearance in Spain. However, the onomatopoeic reason described above should suffice.[20]

Ortiz's argument was intentionally contrived, of course, as it's not clear why one should look for a faraway explanation when the most elegant one would be to derive it from the Latin word *balbus*—still today the accepted etymology of *bobo*. But it was certainly provocative to claim that the several African languages Ortiz quoted participated in an "onomatopoeic universal." Ortiz surely would have provoked philologists who might not have wanted to think of a shared linguistic heritage between Spain and Africa.

Still, Ortiz's emphasis on historical speculation did not go as far as approving of another wildly imaginative thesis on early contacts between Africans and Americans, Leo Wiener's work *Africa and the Discovery of America* (1920). Wiener was not a specialist of Latin American literature or linguistics; he held the chair of Slavic literature at Harvard and was a polyglot, a translator of Leo Tolstoy's complete works, as well as the author of, among others, books on Yiddish literature, Russian tales, and Arabic literature. In this book Wiener proposed that before the arrival of the Spaniards, America had been explored by African peoples who had brought with them cotton and tobacco. Wiener frequently used etymology to argue that African linguistic remnants indicated the pre-Hispanic presence of African cultures. In response to this extravagant thesis, Ortiz took pains in his *Glosario* to refute Wiener, insisting on the conservative reading of clearly Latinate words such as *nabo* (Latin *napus*) or clearly indigenous derived words such as *maíz*.

In his two dictionaries, Ortiz became not only a defender of the impact of historical context on language change but a believer in entangled or "zigzag etymologies," an example of which is his analysis of *guarapo,* a fermented sugar drink popular in Cuba. After citing the Real Academia's generic definition of the word's origin as "American" and Coll y Toste's thesis that it was Quechua, Ortiz proposed that the word came from *garapa,* used in Angola and Congo to refer to a fermented drink made of corn and yuca. But the word *garapa* itself had come from the Portuguese *xarope,* which in Spanish was *jarabe,* derived from the Arabic *xarab* for "drink." Ortiz concluded: "It is then a curious Afronegrism, if we honestly consider its etymology. The original word is not formed by elements of black linguistics; but we say *guarapo* because the word comes to us as is from the African Negroes, who corrupted it, taught by the discoverers, who had learned it from the Arabs. It is a zigzag etymological genealogy: from the Arabic to Spanish and Portuguese, from them to the Congo, and from the Congo another time to the Spanish and Portuguese of the colonies."[21] Even though it might have seemed far-fetched philologically, this argument was persuasive in its historical logic. For Ortiz, the evolution of words like *guarapo* was a testimony to the entangled colonization processes among Spaniards, Portuguese, and parts of West Africa, the Spaniards being the last ones in a long chain of powers exploiting Africans. The idea of zigzag etymologies, like so many other instances in Ortiz's dictionaries where he speaks of cultural contact as fundamental to contemporary Cuban Spanish, might in this way have prefigured Ortiz's theory of the transculturation of Cuban society in his *Cuban Counterpoint,* where he developed his irreverent, long-term view of cultural contact into a fully formed concept.[22]

All in all, Ortiz deployed the toolbox of the philologist to great effect, adding a wealth of historical context to his analyses of language change. He used an impressive bibliography of philological and historical studies, and his work was well received by philologists in Cuba and in Spain, despite its polemical stabs. He inscribed himself in this way in a long line of dictionaries of regionalisms often written by Spanish American intellectuals with little training in philology—the Cuban writer Estéban Pichardo being the first among them to have trained himself on the matter. What's more, in representing Cuban Spanish as a result of multiple cultures coming into contact with each other, Ortiz drafted a multicultural ethos of Spanish as Cuba's national language, a monoglossic ethos, to be sure, but one that was different from the unquestioning acknowledgment of Spanish authority of nineteenth-century lexicologists.

In the same period, Ortiz embarked on yet another adventure in language politics, the creation of a Cuban Academy of Language as a corresponding member of the Real Academia Española. He launched the idea of such an academy in 1925 in a letter to Chacón y Calvo, who was a diplomat at the Cuban embassy in Madrid at the time and who became active on Ortiz's behalf to make the proposal at the Spanish Royal Academy.[23] The project found the support of Menéndez Pidal, Bonilla, and several others. Ortiz then suggested the names of the first eighteen academics in a letter to Chacón y Calvo of October 26, 1925, adding a draft of a letter of invitation to founding members of the Cuban academy (Gutiérrez Vega 47–48). The Academia Cubana de la Lengua was indeed founded in May 1926 in Madrid, followed by a first meeting of its members in Havana, in October 1926.[24] Its first president was Enrique José Varona, with Ortiz as its vice president. The purpose of the academy was to pay attention to all issues of the Spanish language in Cuba, but since it had no building or meeting room of its own and seems to have lacked funds, it did not meet often in the first decades of its existence.

Ortiz's turn toward culture as embracing language but also a shared literature and science can be seen in another institutional initiative he started in the 1920s. In the same year as the founding of the Academia Cubana de la Lengua, there also opened in Havana the Institución Hispano-Cubana de Cultura (IHCC). This institute invited numerous Spanish writers and philologists, including Federico García Lorca, Menéndez Pidal, Américo Castro, and Juan Ramón Jiménez, to Cuba. Its objectives were explicitly, as Ortiz declared in an interview for the *Diario de la Marina,* not to sing "songs to race, language, history, or the empire of Cervantes" but to bring outstanding lecturers to Cuba (in: Naranjo Orovio and Puig-Samper Mulero 26). Ortiz made the IHCC part of a wider network of exchange institutions with Spain, such as the Cultural Institute in Mexico, the University of Puerto Rico, and the Instituto de las Españas at Columbia University in New York. This exchange network also made it possible for Ortiz to reach out during and after the Spanish Civil War and invite Spanish Republican intellectuals to Cuba, thus supporting them.[25] The IHCC's journals, *Surco* (1927–29), *Mensajes* (1928–30), and after Ortiz's return from exile its new incarnation *Ultra* (1936–47), published excerpts of the lectures given by the guests of the IHCC, as well as articles in translation taken from foreign scientific or other publications. The cover of *Ultra* stated that its mission was to present a digest of foreign publications and news, an "encyclopedia of modern ideas." Ortiz in this way strategically made Cuba part of a Hispanic conference and lectures circuit organized independently by non-Spanish institutes in Mexico, Argentina, Puerto Rico, and New

York, replacing the work of the Spanish Unión Ibero-Americana that had supported Rafael Altamira's visit in 1910, along with the Universities of Oviedo and Havana. Ortiz also succeeded in turning attention away from Spain-centered ideas toward the promotion of "modern ideas" through the IHCC and its journal.

From the late 1920s on, Ortiz also began to develop a greater presence in Americanist scientific organizations unrelated to philology. An important moment giving Ortiz international visibility was his participation in the 1928 founding of the Instituto Panamericano de Geografía e Historia, a research institute based in Mexico and dedicated to the integrated study of the Americas.[26] He was invited to join the membership of numerous institutions dedicated to the study of the anthropology, literature, and history of the Americas.[27] In 1943 he also participated in the Primer Congreso Demográfico Interamericano in Mexico. It was there that Ortiz put forward and won the motion recommending the suspension of the so-called Día de la raza in all Latin American states.

Rallying against the Día de la raza

Already in 1923, Ortiz had voiced his opposition to the Día de la raza, decreed only one year earlier in Cuba, as an aside in his introduction to the *Catauro,* where he distanced himself from the patriotic declarations of the Día de la raza, holding up against them the more precise science of philology: "An academic initiative with this purpose would do more for the moral interests of the *raza* than that boisterous patriotic declaration served at toasts in every patriotic banquet. Fortunately, we Iberoamericans have a philological tradition that compares favorably with the Spanish one and with more than a few authorized masters."[28]

By 1929, Ortiz had moved entirely away from using the idea of a Hispanic race. In a lecture delivered at the Sociedad Económica de Amigos del País he pointed out that racism in the name of Hispanism was as bad as racism against Afro-descendants or indigenous peoples, concluding that "culture unites everyone; race only the select few or the cursed ones" ("Ni racismos, ni xenofobias").

In 1942, in an opening speech at the First National Congress of History, Ortiz criticized the Latin American holiday once again, now mentioning Nazi Germany as the enemy and the Spanish philosopher Unamuno as his ally in the struggle against false notions of race:

> Are we to convert these evocations of the discovery of America, as some do, in "feasts of the race"? No, because there is no such race, because this race,

> said the good master Unamuno, was invented on the same day as the feast was invented. And besides, this would only end up deceiving genuine collective emotions, associating them with the shameful and anti-Christian passions of racism whose satanic incarnation is Adolf Hitler's empire of race, which is currently covering the continents in blood. The Aryan race is as mythic as other races are, created to stimulate aggressive noncultures and serve as cover-ups for predatory politics. There is no race whatsoever in the world that would merit special exaltation. The era of racisms has already passed.[29]

By this time many Spanish philologists and writers had left Civil War Spain for the United States and Latin America. Pseudo-scientific theories of race had gained currency in Germany and elsewhere despite anthropologists' efforts to refute them. Ortiz in turn in 1936 had founded yet another society and journal, the Sociedad de Estudios Afrocubanos and its *Revista de Estudios Afrocubanos,* where he gathered a diverse group of scientists, writers, and artists, including the singer Bola de Nieve, with the general purpose of studying "the phenomena (demographic, economic, juridical, religious, literary, artistic, linguistic, and social in general) produced in Cuba by the living together of distinct races, particularly the so-called black and African-origin one and the so-called white or Caucasian one."[30] Like the IHCC, the society invited a number of speakers to give lectures; its *Revista* had a more scientific orientation than *Ultra,* containing original scientific and literary contributions. It folded after having published five volumes. The study of race and culture clearly had become more politicized, so much so that in 1941, Ortiz founded the Cuban Alliance for a Free World, another short-lived institution that was to "defend the ideals of freedom, democracy, and social justice as fundamental for the civilized and pacific lives of peoples" (Barreal xxvi).

Further, in his intervention in the first Interamerican Congress of Demography in 1943, Ortiz used his keynote lecture to propose eliminating the word *raza* from official administrative jargon across Latin America. Along with this, Ortiz proposed suspending celebrations of the Día de la raza (Barreal xxxi). The motion ended in a recommendation only, but Ortiz had succeeded in having the congress give attention to the issue.

In his book *El engaño de las razas* (1946; The deception of the races), Ortiz finally had moved entirely away from philologically inspired arguments about language to a more strictly anthropological approach to race that insisted on properly scientific methods when studying the physical differences between human beings. Associating his position with that of Roosevelt's vice president, Henry A. Wallace, whom Ortiz quoted as having stated that science needed to combat racism, he now argued that "science" was the only way to refute obsolete categories such as race: "It is of the utmost importance that about races, as with diseases, crimes, and economic conflicts, the criteria proposed by science be applied; it is the only way to confront social calamities and reduce them."[31]

Even in this rather combative book, concerned with asserting indisputable facts against ideas of race and racism, Ortiz again used close readings of early histories of racial difference to demonstrate flawed interpretations or arguments, beginning with the biblical story of Ham. He systematically surveyed everyone who ever had written on bodily definitions of race, the idea of the pure and the impure, and the hierarchy of races, quoting anthropologists, psychologists, philosophers, and essayists such as Paul Rivet, Ruth Benedict, Gustave Le Bon, Lucien Levy-Bruhl, Luis Montandon, C. G. Jung, Otto Klineberg, and many others. Instead of a scientific subject, race was to Ortiz now a "specter": "Certainly, one can speak of the 'racial specter' in more than one sense. Races are unreal like specters, but they inspire very strong emotions. That is why racism is so fearsome. . . . We have to achieve the deracialization of humanity, humanity has to be 'deracialized.' The bad spirit that is the racial specter has to be exorcized, freeing us of its dread. The human society that has created 'races' will have to suppress them."[32] *Race* was no longer the wrong term for what should be *culture.* Ortiz perceived it as a dangerous idea that had to be attacked vigorously through ideological critique.

He responded in similar fashion to broad but vague ideas of *mestizaje,* as discussed by essayists and politicians. In his first chapter, Ortiz specifically criticized those Spanish American writers—he mentions José Vasconcelos's *The Cosmic Race*—who lent to the idea of racial mixing a figurative, humanitarian, or cosmopolitan sense. Ortiz insisted that one might distinguish the human "race" from animals, but that the myth of mixed races in Latin American countries obscured real existing social injustices:

> "Race problems" are of great importance in America and are likely to become large and tragic episodes. As the centuries have gone by, a system of social injustices, concealed by the myths of diverse bloodlines, has been created, and it is very unlikely that the idolization of races and the holocausts demanded by such cults may be ended without more confrontation and cruel sacrifice. All of America is feeling the pain. This is so because in this hemisphere, which used to be the new world and which by now needs a total and urgent renovation in order to remain new, there are various human groups defined as races that are in socially intense contrasts, embittered and from day to day less stable.[33]

Rejecting *mestizaje,* Ortiz now spoke of "ethnic essences" and emphasized that it was vital to understand their historical importance: "American history cannot be understood without knowing all the ethnic essences that have melted together in this continent and without appreciating what has been the real result of their mutual transculturation."[34]

While at first Ortiz had confronted Hispanists about the linguistic and ideological uses of the term *raza* in the context of the relationship between Spain and Latin America, he changed course in the 1940s, understanding race as a concept that, no matter if in Spanish or in English, needed to be scientifically contained and linguistically controlled. Ortiz's somewhat nominalist hope was that if only the term *race* could be eliminated from current language use, racism would also be done with and a better understanding of ethnicity and transculturation in Cuban and Latin American societies produced. Yet, he only ended up making race into the dialectic opposite of his argument about transculturation, the specter that he could not make disappear when studying culture.

Networks, National and International

Ortiz was part of a shifting landscape of social and professional networks. It is crucial to look at Ortiz's interaction with different networks of scientists and intellectuals from Cuba and elsewhere to gain an understanding of how he was able to position anthropology as the new science of culture in Cuba. He did this inspired especially by U.S. American anthropologists, staking out a unique role for himself as a mediator between the Cuban scientific discussion on race and culture and U.S. American scientific theories.

As Alejandra Bronfman has shown, different groups of scientists and intellectuals competed in Republican Cuba to reform ideas of racial difference and create a modern nation-state, and Ortiz was not the only one to wield the tools of cultural anthropology as a modern science able to integrate Afro-Cubans into the nation. Ortiz seemed to coexist all too easily, for example, with his fellow Cuban anthropologist and friend Israel Castellanos, who continued to defend a strictly taxonomic approach to Cuba's different ethnic groups, applying the methods of "Lombrosian" criminal and physical anthropology and excluding from his own studies the historical and sociological approach Ortiz had taken. As Castellanos writes in 1937: "The study of witchcraft and *ñañiguismo* determines from the medical and legal point of view naturally the reduction of the topic to its sociological aspect and the broadness of the topic from a strictly scientific point of view. For this reason one must make abstractions of many social, juridical, and historical considerations to pay special attention to those factors and characteristics that are of the greatest interest to the forensic doctor."[35] It was Castellanos's emphasis on the statistics of Cuba's white, mixed, and black ethnic groups, not Ortiz's sociological and historical approach, that was favored by Cuba's subsequent governments of the 1930s through the 1950s, and Castellanos worked throughout this period at the Bureau of Identification, gathering data on black and mestizo Cubans in the judicial and penitentiary system (Bronfman 124–34). Castellanos and Ortiz nevertheless both refrained, from the late 1920s on, from eugenicist or discriminating politics. They managed to divide up their competencies, with Castellanos working as a government official while Ortiz, as the cultural anthropologist that Castellanos was not, sought out for himself a position independent from the state or the university.

Closest in interests and method to Ortiz were two other Cuban anthropologists, Rómulo Lachatañeré and Lydia Cabrera, who similarly worked without academic support from a university or research institution. Lachatañeré came from a mixed-race family in Cuba's Oriente and studied with Ortiz in the 1930s. He, like Cabrera, was a member of the Sociedad de Estudios Afrocubanos and published in the pages of its journal. In the 1930s Lachatañeré studied Cuban santería, eventually publishing two books, *!!Oh mio Yemayá!!* (1938) and *Manual de Santería* (1942; Santería manual), and a number of articles. He left for New York in 1939 to live with his wife in Harlem, tried unsuccessfully to enroll for a master's program in anthropology under Ruth Benedict, and studied Afro-Cuban culture in New York, aside from working odd jobs.[36] He died tragically in a plane crash at the age of forty-two. In the 1920s Cabrera, Ortiz's sister-in-law, studied art in Paris, where she wrote a book of stories inspired by memories of her black wet-nurse, *Contes nègres* (1936; *Afro-Cuban tales,* 2004), later published in Spanish translation. Her masterwork, *El monte* (1954; The forest), a still-current manual of Afro-Cuban religion, collected the magic, religions, beliefs, and folklore of Afro-Cubans in the most comprehensive manner to date, recording the different languages Cabrera had heard when speaking with her subjects. In contrast to Ortiz, whose work relied little on personal interviews with Afro-Cubans, Cabrera and Lachatañeré immersed themselves in individual Afro-Cuban communities, learning their languages and participating in ceremonies. They produced detailed participant accounts of feasts and rituals, using methods that were closer to U.S. American field research methods than Ortiz's methods were. Ortiz,

Lachatañeré, and Cabrera, one can say, were part of the same informal social network of intellectuals, artists, and scholars in Cuba who had frequent exchanges, often outside of an institutional context. While they used different methodologies and narrative strategies, as Emily Maguire has shown, they were also vying for controlling versions of Cuban culture that included Afro-Cuban religious and musical practices.[37] Ortiz, by far older and better known internationally, occupied in this constellation the role of a mentor and translator of Lachatañeré and Cabrera for a nonspecialist readership. He wrote introductions to both of their works, where he emphasized the universal message of their collected stories. Speaking about Cabrera's *Cuentos negros,* Ortiz compared her stories to "Greek, Etrurian or Roman archaic tales" and placed them in the genre of animal fables and myths (in: Cabrera 32). In his introduction to Lachatañeré's *!!Oh mío, Yemayá!!* Ortiz insisted that the book would not be comprehensible to regular readers if not read as part of a long line of Afro-Cuban-themed literature and pointed out the universal themes running through the myths related by Lachatañeré, likening them to those of James Frazer's *Golden Bough* and Cabrera's stories. Lachatañeré, in his own introductory words, reinforced Ortiz's universalizing message, all the while insisting on his own "incorporation of blacks into the national culture" as a main goal (*!!Oh, mío Yemayá!!* xxxi). Cabrera, who herself, like Ortiz, was a member of Cuba's white upper class, does not seem to have had difficulties with Ortiz as her mentor.[38]

When reading Lachatañeré's late *Manual de santería,* however, it becomes clear that as an Afro-Cuban Lachatañeré was not at ease with Ortiz's protagonist role in Afro-Cuban anthropology. In his introduction, Lachatañeré criticized Ortiz for having followed, as late as in his article "La religión en la poesía mulata" (1937), the French anthropologist Lucien Lévy-Bruhl's view that African cultures had a "para-logic" mentality and for not having distinguished clearly enough between individual African religions in Cuba.[39] Lachatañeré wanted Ortiz to accept Afro-Cuban santería as a religious practice, distancing himself more explicitly from his earlier book *Los negros brujos,* where he had called it witchcraft. According to Jorge Castellanos, Lachatañeré's insistence on abandoning his earlier criminologist point of view and using strictly anthropological criteria had perhaps a corrective influence on his former teacher (132–33). Clearly, there was also a certain tension at play between Lachatañeré, as a scientist of color, and Ortiz, as the privileged white senior scientist speaking with great authority about Afro-Cuban culture.[40] This is also Bronfman's argument: "As they became more and more familiar with anthropological theory, intellectuals of color thus contended with the representation of Afro-Cuban culture on its terms. In their valorization of African-derived traditions they vied for greater control over those terms, rather than, as had earlier generations, distancing themselves from such practices" (169).

Ortiz's network of social and scientific contacts remained strong throughout the 1920s and 1930s. The list of members Ortiz proposed in 1926 for the Academia Cubana de la Lengua is not so different from the list of members of the Sociedad del Folklore Cubano, formed in 1923, or of the Sociedad de Estudios Afrocubanos in 1936. Among them in all three cases were the historian Enrique José Varona, the political activist and poet Juan Marinello, the journalist Emilio Roig de Leuchsenring, the diplomat and writer José María Chacón y Calvo, and the historian Ramiro Guerra. The list of members of the Academia Cubana de la Lengua also included, of course, philologists such as Manuel S. Pichardo and Juan M. Dihigo and the writers Alfonso Hernández Catá, Miguel de Carrión, Carlos Loveira, and Jorge Mañach. The associated members of the *Revista de Estudios Afrocubanos,* in turn, consisted of a few anthropologists but many more literary personalities, painters, and musicians, including the anthropologists Castellanos, Cabrera, and Lachatañeré but also Nicolás Guillén as secretary, the poet Regino Pedroso, the historian Luciano Franco, the journalist Gonzalo Roig, and the singer Bola de Nieve. Many of these writers and intellectuals also had formed part of the Grupo Minorista, which in the 1920s had protested unsuccessfully against corruption in the Cuban government of Gerardo Machado. This tightly knit network of white and Afro-Cuban intellectuals, scientists, artists, and writers did not need to agree on all aspects of racial politics in Cuba, but in their overall focus on the study of popular Afro-Cuban culture, and in their political push for integrating Afro-Cubans more into the Cuban nation, they seem to have collaborated.

The Sociedad de Estudios Afrocubanos made an extensive outreach effort to distribute the journal internationally, in the form of subscriptions or exchange relations (*canjes*), which were established with universities and journals in Latin America, the United States, Europe, and Africa. The *Revista de Estudios Afrocubanos* was also sent to a list of distinguished individuals—among them Frank Tannenbaum (Columbia University); Alain Locke (Howard University); Suzanne Comhaire, Jean Price-Mars, and Edmond Mangonès (Haiti); Tomás Blanco (Puerto Rico); Gonzalo Aguirre Beltrán (Mexico); Arthur Ramos (Brazil); and the Cuban writer Alejo Carpentier (Caracas)—and research institutions, such as the Bureau of American Ethnology (Smithsonian Institution, Washington) and the Escuela de Estudios Hispano-Americanos of the University of Seville, among many others.[41] Similar lists of institutional and personal addresses of the Sociedad del Folklore Cubano and the Institución Hispano-Cubana de Cultura indicate the large number of copies of the journals *Archivos del folklore* and *Ultra* that were routinely sent out worldwide to persons or institutions of anthropology and culture. This shows Ortiz's ambition to make Cuban activities concerning folklore and Afro-Cuban culture known internationally.

Yet another testimony to his extended network of contacts in the world of science and literature is Ortiz's correspondence. Ortiz maintained contacts with a large number of Caribbean and Latin Americanist scholars, writers, and politicians, such as Sidney Mintz, Richard Morse, Jean Price-Mars, the Puerto Rican poet Luis Palés Matos, the French anthropologist and Brazilianist Roger Bastide, the Dominican Juan Bosch, the Puerto Rican governor Luis Muñoz Marín, and Gilberto Freyre in Brazil, among many others.[42]

Strikingly, even as they were pursuing parallel interests in establishing an antiracist concept of culture, Ortiz barely interacted with the scion of anthropology in the United States, Franz Boas, at least to judge from the lack of correspondence between them. It is true that in 1938 Ortiz published in *Ultra* an article by Franz Boas on racial prejudice, where Boas comments on what he calls "racial injustice" in the United States, asserting that the prejudices against blacks in the United States stem from their having come as slaves to the country and are therefore socially rather than biologically driven ("El prejuicio racial"). In 1939 *Ultra* published a translation of the "Declaration against racisms" of the American Anthropological Association, protesting the abuse of the terms *Arian* and *Semite*. The statement had perhaps inspired what preceded it in *Ultra,* the declaration of the ephemeral Asociación Nacional contra las Discriminaciones Racistas, titled "Defensa cubana contra el racismo antisemita." The president of that association was, naturally, Fernando Ortiz. But beyond that we have no traces of a dialogue between Boas and Ortiz.

Boas's parallel interest in philology next to anthropology deserves a brief parenthesis, however, for its similarities but also its differences at root with Ortiz. The relationship between the study of language, culture, and race was crucial for Boas, leading up to *The Mind of Primitive Man* (1911), but the way he approached language diverged from Ortiz's approach. Boas's goal was to record and preserve Amerindian languages as completely as possible, chiefly in order to determine to what family of languages they belonged. In 1905, in the letter "The Documentary Function of the Text," Boas wrote, for example, that it was essential to publish and preserve all transcriptions of recordings of American Indian tales and communications. These were necessary to constitute an archive that would eventually allow the reconstruction of their language and culture, just like Indo-European philology had done on the basis of old Indo-European texts (Stocking, *Franz Boas Reader* 122–33). In 1906, in a paper read at the joint meeting of the American Anthropological Association, the Archeological Institute, and the Philological Association, Boas similarly insisted on the importance of the study of history and of language as part of anthropological research ("Some Philological Aspects" 184). Boas here, like Menéndez Pidal and other Spanish Hispanists, was following the idea that in the absence of objectively existing laws, languages had to be recorded and analyzed systematically, in order to document linguistic and cultural changes. This diachronic method, Boas thought, was more promising than the comparative anthropology that had been attempted by James Frazer and other early anthropologists. Indeed, philology became for him a model discipline in its attention to detail and an exemplary way of undertaking the study of history: "We must demand from the serious student the same degree of philological accuracy which has become the standard in your sciences" ("Some Philological Aspects" 185). For Boas, the problem was concretely a matter of understanding and classifying the many dialects spoken by North American Indians, which he considered the very basis of investigating their history and ways of life.[43]

Ortiz, as we have seen, was less interested in studying Cuba's oral culture and storytelling practices, despite his efforts at cataloging *afronegrismos*. Instead, beginning in the 1920s, he edited a book series, "Colección de libros cubanos," of out of print or previously unpublished works and studies of Cuba's pre-Hispanic and colonial period by Cuban, Spanish, and other lettered authors. In this way he republished Alexander von Humboldt's *Ensayo político sobre la isla de Cuba* (1930; *Political Essay on the Isle of Cuba,* 2011); several works by José Martí; selected poetry by Julián del Casal, José María Heredia, and Plácido (Gabriel de la Concepción Valdés); two short novels by Cirilo Villaverde; and important historics of Cuba by José Antonio Saco, Antonio Bachiller y Morales, M. R. Harrington, and others.

More than with Boas, we know that Ortiz interacted with Bronislaw Malinowski, a representative of the British school of social anthropology, who lived and taught at Yale University from 1939 until his death in 1942. Malinowski visited Ortiz in Cuba and exchanged a number of letters with him, where the two conversed about cultural contact. Malinowski, feeling isolated in the United States, was enthusiastically supportive of Ortiz's theory of transculturation. One result of their meeting was Malinowski's famous introduction to Ortiz's *Cuban Counterpoint* (1940), translated into English by Harriet de Onís in 1947.[44]

The broader discussion of cultural contact had been started by Robert Redfield, Ralph Linton, and Melville J. Herskovits in their "Memorandum for the Study of Acculturation" (1936), published in the *American Anthropologist,* the journal of the American Anthropological Association. There, the group defined acculturation as "comprehending those phenomena which result when groups of different cultures come into continuous first-hand contact, with subsequent changes in the original cultural patterns of either or both groups," a concept distinct from culture change, assimilation, or diffusion (149). Herskovits further explained his point of view in his *Life in a Haitian Village* (1937), where he argued that Haitian society was a result of the mutual dependence of slaves and masters in the past and that Haitians therefore needed to be studied using both ethnological and historical criteria. Herskovits opposed to the British functionalist method, which focused on the synchronic analysis of "simple societies," his own view that every culture was situated in a unique historical continuum, based on definitely ascertainable historical contacts with others. Malinowski, feeling accused unjustly, responded to this critique in several book publications, among them his *Methods of Study of Culture Contact* (1938), *The Dynamics of Cultural Change, Acculturation: The Study of Culture Contact* (1938), and the posthumous *An Inquiry into the Nature of Race Relations in Africa* (1945). Herskovits, however, found a strong following especially in Latin America; in Brazil, where Arthur Ramos's *A aculturação negra no Brasil* (1942; The acculturation of blacks in Brazil) helped to spread his ideas; and in Mexico, where Gonzalo Aguirre Beltrán's *La población negra de México, 1519–1810* (1946; The black population of Mexico) made use of his method. Aguirre Beltrán also later published a lucid account of acculturation as a method and the role it had played particularly in Mexico, *El proceso de aculturación* (1957; The process of acculturation).

Ortiz's own intervention in the debate was certainly idiosyncratic. In writing a history of two economic products, tobacco and sugar, instead of an anthropological study of an ethnic or cultural group, Ortiz shifted the argument away from by then established anthropological methods of field study and participant observation to the terrain of national macroeconomics, defining *transculturation* first in relation to economic products and only by inference to a human group. Ortiz also kept his discussion of the concept of transculturation relatively short, not dwelling much on the controversy that had formed around acculturation. It was perhaps because of this that Ortiz's proposal was only moderately successful on the international anthropological scene. Malinowski would only use the term on two occasions in his later works, and Ortiz still today appears little in anglophone or francophone discussions of cultural contact.[45]

All in all, Ortiz's efforts to establish culture and transculturation as new scientific objects of interest, instead of race, were successful on a national scale, going in step with trends happening on an international scale, where cultural anthropology and studies of acculturation only slowly established themselves. In Cuba, the new emphasis on culture was noticeable in the classes Ortiz himself taught, beginning in the 1940s, with a series of summer classes labeled "Races and historical cultures that have formed the Cuban people. Cultural factors of Indians, Africans, Europeans, and others: The phenomena of their transculturation" (1941–45). From 1943 on, he and a few others close to him, like the exiled Spanish philosopher María Zambrano, taught ethnography at the Instituto Universitario de Investigaciones Científicas y de Ampliación de Estudios at the University of Havana, teaching foreign students (Díaz).[46]

One central point of convergence among Latin American, European, and U.S. American anthropologists was surely the Americanist conference organized precisely on the topic of acculturation in 1948 in New York.[47] For Elazar Barkan and for George Stocking, this shift amounted to a scientific revolution.[48] And to be sure, anthropology was moving all over the Americas, from the learned societies and museums of the nineteenth century to universities, bringing with it the professionalization and the increasing specialization of anthropologists.

Ortiz's *Cuban Counterpoint*

Why did Ortiz, given his evident desire to establish a science of culture in Cuba that was conversant with other cultural anthropologists, write a scientific essay that was conspicuous for its rhetorical brilliance and the allusion to the musical notion of counterpoint? The structure of *Cuban Counterpoint,* it has often been remarked, is unusual, as the first part of it tells a fable about two luxury items produced in Cuba, whereby tobacco becomes Don Tabaco and sugar Doña Azúcar, and only the second, larger part loosely adopts a scientific format. Some therefore read *Counterpoint* as a literary essay similar to the essays of José Carlos Mariátegui, Pedro Henríquez Ureña, and Alfonso Reyes, rather than as an ethnographic study or history, which is what it promises to be in the title that precedes the additional chapters: "The History, Ethnography and Transculturation of Havana Tobacco and the Beginnings of Sugar and of the Slavery of Blacks in America." However, if the first chapter of eighty or so pages indeed is a literary masterwork, the additional chapters have no rhetorical ambition or continuous argument. Indeed, they read more like dictionary entries or glosses of terms, similar to the dictionaries that Ortiz had written in the 1920s. The work, in short, is uneven, and its anthropological ambition, signaled by Malinowski's introduction, seems at odds with its form.

As Fernando Coronil has argued, Ortiz playfully deviates from scientific discourse to offer an alternative vision of Latin America that draws from the allegorical mode popular in the nineteenth-century national romances studied by Doris Sommer in her *Foundational Fictions*. In Coronil's opinion, Ortiz, while not giving in to a subaltern perspective vis-à-vis the United States, enters into a "dynamic exchange between subaltern and dominant anthropologies" (in: Ortiz, *Cuban Counterpoint* xlii). For Coronil, Cuban anthropology is a more "literary" than metropolitan anthropology precisely because it is in a position of marginality. While this point is well taken, I still find that it does not explain the existence of the additional chapters, which are together more than three times the length of the first essay.

My own explanation of the conundrum of the excessive chapters is that Ortiz's *Cuban Counterpoint* was written in response to the two formative influences on Ortiz's career, philology and anthropology. In the additional chapters, Ortiz uses historical documents, chronicles, and literary texts to analyze technical terms and situations relating to sugar and tobacco and to comment on them, using philological methods that complement his anthropological-literary analysis. He forges in this way an anthropology sui generis that is conversant with social science methods and humanistic methods but that also maintains a strong, almost nominalist emphasis on precision of language. We can see this in several of the additional chapters of the original Spanish edition, where Ortiz explains the differences among specific Spanish terms used in the sugar and tobacco economy.[49] Many of the other additional chapters offer long quotes that expand on a topic discussed in the opening essay, complementing or authorizing it, with relatively little comment from Ortiz—this happens in chapters 12, 14, 16, 20, and 23. That is, the philological apparatus offered here functions like an additional archive that expands and adds references as if in a manual or a dictionary.

Race continues to play a significant role in Ortiz's long opening essay, but his focus on products instead of human beings makes it possible for him to avoid entering into any discussion about the meanings of race or culture. Race is used only in reference to the work of specific groups, not their physical characteristics. What is more, in anthropomorphizing "Don Tabaco" and "Doña Azúcar," Ortiz plays with the idea of race as attached to those products, only to question right away even the possibility of attributing any sort of stable characteristics to either one of the two. Tobacco in his analysis represents the locally driven economy that Ortiz seems to yearn for, whereas sugar stands for the large-scale, foreign-owned economy that was introduced by the Spaniards and was now largely in the hands of U.S. companies. Even beyond distinguishing between Spanish and "foreign," he also characterizes sugar as "mulatto," an economy where African slaves worked for white plantation owners, and tobacco as always having sought "purity," being a business conducted mainly by Spanish immigrants, but also possibly alluding to the racist nineteenth-century idea of "pure" races. Each position, however, should not be taken too seriously since Ortiz notes that "the union between sugar and the Negro has nothing to do with race and rather with the slave" (60). He also points to other "foreigners" such as the Jew and "Marxist" Luis Marx, who invented in Cuba the technique of obtaining high-quality tobacco leaves by covering them (28). In this way, Ortiz destabilizes any essentializing argument about sugar and tobacco as inherently black and white, African and Spanish, leaving us with the impression that each of these products has a distinctly mixed or "transculturated" quality: sugar and tobacco exist only as commodities, products that shape a culture through the type of labor and market that they require; they represent a culture that constantly reinvents itself by means of the mixing and blending of its different elements.

Martí's Races

Ortiz intervened in several instances in the discussion of contemporary "mulatto poetry," which lasted in Cuba for several years, from Nicolás Guillén's publication of *Motivos de son* in the Cuban press in the late 1920s through the 1930s (Cairo Ballester). In agreement with Guillén's notion of "mulatto poetry," Ortiz claimed in several essays published in *Revista Bimestre Cubana* that there was no "black poetry" in Cuba, since the language of communication had from early on been Spanish, but that there were typical characteristics that historically characterized the figure of the black woman or man in poetry.[50] In 1941, one year after *Cuban Counterpoint,* Ortiz published what was to be perhaps his most important essay specifically on race. "Martí y las razas" (1941), republished on several occasions and translated into English, was as much a statement of his anthropological understanding of race and culture as it was a work of literary criticism.[51] In it, Ortiz presented an analysis of the passages where Martí had either spoken about race or used racially marked characters in his literary works. Martí becomes his model as both a Cuban nationalist and a man of good judgment, who distrusts the "library races" that early anthropologists had invented in the nineteenth century. Finally, Martí is to Ortiz the writer whose imagination of Cuban race relations is as instructive as his political analysis is.

It is clear that Ortiz emulated Martí, not only his good judgment in regard to European race theories but also his rhetoric, and indeed, Martí's fragmented, "brilliant" style might well have been one of Ortiz's inspirations in writing *Counterpoint:* "Martí's written work is not a didactic treatise, nor is it a systematic production, but rather a fragmentary output, almost always dispersed in verses, articles, speeches and manifestos; but throughout the work of his genial spirit, inspired by a single dominant ideal, sparkle brilliant concepts and scintillating sentences, like sparks from the torch which he carried aloft all his life" (Ortiz, "Cuba, Martí and the Race Problem" 259). Even more, what Julio Ramos calls Martí's "overwritten" style is for Ortiz the "sparkle" that lends authority to his argument about race.[52]

But Martí was to Ortiz also an intellectual, more so than a scientist, who was well informed about nineteenth-century ideas of race yet who knew to take the right distance toward them:

> And there is no doubt that he was acquainted with libraries where these phantom races of anthropological alchemy appeared just as in former times demons had been manufactured. On reading Martí, one sees him treating the anthropological societies, the American congresses, the pre-Columbian civilizations and the sociological texts most in vogue during his time, even including Spencer and Ribot. Above all, Martí understands the decisive importance of those problems, the fallacy of their treatment, and he is seen to be most interested in studying objectively the human types considered racial and their repercussions on society. (Ortiz, "Cuba, Martí and the Race Problem" 261)

Ortiz reads Martí not as an enemy of anthropology as such, but as an opponent of evolutionist theories (Ribot and Spencer). Martí is invested in social contexts rather than in the analysis of types.

Ortiz then qualifies Martí's famous statement that there are no races in two ways. First, he points out that when Martí speaks of races, he is in fact using the term "in its improper and vague but very current connotation," when he is really thinking of groups sharing "accumulated characteristics." ("Cuba, Martí and the Race Problem" 264). Second, especially with respect to Latin America, Martí does not identify "our America" with "our race" but rather thinks of it as a culture: "In the above instance, 'race' means 'culture' as one would say today; but this connotation was not yet in use sixty years ago when Martí was writing" (264). Ortiz, in typical philological fashion, contextualizes Martí's language in its time and then compares it to current language, suggesting that Martí uses the common language of his time but that in fact he would agree entirely with the contemporary shift from race to culture.

Ortiz in this way appropriates Martí's ideas while transforming his language. All the problems related to the indigenous populations of the Americas are social, not anthropological, insists Martí via Ortiz. Similarly in Cuba, Ortiz argues, quoting Martí's letter to Antonio Maceo: "The solution to the Cuban problem is not political but social, and this cannot be effected without that mutual love and pardon of both races and that prudence ever appropriate and generous by which I know its lofty and noble heart is animated" (Ortiz, "Cuba, Martí and the Race Problem" 268).

Ortiz ends his argument by using Martí's literary and essay drafts that had been made available in an edition of Gonzalo de Quesada, *Papeles de Martí* (1933; Martí's papers). He proceeds to argue that Martí's use of protagonists of color in his dramas and notes signals his central preoccupation with race relations in Cuba.[53] Even while Martí was organizing the revolutionary movement in Cuba, Ortiz writes, he was aware of the race question and its social repercussions, confronting racism among whites and blacks. Martí's program of a raceless Cuban society therefore was one of his most earnest concerns, expressed even as late as in his "Montecristi Manifesto," written shortly before his death.

In making Martí's words on race his own, Ortiz displayed as much the skills of a philologist as those of an anthropologist, selectively rereading Martí and recasting his terms so that they would fit his own theories. Ortiz's passage from the anthropology of race to philology to cultural anthropology was then an exemplary trajectory in the sense that Ortiz transitioned through the hegemonic fields of knowledge of his time as they were undergoing fundamental changes. In Ortiz's own work and in the work of his circle of allies and friends, however, these different fields of knowledge continued to coexist in polarized figures such as Israel Castellanos and Rómulo Lachatañeré, producing tensions among them, to be sure. But given the tenuous informal existence of many of the institutions, journals, and lecture circuits in which they rallied, their shared conviction about the importance of an antiracist science of culture—however defined—was a strong enough bond among them, producing a uniquely rich environment for the study of culture.

2 Paul Rivet's Museum Matrix and the "Drama of Inadaptation"

> Toward the end of the nineteenth century one inquired usually with biologists about the philosophy of humankind and the world; then, one turned toward sociologists, historians and philosophers themselves. But for a few years now anthropology has taken on that role, and it is from anthropology that we await the great syntheses as well as reasons to live and to hope.
>
> —Claude Lévi-Strauss, "La crise moderne de l' anthropologie"

THE NAME of the anthropologist who came to represent the comprehensive study of the Americas more than anyone else in the first decades of the twentieth century is only rarely mentioned in the many cultural histories of Latin America that were published in the time between the wars.[1] Yet, Rivet was a pioneer of Americanism, renowned not only in France but in Latin America as well. Alejo Carpentier called him the second Americanist after Montaigne, recognizing the long tradition of French intellectual and scientific interest in the Americas ("Paul Rivet"). Rivet, indeed, helped shape the study of Latin America in Europe and Latin America in important ways, most notably through his focus on the earliest history of the Americas and on the comparative ethnography of all populations living there.

A prolific writer and editor, Rivet was from 1922 on the general secretary of the Société des Américanistes, in charge of editing the society's prestigious *Journal de la Société des Américanistes,* and he was instrumental in closely associating the Institut d'ethnologie, the first academic research institute in France dedicated to anthropology, with the Musée d'Ethnographie and its later sequel, the Musée de l'Homme. Distinct from U.S. American anthropology, which had become separated entirely from museum practice since Franz Boas, Rivet and his students kept together the research and teaching of anthropology and the museum exhibition of objects, in order to study the past and present of individual cultures as completely as possible (*Paul Rivet. Fondateur* 26). Rivet's focus on what has been called "rescue anthropology," collecting and classifying objects and languages of cultures that were at risk of extinction, ended up reinforcing in Latin Americanist anthropology a focus on material culture, on the earliest indigenous heritage of the Americas, and on long-term history in general. While Rivet and his students were not concerned primarily with race, the "drama of inadaptation" of American indigenous populations, as Rivet's student Alfred Métraux put it, impacted their research, greatly contributing to the humanistic anthropological turn of Rivet and a number of his friends. In this chapter I will discuss Rivet's own anthropological and linguistic contributions and those of his student Alfred Métraux during the time when he worked as an anthropologist in Tucumán, Argentina. I look closely at some of the misunderstandings about race and culture that Rivet experienced while in exile in Colombia and Mexico. I end by discussing the Mexican journal *Cuadernos Americanos* as one instance where Rivet's humanistic anthropology clashed with the antiscientific, literary turn of some writers.

The Museum Matrix: From Learned Societies to the Science of Man

French Americanism has a long history, originating in the middle of the nineteenth century in several learned societies that became interested in the pre-Hispanic past, taking "American" culture to be that of indigenous communities before they had come into contact with the West. The Société des Américanistes, founded in 1895, was one of them.[2]

Rivet's own research was marked early on by his stay in Ecuador, from 1901 to 1906, as a member of the French geodesic mission, from which Rivet returned with a large collection of objects, his Americanist vocation decided. He went on to classify the collection for the Geographic Service of the Military and published articles on his findings. In 1908 he received his first permanent position as an anthropologist at the National Museum of Natural History in Paris. It was a time of political polarization and diversification in anthropology, whereby the Museum of Natural History and the Société des Américanistes became associated more and more with a social and cultural approach to anthropology, and the Société d'anthropologie focused on physical anthropology. Rivet founded a new institute, associated with the Museum of Natural History, the Institut francais d'anthropologie (IFA), to unite "specialists of diverse sciences who together constitute the science of man," as opposed to the exclusive focus on physical anthropology and anthropometrics practiced in the Société d'anthropologie (Laurière, *Paul Rivet* 203). For the first time Lucien Lévy-Bruhl, Marcel Mauss, and Rivet collaborated, along with linguists like Marcel Cohen and Antoine Meillet, working to develop a new inclusive anthropology that included ethnography, sociology, and linguistics, among other fields (Laurière, *Paul Rivet* 202–9).[3]

In France, the academic study of anthropology was separated out from sociology only in the 1920s.[4] Lévy-Bruhl became in 1925 the founding director of the Institut d'ethnologie at the University of Paris, together with Rivet and Mauss as his general secretaries. The institute was the first step in a process of academic consolidation of ethnology, making the institute itself part of the Université de Paris. Financed entirely by the Ministry of Colonies, its goals were not purely academic in principle but also aimed at assisting colonial administrators, as can be seen in the notice announcing the goals of the new institute:

> The Institute of Ethnology, supported exclusively by funds voted on for the budgets of the diverse colonies, will have three goals: to form, in using existing courses or by creating new classes, trained and informed observers for the study of the indigenous; to give to the travelers and colonial citizens, when they return to the metropole, the means and the facilities to enhance their collections and notes; to publish in the form of carefully edited and illustrated monographs the studies of these collaborators. The new institute will be, as is natural, more specifically focused on the French colonies, but this legitimate specialization does not exclude at all the possibility of inquiries and studies that exceed that frame.[5]

Yet, none of the three directors of the Institut d'ethnologie was in a direct relationship with the ministry, and there were few if any connections between the Ecole Coloniale—an older institute where some professors of anthropology had delivered lectures—and the Institut d'ethnologie (Dias 72). Even though it can be argued, as Benoît de l'Estoile has done, that French anthropology in the first half of the twentieth century was generally dedicated to rationalizing colonial domination, the goals of the three directors of the Institut d'ethnologie were certainly more complex than that (de L'Estoile, "Rationalizing Colonial Domination"). It is particularly striking, for example, that it was the Americanist Rivet who became the director of the Musée de l'Homme, since in the twentieth century France had no colonial possessions in the Americas. Rivet, furthermore, was a member of the French socialist party and an elected member of Parliament for the Popular Front in the 1930s. He certainly had no strong colonialist convictions but rather agitated in favor of international collaboration and antiracism.[6]

The institute established a curriculum with a rather traditional layout of classes in physical anthropology, as well as ethnography and linguistics.[7] It was admittedly a discipline that still retained much of the older traditions. As Alice Conklin writes:

> It would be a mistake to see ethnology at this moment as a discipline disentangled from the older traditions and structuring concepts of French museum-based ethnography or nineteenth-century physical anthropology, or the Institut d'Ethnologie faculty as having the professional field to themselves. As the new Institut d'Ethnologie's curriculum revealed, Mauss and Rivet continued to sanction tried-and-true indirect observation methods (questionnaires, collections of artifacts and bones) inherited from their predecessors, alongside the more novel task of preparing students to study social structures in situ in imitation of their foreign colleagues. (97)

What Conklin sees as an unfortunate entanglement between the museum and the research institute can on the other hand also be regarded as a unique feature or even advantage of French anthropology vis-à-vis the Anglophone tradition of an anthropology separated strictly from the museum. The greater integration of the Institut d'ethnologie with the larger matrix of ethnographic museum studies was, in any case, the desired outcome of Rivet's promotion, in 1928, to the position of a professor of anthropology at the Museum of Natural History and the director of the Museum of Ethnography at Trocadero. In the following years, the seat of the Institut d'ethnologie was transferred to Trocadero, along with the learned societies associated with anthropology, among them the Société des Américanistes. At Trocadero, classes were taught, there were museum "laboratories" and exhibition rooms, and there was the library, which quickly grew to over one hundred thousand books. Trocadero was also where Rivet himself had his apartment and where he held an open house every Saturday evening (later Sunday afternoon) (Ronze). Sarah F. Deleporte has called it Rivet's "Trocadero matrix": he made it his mission to unite in one building the museum, the research institute, and the "laboratory," where collections were classified and organized.[8]

Rivet considered the Musée de l'Homme at Trocadero his most important creation. It differed from the old Musée d'Ethnographic in Trocadero in that it now differentiated strictly between the aesthetic value of indigenous objects and their scientific interest. Contrary to the chaotic presentation of objects in the old Trocadero museum, the Musée de l'Homme followed a Modernist aesthetic of light, straight lines and steel vitrines that was meant to bring alive the objects almost as if they were Durkheimian "social facts" (de L'Estoile, *Le goût des autres* 183). As Rivet wrote, "It is important to know all aspects, or at least the average outlook of a civilization, not the exceptional aspect that it exhibits among the privileged classes."[9]

While remaining focused on "primitive" or illiterate cultures, this new conception of anthropology placed an emphasis on popular culture and folklore in general, with the Musée de l'Homme accompanied, in a second wing of the Palais de Chaillot at Trocadero, by the Musée des Arts et Traditions Populaires, focused on rural France and its traditional culture. Thanks to this comparative approach to anthropology, young anthropologists were sent to unknown corners of France and around the world to collect objects that would fit into and complete the existing collections, the goal being eventually to represent the entire world in the space of a museum. And indeed, when it opened in 1938, the museum offered a dazzling display of objects for audiences of all kinds. As Carpentier writes, for him and his artist friends, Rivet gave scientific depth to their fascination with America ("Paul Rivet" 54). To Georges Bataille it was the world turned into a spectacle, looking at itself through the lens of a museum.

Rivet's ambition for the Musée de l'Homme was to turn it into an institute of mass education where visitors could not only learn about foreign cultures but also begin to value their own popular culture. Rivet opened the museum in the evening, so that working-class people could visit. He also initiated an "Association populaire des amis des musées," which published between 1937 and 1940 a promotional bulletin, *Le Musée Vivant* (The living museum), that included announcements of educational activities, brief essays, and reports. For the anthropologist Jacques Soustelle, who wrote for the opening issue, it was indeed important in France and in its overseas territories to create local museums where communities could identify with their history and popular culture: "The regional populations of continental France and those from overseas must have at their disposal local museums, open air museums in the regions and the colonies where they will see their history and popular art come to life in concrete expositions, making them understand at the same time what connects them to the entire country and what makes them distinct."[10] For the writer and anthropologist Michel Leiris, the Musée de l'Homme was for that reason at the foundation of a "new humanism" whose arrival every independent spirit could only desire.

French Science, According to Rivet

Rivet expressed his humanist vision of anthropology in several instances, most comprehensively in the *Encyclopédie Française,* edited by Annales historian Lucien Febvre, volume 12 of which, *L'espèce humaine* (1936; The human species), had been edited by Rivet. The introduction to this volume summarized Rivet's approach to anthropology as a human science (not a natural science or a separate social science), and it seems to have been widely read in Latin America.[11] Ethnology, used in French as a term standing for the more common English *anthropology*, for Rivet was the most comprehensive and important of all branches of the sciences, and he carefully built it as a science that included physical anthropology, among several other branches, as suggested by Armand de Quatrefages, the first professor of anthropology (Rivet, *L'espèce humaine* 7.06–6).[12] To Rivet, ethnography, that is, the description of a culture on the basis of texts and other material artifacts, could only be comparative, because there was no use in describing and inventorying collections if they were not considered in the larger context of their neighboring cultures (7.08–10). Convinced that cultures grew by way of diffusion and contact with other cultures, Rivet defined them not as autonomous entities, but by way of traits that converged or diverged from neighboring cultures. He was interested in establishing travel routes and genealogies for one culture in relation to another. The "diffusion" of an instrument such as the boomerang, for example, was deeply interesting to Rivet, who was rearticulating the idea of a "culture area," first formulated by Fritz Graebner in Germany and by Clark Wissler and Alfred Kroeber in the United States, only slightly changing his focus to what he called "centers of irradiation" and their cultural production and relative chronology. History was thus mapped out and reconstructed according to the material fragments found and their distribution in physical space. For Rivet, the object of ethnology was ultimately to distinguish between the universal laws of humanity and the achievements of individual culture areas (7.08–15). The task of the anthropologist (or ethnologist, in Rivet's words) was demanding, in that she or he had to combine, as in a jigsaw puzzle, all existing fragments of the material culture, as well as the text documents, if existing, of a given geographic space, comparing them to other contiguous areas and delimiting distinct cultures in this way. It was an approach common to early-twentieth-century anthropologists, with only Franz Boas taking his distance from the diffusionist comparative study of cultures, finding it in the end too cumbersome and preferring to focus on the study of individual cultures instead.[13]

While his diffusionism represented broadly accepted views of the field, Rivet's emphasis on anthropology as a historical discipline distinguished him from his colleagues in other countries. This can be seen in the two-volume reedition of *La science française* (1938; French science), a work that had been published first in 1915 on the occasion of the Universal Exhibition in San Francisco. One of the important changes of this second edition was that the section "Prehistory" now received additional chapters on ethnology, "anthropology" (Fr. physical anthropology), and "Americanism and France," with Rivet authoring the article on ethnology. Ethnology and physical anthropology were now recognized as independent areas of research next to sociology, the only science of the three represented in the first edition, with a chapter authored by Durkheim. There are, however, some tensions evident in the new articles written for the volume. The section "Americanism and France," the field in which Rivet had been most active and most published, was given to Raoul d'Harcourt, a Peruvianist who wrote an article with clearly nationalist undertones, focusing entirely on France's attempts to extend its colonial empire to the Americas and listing early explorers, French Caribbean pirates, and French possessions in Canada and Louisiana as examples of French Americanism. Whereas Rivet had in his own work done everything to represent French Americanism as an idealist, purely scientific endeavor, this article made clear the cultural politics motivating other researchers like d'Harcourt.[14]

Rivet's "ethnology" was an effort to create a modern science of humankind, combining physical and cultural anthropology, sociology, and linguistics. As such, it attracted a number of artists and intellectuals interested in studying culture sometimes from an avant-garde point of view and achieving what James Clifford has called "ethnographic surrealism."[15] It was this type of humanist, engaged anthropology that also led the communist Haitian writer Jacques Roumain to come study with Rivet. Rivet, however, was increasingly opposed by conservative anthropologists grouped under the leadership of Louis Marin at the Ecole d'Anthropologie—among them the Swiss anthropologist and later Vichy collaborator George Montandon.[16] It was this latter branch of anthropology, focused on the distinction between pure and mixed races in France and elsewhere, to which Haitian anthropologists Lorimer Denis and François Duvalier were drawn.

The Origins of American Man: Anthropology as History and Human Science

In contrast to the interest cultivated by Latin American writers in indigenous cultures immediately before the conquest and in the Hispanic colonial past, Rivet went even further back, to the earliest centers of Amerindian civilization from which languages and cultures had originated. While Latin American writers sought to reconstruct national origins and contemporary Latin America's cultural specificity, Rivet sought for many years to investigate how the population of the Americas had arrived and from where they had come.

Interestingly, Rivet's anthropological diffusionism bore more than one affinity with the linguistic theory of the *Ursprache,* which had been developed by Indo-European linguists in the nineteenth century. Disillusioned with the uncertain results of the study of physical races, Rivet became persuaded that human societies originated in and then spread from relatively few centers, just like Indo-European languages had come from Sanskrit and then divided into linguistic branches and subbranches, among them the Romance, the Slavic, and the Germanic language families. Rivet, as Laurière points out, can be blamed in this regard for having overextended, making implausible inferences from linguistics to culture. Yet his work resulted in valuable studies of individual language groups, like his *Bibliographie des langues aymará et Kičua* (1951; Bibliography of the Aymara and Kičua languages), where Rivet displayed a full bibliography of books and manuscripts using the Aymara and Quechua languages, demonstrating the resilience and long survival of these ancient languages of the Inca Empire (Laurière, *Paul Rivet* 211–49). It was his hope, he wrote in the introduction to the *Bibliographie,* that the study of indigenous American languages would produce rising interest in the Americas at large, as had happened before with the study of other non-European cultures like Africa and Oceania (Rivet and Créqui-Montfort xviii). As Laurière tells it, it was indeed his publications in Amerindian linguistics that gave Rivet international recognition, even though today the analogies suggested by Rivet between language families and culture areas have been largely disproven.[17]

As a result of his scouring of historical sources for Amerindian vocabulary, Rivet published several unknown and previously unpublished manuscripts and encouraged his students to pay attention to colonial document sources. It was in this area of research into colonial history that he most closely coincided with Latin American scientists like Ortiz and

Freyre, who had begun to publish series of little-known manuscripts and book editions.

The most important initiative to this effect was the series "Travaux et mémoires de l'Institut d'ethnologie" (TMIE), edited at the Institut d'ethnologie, in which, out of a total of forty-seven volumes published between 1926 and 1946, seven were written about Latin American topics. They were Louis Baudin's *L'empire socialiste des Inkas* (1928; The Inca socialist empire), an ambitious argument comparing the Inca Empire to modern socialism, relying entirely on readings of colonial texts by the Inca Garcilaso de la Vega and Pedro Cieza de León, and Nicolao de Albenino's *Verdadera relación delo sussedido en los Reynos e provincias del Peru . . .* (1930; A true account of what happened in the kingdoms and provinces of Peru), a text written in 1549. The latter was a facsimile edition of a little-known document about the death of Gonzalo Pizarro in Peru. Robert Ricard's *La conquête spirituelle du Mexique* (1933; The spiritual conquest of Mexico), another landmark study, analyzed the strategies employed by the Catholic Church and monastic orders in colonial Mexico to convert the indigenous populations of Mexico. Ricard, like Baudin, made good use of written colonial documents and emphasized the necessity to bring together the study of pre-Hispanic civilizations, colonial history, and the present time (Ricard xiv). Jacques Soustelle's book *La famille Otomi-Pame du Mexique central* (1937; The Otomi-Pame family in central Mexico), a linguistic study of the Otomi-Pame indigenous peoples living in Mexico, argued that the Otomi-Pame had been in contact with western civilization for a long time but that their language had remained untouched by western influence (v). Rivet's study *La métallurgie en Amérique précolombienne* (1946; The metal-working industry in Pre-Columbian America) in turn was a study of the metallic objects in the collection of the Musée de l'Homme. By far the most influential publication edited by Rivet for the TMIE proved to be the facsimile edition of Felipe Guaman Poma de Ayala's 1617 chronicle *Nueva corónica y buen gobierno. (Codex péruvien illustré)* (1936; *The First Chronicle and Good Government,* 2009). This manuscript, which had been hidden away in the archives of the Danish Royal Library, had been discovered by the German scholar Richard Pietschmann in 1908. It was a lavishly illustrated document of 1,189 pages, and even though it was mainly written in Spanish, it was full of terms taken from the Quechua and Aru dialects that Guaman Poma knew. Having received scholarly attention only from the 1970s on, Guaman Poma's book has since become one of the most studied documents of early indigenous expression from the Andes.[18]

Rivet shared with the so-called Annales school of history the desire for writing a *long durée* history that comprised not only specific events and heroes but a more complete overview of the workings of history as such.[19] This entailed for both his ethnological school and the Annales school a sustained interdisciplinary effort, whereby Rivet included in his anthropology fields such as archaeology, linguistics, physical anthropology, and sociology; similarly, Marc Bloch's "histoire" studied the connections among religion, law, and geography and "atmospheric" changes alongside concrete political events (M. Bloch 154–55).[20] Both had given up a teleological view of evolutionary history, focusing instead on everyday life in its relation to contemporary life (M. Bloch 23–39). Both studied the reconstruction of a milieu, a way of living, and a technique instead of an outstanding event or object.[21] Like Rivet, Marc Bloch defined the object of history as people: "Long ago, indeed, our great forebears, such as Michelet or Fustel de Coulanges, taught us to recognize that the object of history is, by nature, man. Let us say rather, men. Far more than the singular, favoring abstraction, the plural which is the grammatical form of relativity is fitting for the science of change" (21–22). Seen from this perspective, history and anthropology were indeed two complementary sciences, where history is concerned with changes in human society and anthropology with the continuity of humankind.

When looking at Rivet's idea about anthropology as a human science, it is instructive to compare his views with one of Boas's first publications, "The Study of Geography" (1887), where Boas distinguished between the methods employed in the natural sciences and those employed in the study of geography. In the natural or "physical" sciences, he argued, the single fact was less important than the general law that governed it. For the scientist of Alexander von Humboldt's type, on the other hand, every phenomenon was worthy of being studied for its own sake. For Boas these two approaches formed two branches of science. That of the natural sciences was aesthetic in its nature, inspired by the desire to systematically arrange and clarify the observed phenomena. The other branch—the human sciences—belonged to an "affective impulse" in humankind, as it derived its interest from the truth of that phenomenon, not from the connections established by the scientist between one fact and another (Boas, "Study of Geography" 12–13). The natural scientist resolved the object into its elements and analyzed them separately, whereas the human scientist had much in common with the arts, because he focused on the object in its relation with the observer (14–15). The student of culture, Boas argued, had to analyze cultures across time and space, adopting the methods of the human sciences.

Rivet and Boas then were envisioning the human sciences with anthropology and history as central fields of inquiry. Philology as the science of texts and linguistics as the science of language were instrumental but by no means irreplaceable in their pursuits. The function that philology and linguistics had for them, however, was slightly different. Whereas Boas focused on applied knowledge, on the linguistic competence of his students, on fieldwork and "philological" precision in recording oral testimonies of North American natives, Rivet was impacted by the idea of linguistic families living in clearly demarcated cultural areas. Rivet also focused more on existing written archives in Latin America, being a comparatist at heart and encyclopedic in his ambition. Similar to Ortiz, he continued to emphasize the study of textual documents and material objects in Latin America.

Alfred Métraux's Drama of Inadaptation

The students of Rivet who went to Latin America to do fieldwork and in some cases found institutions similar to Rivet's museum matrix were many.[22] This was partly a consequence of Rivet's travels and of the exchange programs and sister institutions he created,[23] including an exchange program with Mexico and the Institut français des hautes etudes brésiliennes in Brazil.[24] While the institutional and professional network cast by Rivet and his students in Latin America was often ephemeral, the experience of living in Latin America for a prolonged time considerably impacted the method and outlook of individual anthropologists and their acquaintances and helped them form new ideas about culture and acculturation. A case in point is Alfred Métraux.

One of the first advisees of Rivet to do work in Latin America, Métraux, of Swiss origin but partly raised in Argentina, was hired after defending his dissertation under Rivet by Juan B. Terán from the University of Tucumán (Argentina) to come there and build a museum and an institute of ethnology, from 1928 to 1936. This he did, with some assistance from France, it seems, also founding a journal, the *Revista del Instituto de Etnología* of the National University of Tucumán. While in Tucumán, in order to fill his museum, Métraux began to study the indigenous populations of the Gran Chaco area, a semiarid plain to the north of Tucumán where various indigenous populations lived. But he soon found the method of collecting objects for the purpose only of classifying and exhibiting them unsatisfactory. On March 10, 1929, he wrote to Rivet from Cuevo (Gran Chaco), expressing his regret about not interacting more with people in the Chaco: "I regret that the imperial necessity to collect the greatest number possible of objects hinders me from making longer stays with the Indians, and prevents me from doing intensive ethnography, but I am tormented by the memory of my empty exhibition room, which I have to fill as quickly as possible and as best I can. I hope that that will gain me the right to live one day with my friends in the Chaco."[25] Métraux's dilemma was that while, as a human being, he empathized with the people he met during his trips—the Argentinian Chaco is still today one of the poorest provinces in the country—as the director of the Ethnology Museum in Tucumán, he wanted to build his museum. Métraux at this point was entirely focused on preserving in the museum the objects of indigenous cultures that were about to disappear and already essentially belonged to the past. His method of collecting and presenting objects, he wrote, using an unfortunate metaphor, was able to offer the "skeleton" of a past culture, allowing museum visitors to understand its present uniqueness ("El museo del indio sudamericano en Gotemburgo"). Métraux built his collection in Tucumán relatively quickly, on the side assisting Rivet's research in France, communicating to him the vocabulary of indigenous languages and sending him, through a visitor, a small collection of objects.[26] Rivet in turn reported in the *Journal de la Société des Américanistes* that several indigenous languages had already been "rescued" (in: Monnier 66–67). After four years in Tucumán, Métraux concluded, in an article published in the newspaper *La Nación* (Buenos Aires), that his institute was a success ("El Instituto de etnología de la Universidad de Tucumán").[27]

The *Revista del Instituto de Etnología,* too, garnered a certain success, drawing foreign collaborators, among them in 1932 Rivet himself and several professors from the University of Geneva, and several articles by contributors from the museum in Goteborg. The third and last volume under Métraux's editorship (1933) contained only four articles, however, all of them by Métraux, with a focus on linguistics and the presentation of the results of field trips.

Yet, while Métraux accomplished everything that he had been expected to do, from the point of view of Rivet's outreach and network, it is striking that he built very few local connections with Argentinian anthropologists. Only one article by the Argentine anthropologist Enrique Palavecino was published in his journal, and after Métraux's departure, the institute as well as the journal changed names and became, respectively, the Instituto de Antropología and the *Revista del Instituto de Antropología*, adopting the more customary American term *anthropology* over the French *ethnology*. The new series begun by the Instituto de Antropología focused on anthropometric studies under its director, Radamés Altieri. While Métraux was a candidate for a position at the Museo de La Plata, this prospect never became concrete. There are several possible reasons for his rejection by local anthropologists.

One might have been Métraux's principled defense of the Chaco indigenous population, joining a committee proposing reservations for them, but without success. Already Roberto Lehmann-Nitsche, the German-born director of the Museo de La Plata until 1930 and a noted anthropologist and folklorist, had criticized the treatment of the indigenous population but found little interest in their present plight among his anthropologist colleagues. As Carolyne Ryan Larson discusses, the ideology of anthropologists at the Buenos Aires Museo Etnográfico, for example, emphasized a national narrative of indigenous heritage belonging to ancient high cultures, all the while forging a discourse of Argentine creole identity as distinct from modern mass immigration. The poverty and simple life of Chaco indigenous peoples did not fit this model. For Santiago Bilbao, part of the problem was also the discrepancy between Métraux's relatively good working conditions and external funding in Tucumán, allowing him to publish the *Revista del Instituto de Etnología* in French, oriented toward European anthropologists, and the much lower funding of museum directors and anthropologists in Argentina's metropolitan centers.[28] Métraux ended up publishing his research on the Chaco in English, after having accepted employment in the United States, where his collections of myths from the Chaco found great interest.[29]

Métraux was quite well liked, however, by Victoria Ocampo, the editor of the most important cultural magazine in Argentina, *SUR*. As Métraux describes it, she had an unusually keen interest in anthropology, when it was not yet well respected, and made it part of her vision of Argentine and, more generally, American culture ("Victoria Ocampo y la etnología"). In publishing in *SUR* two reports by Métraux from the Chaco, Ocampo offered him a forum of great visibility in the Latin American intellectual world, which he used to draw a bleak picture of Argentine indigenous history. In these two essays, Métraux proceeded to tell the stories of three indigenous groups, following a basic plot of rising and decaying civilizations. In his "Un mundo perdido. La tribu de los Chipayas de Carangas" (A lost world: The tribe of the Chipayas of Carangas) he evoked the Chipaya indigenous group as a people that at one point had come from the Amazon River and become part of the rural class of the Inca Empire but had long since been defeated by the Aymara and never recovered their old strength ("Un mundo perdido"). The mood of this story was one of tragic failure and nostalgia for a lost world. In his second essay for *SUR,* "El universo y la naturaleza a través de las representaciones míticas de dos tribus salvajes de la Argentina" (The universe and nature as seen in the mythical representations of the savage tribes of Argentina), Métraux yet again emphasized the primitiveness of the indigenous groups living in Argentina and gave an account of the creation mythologies of two groups living in the Chaco, as they had been told to him. While he wished to convey the cultural richness of a society whose survival was at risk, he also spoke of its present-time cultural value as broadly human. As he wrote, referring to anthropology: "This science has imposed itself in all the domains that are humanely interesting, and thanks to the widening of our artistic sensibility, it has been incorporated into the culture of every civilized man. There is, however, a poorly known and little explored region of which we can expect new enrichments, for science as well as for literature. This unexplored material is that of primitive representations. I am referring to the world of ideas that civilized people have of the universe."[30] As Métraux argued, indigenous cosmologies, rather than being documents of cultural difference, are part of a universal human patrimony. Beyond anthropology, Métraux opened to Ocampo and her readers and friends a new world, that of the indigenous, rural populations, which they hadn't known before; it was those readers who came to appreciate his work in its humanistic dimension.[31]

His writings for *SUR* then represent a transition in Métraux's work, from a purely historical and documentarian interest in indigenous cultures to their humanity and present-time concerns. This can also be seen in the review he wrote for *SUR* in 1939 of the Spanish translation of Ruth Benedict's book *Patterns of Culture,* where Métraux most explicitly discussed the relevance of anthropology for the present time. Benedict, a student of Franz Boas, had undertaken a field study of three different cultures—the Pueblos of New Mexico, the Dobus of New Guinea, and the Kwakiutl of the American Northwest—and proposed in her book a rethinking of the notion of culture itself. For Benedict, anthropology as a science had to overcome the distinction between "civilized" and "primitive" and instead study the individual themes or preoccupations of individual cultures. Benedict argued that anthropologists had focused for too long on the analysis of culture traits; they should instead consider cultures as articulated wholes or patterns (48). Métraux, in his review, agreed with Benedict but preferred a more malleable image when speaking of culture, proposing that rather than "patterns" of culture, their "plasticity" was even more characteristic ("El problema de la civilización" 10). In focusing on cultural change rather than on cultural patterns, Métraux alluded to the debate on cultural contact initiated by Herskovits, Ortiz, and Freyre, but he also remained true to his mentor Rivet's emphasis on history in anthropological research. While Benedict emphasized individual themes particular to every society, like, for example, technology, Métraux claimed that no individual in any given society was entirely determined by his or her circumstances. Instead, "indadaptation" was a major problem of the individual in modern society:

> The drama of inadaptation presents itself incessantly to us. Our society is one of the most changeable ones that has ever existed. Modalities and attitudes are transformed rapidly and provoke daily conflicts between those who are delayed and those who are advanced in time. In spite of this uninterrupted movement we obstinately consider the trend of the moment as eternal and necessary to life itself. Our civilization has not yet incorporated the notion of change into the number of its strong ideas, and since it denies the evidence it insists on accumulating human suffering that is perfectly useless.[32]

To Métraux then the drama of indigenous peoples was to some degree the drama of modern society, and his pessimistic view of the Chaco indigenous population was less a product of his idealization of a "primitive" society than it was part of his reflection on both cultural patterns and change. Benedict in contrast focused less on problems of adaptation than on the question of value judgments of cultures.

Surprisingly, Métraux's Argentinian stay became much more than the exploration of yet another unknown indigenous culture mapped out for museum purposes. It was an introduction to broadly humanitarian concerns about indigenous groups and a first reflection on the effects of culture contacts between indigenous and modern cultures. Both Métraux and Benedict also became politically active against scientific racism in the 1940s. During World War II Benedict published two books refuting racism, *Race: Science and Politics* (1940; *Raza: ciencia y política,* 1941) and, together with Gene Weltfish, the pamphlet *The Races of Mankind,* working between 1943 and 1945 for the American Office of War Information. Métraux, after research stays on the Easter Islands, in the United States, and in Haiti, began to work for the United Nations Educational, Scientific and Cultural Organization (UNESCO) at the end of World War II, from 1947 on as a permanent member of its Social Sciences Department.

As such he participated in the Hylean Amazon project, designed to protect the indigenous populations and the natural rain forest of the Amazon area, in a study of poverty in Haiti's Marbial Valley, and on UNESCO's committee on race relations.

Rivet's Exile and the Cultural Politics of *France Libre*

In the 1930s and 1940s, as more European scientists and writers arrived in Latin America, the networks between European and Latin American anthropologists and writers became more entangled. Rivet's own contact with and later exile in Colombia is a good case in point for how such impulses produced often complicated results.

Rivet's museum matrix was being emulated in more than one Latin American country by the time he had to flee occupied France in 1941. He had been in contact in particular with President Eduardo Santos of Colombia since 1938, recommending the creation of an institute and museum of ethnology able to preserve Colombia's indigenous heritage and establishing, from 1939 on, a student exchange program with Colombia similar to the one in Mexico, with the archaeologist Gregorio Hernández de Alba coming from Colombia to study for two years in Paris and Henri Lehmann traveling to Bogotá (Laurière 569–72). In 1941, when a resistance network was discovered at the Musée de l'Homme, and Rivet had to leave France overnight, he accepted Santos's invitation to live and work in Colombia for several years. There, together with Hernández de Alba, he founded the Instituto Nacional de Etnología (INE), whose director and fundraiser he was for several years and where he taught, along with other exiled European anthropologists, such as Justus Wolfram Schottelius, Gerardo Reichel-Dolmatoff, Pablo Vila, Henri Lehmann, and José de Recasens. Several of these exiles stayed on after the war, with the Spanish architect and anthropologist José de Recasens directing the INE after Rivet's departure for Mexico in 1943 and seeing to the founding of other regional institutes in Colombia. Gerardo Reichel-Dolmatoff, a German exile, also remained in Colombia, where he established a periodization of indigenous cultures; today he is recognized as one of the founders of Colombian anthropology, albeit a particularly problematic one, next to Hernández de Alba, Rivet, and Recasens.[33] Rivet's methods helped to balance Colombian anthropology between what Clara Isabel Botero calls a "nationalist Colombian tendency" toward archaeology and a French or European emphasis on ethnology, that is, the study of distinct indigenous groups and their history (286). His influence on the institutionalization of anthropology in Colombia was considerable, as the work of his disciples continued to place a prime value on a four-branch anthropology (physical, cultural, archaeological, and linguistic), on rigorous research methods, and on publication (Botero). Rivet also continued his scientific explorations in Colombia, heading to the southern provinces with a team of researchers. It was during his tenure that researchers compiled the important archaeological collections and linguistic data that Colombia holds still today and that were published in the institute's own journal, the *Revista del Instituto Etnológico Nacional.* According to Carlos Uribe, these collections remain obligatory reference points today, with very little added to them later on (286).

However, similar to the discrepancy Métraux had perceived in Argentina between the collecting of objects and the study of living indigenous populations, Rivet's method had its limitations and was not universally acclaimed in Colombia. Fairly soon after its opening, the Instituto Nacional de Etnología was criticized for not being sufficiently involved with the cause of the living indigenous populations. In this dispute, there were certainly also personal animosities and rivalries at play. It was Gregorio Hernández de Alba, who had become estranged from Rivet and resigned from his post at the INE, who in 1941 founded the Instituto Indigenista, which adopted a hostile attitude toward the INE. In response, Rivet defined his position toward *indigenismo*, not arguing for or against the attempt to integrate or isolate indigenous communities but instead claiming that the study of the past helped researchers understand and better respect indigenous contributions to contemporary society:

> What is not a dream, in turn, is to harmonize in every American milieu the aspirations of the two races or contemporary peoples, and to profit from their specific qualities to the advantage of all. But, some will say, what can we expect from the indigenous race? The archaeologist will answer them that it should not be judged only from its current state but also from what it was able to realize by its own efforts, before the Conquest paralyzed it momentarily. The past of a people corresponds to its possibilities in the future. For that reason it is good to remember who the American Indian was and what their contribution to the progress of humanity was.[34]

Despite Rivet's goodwill, however, such a speech let his interlocutors know that he was less interested in studying contemporary indigenous peoples, focusing instead on what could be found out about their life before the Spanish conquest. Rivet's unfortunate separation of the indigenous past from the present time also meant that he was not sought out by intellectuals like Raúl Haya de la Torre, the Peruvian leader of the

Aprista movement, who, inspired by the ideas of Martí, Rodó, and José Vasconcelos, spoke of Indoamérica as the common culture to which all Americans belonged. Rivet, all the while intending to give Colombians reason to be proud of indigenous achievements, made it difficult to apply anthropological knowledge and integrate it with contemporary lives.

Rivet's own political call came when, after two years in Colombia, he went to live in Mexico City (1943–44), to work for Charles de Gaulle's *France Libre,* promoting de Gaulle's ideas through a number of initiatives (*Paul Rivet. Fondateur du Musée de l'Homme* 32). He formally became de Gaulle's cultural attaché for Latin America and founded, with the support of a number of French refugees, the Instituto Francés de América Latina (IFAL) as an institute both serving research purposes and promoting French culture abroad, through conferences, a movie program, and in the journal *Tierras Latinas/Terres Latines,* which appeared for several years after the war. Behind the institute was the attempt to defend the ideas of humanism and democracy, dear to those who had left totalitarian states and a Europe at war (Bataillon 29). Under the supervision of Rivet, a French bookstore, the Librairie Française, was opened. Rivet even became the coeditor, with Evelyne Hassin, of a French textbook, *Anthologie de la littérature française* (1944; Anthology of French literature).

His stay in Mexico also led Rivet to improvise thoughts on the values that united Latin American cultures with "Latin" European nations like Spain and France. In a lecture delivered to the Centro republicano español in 1944, "Socialismo y unidad latina," Rivet argued that racial and linguistic ties, as well as common habits, were the basis of European "Latin unity," to which Latin America could be easily joined:

> We have to establish zones of coincidence within which no country will lose the attributes of its sovereignty. Between the countries that I just mentioned there exists precisely that coincidence marked by geographic proximity, the racial origin, the linguistic root, and the similarity of customs and habits. To that Latin union we may add then the brother peoples of Latin America, taking advantage of the excellent trampoline that Western Africa offers us. We also find in Latin America all the same elements that form such a close and evident tie between the European Latin peoples.[35]

Rivet's Eurocentric though avowedly humanistic vision of a pan-Latin unity was also to dominate the journal *Tierras Latinas/Terres Latines,* edited by IFAL between 1945 and 1948—Rivet himself returned to France after its liberation in 1944. The publication featured a host of exiled and local scientists and writers, among them Henri Lehman, Ramón Xirau, Gabriela Mistral, Jean Guehenno, poems by Paul Eluard, Robert Desnos, Max Jacob, Vicente Huidobro, Miguel Angel Asturias, Francis de Miomandre, Alfonso Reyes, Carlos Pellicer, Bosch Gimpera, Darius Milhaud, Francois Chevalier, Ivan Goll, and Roger Caillois.

Their shared spirit of solidarity quickly waned with the end of the war and the return of most exiles to France. In its fifth issue, the new editorial team under Jean Camp announced optimistically that it wanted to unsettle the perception that Europe and particularly France and Spain were defeated or that Latin America had to offer only a weak imitation of Europe, seeking to redefine the relationship between Latin America and Europe as one where the former "master and his pupils" mutually learned from each other: "Cultivons nos ressemblances et nos différences s'épanouiront comme de grandes fleurs d'or" (Let us cultivate our resemblances, and our differences will blossom like big golden flowers) (Camp)." Issue number 6 gave further precision to the ambitions of the editors: the journal aimed at becoming "une grande Revue internationale," with editions in Europe and South America, the central organ of expression for all Latin peoples, independent of their races, and including "Aztecs, Mayans or Incas, Gallics, Romans or Greeks" (Escarpit). Before this could happen, however, the French government cut its funding drastically, and despite a brief partnership with the Mexican journal *Cuadernos Americanos,* the journal ceased to exist upon Jean Camp's return to France in 1948.

Rivet's own journey from France to Colombia and Mexico, and from Americanist anthropology to foreign cultural politics, culminated back in France with his involvement with UNESCO, where he became part of the French delegation. French cultural politics in Latin America and anthropology's involvement in it, however, came to a definitive end with the close of World War II and the onset of the Cold War.

A New Humanism: *Cuadernos Americanos*

Culture as an anthropological notion, and at the same time as practiced humanism and another term for civilization, became more and more of a central notion for Latin American intellectuals eager to dismiss older notions of race during and after World War II. The most prominent cultural journal to be founded during the war years in Latin America was *Cuadernos Americanos,* which began its run in 1942 in Mexico City, continuing until today. The concept of culture was here mobilized again with the participation of exiles; however, the tradition on which it relied was mostly Hispanic, not French. By promoting an organic notion of culture that included history, science, literature, and the arts and that was vaguely inspired by Oswald Spengler's philosophy of history, *Cuadernos Americanos* continued the tradition of Hispanic thought begun by José Ortega y Gasset in the *Revista de Occidente. Cuadernos Americanos* presented itself as a "work of friendship" and a purely spiritual and idealistic enterprise. Founded by the economist Jesús Silva Herzog, the poet Bernardo Ortiz de Montellano, and the exiled Spanish writers Leon Felipe and Juan Larrea, its central preoccupation was a humanism that included science as only one among several fields of thought, next to literature and the arts.

Silva Herzog, in his opening article "Lo humano, problema esencial," drew a pessimistic portrait of world history and concluded that the progress of history and capitalism had reached its limit. Partly, in his view, this was due to the separation between the spheres of science and art, which had let the broader concerns of humankind sink into oblivion: "Let them not speak to us of science for science's sake or of art for art's sake, but of art and science in the service of mankind. Let them not speak of progress, of culture, or of civilization while holding off from concrete interest in the human species."[36] Silva Herzog thought of humankind as plural, but unlike Boas, he defined it not as a plurality of cultures, but as a plurality of interests that had to be integrated in a holistic enterprise dedicated to the aspects shared by every society:

> When speaking of mankind, we think in plural and don't refer to the economic, metaphysical, or biological mankind, because these are merely abstractions; we refer to man in all his various aspects and multiple contents, to man in his total integrity. And to the well-being, the happiness, and the superior destinies of this complex and contradictory human being, all creative activity has to be subordinated: the economic structure, the political and social systems, scientific investigation, and the work of art. We have to seek out in a new humanism the materials to build the world of tomorrow.[37]

This new humanism also showed through in several essays in *Cuadernos Americanos* by writers of the Hispanic tradition of philology. Alfonso Reyes's essay "América y los *Cuadernos Americanos,*" for example, made the point that America had received a special call to reflect on humankind in an international and regional context. Reyes understood "culture" in its general, nonscientific sense, as the preservation and advancement of "la religión, la filosofía, la ciencia, la ética, la política, la urbanidad, la cortesía, la poesía, la música, las artes, las industrias y los oficios" (8). America, in turn, since it was made up of multiple ethnicities and cultures—Reyes called them the "international," the "Iberian," and the "indigenous context"—was the space of a utopian world, in stark contrast to Europe's destroyed "old" world. In yet another essay, "Posición de América," Reyes dismissed concepts of race and language outright, claiming that "para América no hay más raza que la raza humana." Reyes and Herzog created in this way a notion of Hispanic culture that was distanced from strictly scientific definitions of culture or race, as well as from the reactionary notion of Hispanidad that by then was beginning to be promoted by Franco's regime in Spain and in the Americas through the Instituto de Cultura Hispánica.[38] This culturalist position also differed from Waldo Frank's more politically engaged hemispheric Americanism, expressed in a piece likewise published in *Cuadernos Americanos,* which emphasized the need for a common military and economic defense of the "continuity of Western civilization" (Frank 29).

Anthropology, and in particular Rivet's anthropology, played a small but significant role in *Cuadernos Americanos.* Of the journal's four sections, one, "Presencia del pasado," was almost entirely dedicated to history, archaeology, and anthropology, whereas the others were concerned with contemporary issues and international relations ("Nuestro tiempo"), philosophy and science ("Aventura del pensamiento"), and literature and the arts ("Dimensión imaginaria"). This was, in the view of Ana González Neira, highly unusual for a Mexican cultural journal, yet it seemed to enhance the larger regional interest of the journal (González Neira 22).

Rivet's principal work of anthropological scholarship, *Los orígenes del hombre americano* (1943, The origins of American mankind), published by *Cuadernos Americanos*'s publishing house, received two reviews in the journal.[39] Rivet had by then worked for decades on the question of the origins of the peoples living in the American hemisphere, and the book presented a synthesis of the research he had pursued over numerous journeys.[40] To reconstruct the origins of the societies living in the Americas was a central question at the time for anthropologists and more broadly for humanists, as it entailed not only the question of the periodization of American cultures in relation to other world cultures—a question that had preoccupied Oswald Spengler as well—but also the question of whether or not the American hemisphere was historically isolated in comparison to other world cultures.[41] The argument Rivet ended up putting forward in 1943 was not conclusive and was somewhat inflected by

Rivet's Americanist ethos. As Rivet pointed out in his historical introduction and then again in his concluding remarks, there was no dividing line between the "old" world and the "new"; in fact, the Americas had a history reaching back just as far as Europe's and Asia's. Rivet, rejecting previous European theories about prehistoric connections between the classic civilizations of Egypt and Greece and the Americas, argued that there had been multiple contacts among Melanesian, Polynesian, Asian, and American societies even before the arrival of Normans on American soil. The Americas, in attracting migrations from the other peoples of the Pacific, had turned into a repository of humanity:

> Definitely, the Pacific should not appear to us anymore as an immense empty expanse, an impassible barrier between the Old and the New World. Human migrations have crossed it, at the cost of innumerable efforts and dramas, to arrive in America and colonize it; there were then daring traders who criss-crossed it more or less regularly until the period of the discovery, and these crossings certainly went in both directions. Long before the ships of the great European discoverers, the surprising Melanesian and Polynesian canoes, and perhaps also the primitive Peruvian rafts, had cut through this immense marine desert. An emotional anonymous epic preceded the great historical epic. It is the entire history of Humanity.[42]

In studying American indigenous populations, Rivet claimed, one came to shift one's perspective away from Europe toward America's position between the Atlantic and the Pacific. This could only produce a greater sense of solidarity among peoples of all colors and origins: "The sense of the great human solidarity has to be exalted and fortified today more than ever. Every man has to understand and know that in all latitudes and longitudes, other beings, brothers no matter what their skin color or the shape of their hair, have contributed to make life sweeter and easier."[43] Rivet argued less on the basis of intellectual history and philosophy, and more on the basis of material cultural artifacts. The individual chapters of his book were dry for the nonspecialist, focusing on American geology; the first traces of Eskimo populations; and anthropological and linguistic "proofs" of the presence of Australians, Melanesians, Polynesians, and Normans in the Americas, consisting of bone fragments, tools, statues, and word comparisons.

The book had been published under difficult circumstances: it had been finished in 1940, but Rivet, unable to publish it because of the German occupation of France, had it translated into Spanish and published in Mexico. Even though he claimed to have made updates to it between

1940 and 1943, the book omitted a number of studies from the United States, as Robert Wauchope pointed out, and it also neglected recent Mexican anthropological findings, noted by Rivet's Mexican reviewers in *Cuadernos Americanos*. It combined geology, paleontology, and anthropological and linguistic methods, offering a synthesis of all the available knowledge about American prehistory, yet its immediate purpose was evidently a political and humanistic one. In his preface to the first edition, Rivet placed his argument definitively in the context of an antinationalist and antiracist science, proposing a nonisolationist interpretation of relations between the Americas on the one hand and Asia, Australia, and Melanesia on the other. This led him to argue sometimes hastily, based on word lists, for the existence of language affinities, when more conclusive evidence would have been needed.[44]

In *Cuadernos Americanos,* Rivet's book was received with little patience for the humanist component of his argument and resentment of his negligence of Mexican anthropology. One year earlier, Mexican anthropologist Pablo Martínez del Río had published his own *Los orígenes americanos,* a book that carefully revised Rivet's ideas, as he had proposed them in earlier publications. He had received a favorable review by J. Bosch Gimpera in *Cuadernos Americanos*. The two reviews of Rivet's book in turn acknowledged Rivet's prestige as an Americanist but contested Rivet's views on several points. Daniel F. Rubín de la Borbolla's review was written from a strictly anthropological point of view by one of the founders of the Mexican Escuela Nacional de Antropología e Historia (ENAH). Rubín de la Borbolla indicated that the topic of *Los orígenes* was central to the field and, like José L. Cossío, the second reviewer, lauded Rivet's comparative method and use of not only geological and archaeological arguments but ethnographic and linguistic data. However, Rubín de la Borbolla contested Rivet's idea of the American Man as a product of mixed Asian and Australian and Melanesian origins, as well as his thesis that the "American Man" was much older than commonly assumed. He argued that Rivet's thesis was extreme because it claimed that Australians and Melanesians had not come via the Bering Strait, like other Asian peoples, but separately, following cultural and commercial exchanges by sea. Rubín de la Borbolla considered this rather unlikely. Also, while these three separate migrations, according to Rivet, were first the Asian one, then the Australian, and then the Melanesian, Rubín de la Borbolla quoted evidence of craniometric analyses to the contrary. Finally, Rubín de la Borbolla accused Rivet of using too much jargon and not giving enough of a historical introduction. José L. Cossío's review sounded a more positive note. Cossío lauded Rivet's thesis as a refreshing refutation of abstruse nationalist theories on the origin of American man in the Caribbean and elsewhere, emphasizing again Rivet's rigor and method.[45] Cossío too, however, had doubts about Rivet's argument that an Australian immigration occurred not via the Bering Strait but instead over the Pacific and further criticized gaps in Rivet's argumentation, mainly with respect to recent Mexican findings. For example, against Rivet's argument that the wheel, and more particularly the potter's wheel, did not exist in America before the conquest, Cossío pointed out that in fact they did exist in Mexico. Also, with respect to bronze and copper, they were used not only in Bolivia but also in Mexico, and gold crafting was found in Colombia as well as among the *mixtecas*. Overall, Cossío found that Rivet, while having exhaustively researched American prehistory, had not looked closely enough at individual pre-Hispanic civilizations and had therefore missed several clues. Neither of the two reviewers commented on the humanitarian, politically committed aspects of Rivet's book; instead both focused on the unique traits of Mexican high cultures preceding the arrival of the Spaniards.

To get a sense of the cultural gap separating Rivet from Mexican anthropologists at the time, it is interesting to compare these two Mexican reviews with the one published by Claude Lévi-Strauss in the American journal *Renaissance*. Lévi-Strauss had never been a student of Rivet in France but had been in contact with him on numerous occasions. His review, more so than those by Rivet's Mexican reviewers, emphasized the war years as a backdrop of Rivet's book and succeeded at putting into perspective some of Rivet's most controversial statements. Lévi-Strauss recalled historical European perceptions of South American Indians as "natural" or "pure" and argued that Rivet's book showed precisely the contrary, namely that Americans, just like Europeans, were the products of racial mixing. Against the controversy over whether prehistoric migrations from Australia or Polynesia really had been as important as Rivet claimed, Lévi-Strauss pointed out the importance of noticing that they had taken place at all, much earlier than the Norman expeditions to the "New World." Whereas the reviews in *Cuadernos Americanos* had criticized the scientific jargon in Rivet's book, Lévi-Strauss defended it as a contribution that was not meant to be read only by specialists but was accessible to everyone and really was the work of a politically committed scientist.

Rivet himself would write one article for *Cuadernos Americanos*, "Reflexiones sobre la América Latina." This article, written for a general Latin

American readership, made an argument for the universal relevance of better knowledge about Latin America's cultures. Rivet did not hesitate to compare the "physical anarchy" of races in Latin America with that of Europe in earlier times, concluding that *mestizaje* was the basis of all cultures and that no one area in the world was older than another. For Rivet, it was not *mestizaje* that posed a problem for the consolidation of Latin American cultures; rather, nature impeded better communication among them: "If this national, cultural, and physical unity is not yet realized, this does not have anything to do with the systematic opposition against *mestizaje* that can be found in North America in relation to blacks, but instead with the obstacles that Nature presents to the goodwill of men."[46]

It is not clear how much Rivet was heard in Mexico, with his attempt to integrate Americanist anthropology into a larger argument about humankind, *mestizaje,* and a more careful thinking about the importance of the prehistoric past to the present time. The Mexican discussion of culture and race certainly took on a different dynamic during and after the war, one that was closer to the original direction of *Cuadernos Americanos,* whereby Mexican writers like Alfonso Reyes and Alfonso Caso forged a discourse of Latin American culture that was more humanistic and literary in nature and moved away from anthropology toward a "republic of letters," privileging the Mayas and the Aztecs and looking in particular at the moment of encounter with the Spanish colonizers as nation founding (Conn 160–67). The official and literary discourse about Mexico as a mestizo nation, in turn, seemed to seamlessly integrate racial and cultural elements, often disempowering rather than empowering indigenous groups, who were thought of as tragically but irrevocably losing their indigenous ways of life.[47]

The Aftermath: Claude Lévi-Strauss's Structuralist Anthropology

Rivet's museum matrix did not survive him, even though he resumed his directorship of the museum and the Société des Américanistes on his return to Paris in 1944, until his retirement. The Musée de l'Homme came to be seen as a "museological disaster area" because of a chronic lack of guidance and funding after the war (Price 83–87), and new institutional structures were created outside of Rivet's purview. Claude Lévi-Strauss, arguably the most important French anthropologist after 1945, identified more closely with Marcel Mauss's sociology and with the U.S. American anthropological tradition, which he had encountered while living in exile in New York.[48] Lévi-Strauss created his own institution, the Laboratoire d'Anthropologie Sociale, and chose not to be involved with the Musée de l'Homme. It was also Lévi-Strauss, not Rivet, who received a chair of social anthropology at the prestigious College de France (de L'Estoile, *Le goût des autres 132–34*). Finally, in 2006 the Musée du Quai Branly, Paris's new state-of-the-art anthropological museum, opened, and the Musée de l'Homme closed its doors.[49]

The differences between Rivet and Lévi-Strauss regarding the historical and the structural study of culture arose early on, while both were still in exile. Already in a 1945 article published in the journal *Renaissance,* of the Ecole Libre des Hautes Etudes in New York, "Le dédoublement de la représentation dans les arts de l'Asie et de l'Amérique," Lévi-Strauss dismissed diffusionist studies of "primitive" art as too quick in drawing conclusions about mutual influences. His own comparison of objects from different geographic areas and periods focused instead on representations of symmetry or duplication. Lévi-Strauss concluded his study by affirming that these representations had to be considered first for their meaning in the society to which they belonged, even though this did not preclude the possibility of contacts between one society and another. Isolated objects or styles had not traveled; rather, what had migrated were organic ensembles whose social organization, spiritual life, and aesthetic conventions were interconnected.

Lévi-Strauss's programmatic introduction to *Anthropologie structurale* (1958), published in the year of the hundredth anniversary of Durkheim's birth and also, it turned out, the year of Rivet's death, made clear his perspective on anthropology properly speaking. Here, Lévi-Strauss established links not only with the English tradition of anthropology, defining anthropology, ethnography, and ethnology as branches of sociology, but also with ethnology, as what in English is called social or cultural anthropology. The relationship between anthropology and history was now for Lévi-Strauss ancillary, just like the Boas school's attempt to reconstruct the historical evolution of cultures had become ancillary to Malinowski's functionalist approach to culture. Following Swiss linguist Ferdinand de Saussure's distinction between diachronic and synchronic perspectives of language, Lévi-Strauss turned to a "synchronic" perspective on culture, different from that of the historian of culture.[50] Anthropology and history had much in common, both analyzing societies that were distant either in time, space, or character, but to Lévi-Strauss, history was based on documents and on the conscious expression of a society, whereas anthropology analyzed the unconscious expressions of social life, the "grammar" of social relations. With this reformulation of the goals of anthropology, Lévi-Strauss turned his attention away from Boas's emphasis on history, as well as Rivet's diffusionism, toward structuralism, psychoanalysis, and Marxism. In fact, the only mention of Rivet occurred in a footnote to this introduction, where Lévi-Strauss distinguished archaeology from ethnology, mentioning in passing that Boas as well as Rivet had done important research in that field, which he qualified as properly historic, not ethnographic (*Anthropologie structurale* 19).

The end of World War II then marked a major change for French anthropology, inaugurated by Lévi-Strauss, away from regional specializations on the Americas to the focus on kinship relations and myths, away from philological text editing and analysis and archaeological excavations to prolonged stays in the field, and away from a focus on rescuing cultures of the past toward the analysis of present-day communities. This shift was further enhanced in the United States and Latin America by the rise of studies of acculturation. Rivet himself emphasized in subsequent years the continuities between the study of prehistory in the Americas and the study of acculturation, which had become associated to a large degree with Melville Herskovits. In his speech in the second Americanist Congress after the war, dedicated to acculturation (New York, 1949), he emphasized the universality of processes of acculturation in the Americas and elsewhere, repeating that the nature of the social organization of mankind in America and Europe was fundamentally the same. And he proposed that while Americanism had begun as a European discipline, Spanish Americans had undertaken their own Americanist studies, profiting from the methodical work that had been done before ("Proceedings of the XXIX International Congress of Americanists"). The congress was hailed by the anthropologist Sol Tax as a turning point for anthropologists: "It is a sign of the times that out of a Congress of anthropologists traditionally concerned with separating out historical threads and reconstructing past cultures should come a volume dealing with current problems of acculturation and social change" (v). Anthropology in Latin America turned from the 1940s on to studies of acculturation, or "folk-cultures," in the vein of Robert Redfield's publications in the early 1940s and 1950s, and to the Lévi-Straussian structuralist study of culture (Nutini). After the war, Latin American literature and history came to be studied by a new generation of historians and philologists, such as John Murra, Lewis Hanke, Enrique Anderson Imbert, and others. The two fields of literature and anthropology were now definitely separated. Still, while Rivet's diffusionist approach proved not to be useful, the infrastructure he established, and the institutes and museums that he promoted in Latin America, remained junctures, for a while at least, for anthropologists and intellectuals discussing notions of regional and national identity.

3 Jacques Roumain, Haiti, and the Margins of Latin America

> To take up the cause of science, of scientific philosophy, is not to adopt an abstract attitude; it means that one takes the debate concretely toward the transformation of the world: it means that one chooses between misery, war, Fascism, anti-Semitism, racism and the social reconstruction which thanks to the unlimited potential of the sciences will bring to all human beings safety, abundance and culture.
>
> —Jacques Roumain, "Réplique finale au Révérend Père Foisset," *Oeuvres complètes*

The Haitian writer and anthropologist Jacques Roumain is today widely known for his novel *Masters of the Dew*. And yet, for Roumain, his political commitment as a founder of the Haitian Communist Party and supporter of the cause of the poor in Haiti led him to seek training under Rivet and work as an anthropologist. As such, he became the founder of the Institute and Museum of Ethnology in Haiti and a defender, despite his Communist persuasion, of vodou. Already before Roumain, anthropologists in Haiti had studied vodou as a religion and not a superstitious practice, making way for a folklore movement that celebrated Haitian oral storytelling, dance, and music alongside the collection of vodou objects and recording of rituals. A practice long prohibited, vodou became, thanks to this burgeoning literary, anthropological, and folklore movement, identified with the Haitian masses that had been neglected for so long. Roumain's own contribution to this movement was his emphasis, in his anthropological and literary writings, on "science," a science that stood in his view for a secular, analytical approach to a popular religious practice like vodou, recognizing its cultural value for the majority of Haitians.

The controversy over vodou coincided with Haiti's opening up to the world, after almost twenty years of U.S. American occupation ended in 1934. In the war years of 1939–45, Haiti profited from a host of visitors from Latin America, the United States, and Europe who came to visit the island for one reason or another. Pierre Mabille, a French surrealist writer, was the cultural attaché of De Gaulle's France Libre in Haiti from 1940 to 1946 and wrote about Haiti. It was he who invited André Breton to come and visit in 1946, an occasion upon which Breton imparted two inspirational lectures to Haitian students that, when published in the Haitian journal *La Ruche*, provoked the arrest of the journal's editors, followed by a rebellion of students and workers and the eventual abdication of president Élie Lescot (Nicholls 183–84). Alejo Carpentier in turn visited Haiti in 1944 as part of a Cuban delegation and claimed to have discovered there a quintessentially Latin American phenomenon, the "real marvelous," when seeing the ruins of Sans Souci and Citadelle La Ferrière.[1] The Cuban painter Wifredo Lam exhibited his work at the Centre d'Art, founded by the American painter Dewitt Peters in 1946 (Depestre 20–21, 42–43). The curiosity of these visitors was driven in no small measure by anthropological studies of Haitian peasant culture and vodou rituals. In the 1930s the U.S. American anthropologist Melville Herskovits and the folklorist Harold Courlander did fieldwork in Haiti and wrote accounts of Haitian peasant life and music that sharply contrasted with the sensationalist traveler narratives, films, and novels that had been produced during the American occupation—one reason for their interest being perhaps the racial segregation under discussion in the United States, as Michael Dash suggests (*Haiti and the United States* 73–100).[2] They were followed by the anthropologists Alfred Métraux and Rhoda Métraux, who first visited Haiti in 1941 during their honeymoon, having read Herskovit's *Life in a Haitian Valley*. Others combined anthropological and literary or artistic pursuits, as with Katherine Dunham, who came to learn about Haitian dance, and the writer Zora Neale Hurston, who did fieldwork in Haiti in the 1930s. The Martinican poet Aimé Césaire and his wife, Suzanne, taught at the Institut d'ethnologie, while Breton gave his lectures on surrealism and discovered Haitian naïve art for himself, promoting it on his return to France. Haiti became for them a place where artistic and literary creativity was inextricably interwoven with the anthropological interest in Haiti's African-derived religion and folklore on the one hand and racial and social politics on the other. After World War II, Alfred Métraux created a UNESCO project in the Marbial Valley, continuing in this way to include Haiti in the studies of relations between poverty and race that were taking place across the hemisphere.[3]

This chapter discusses how different factions in Haiti used anthropology and literature in order to create a new discourse about Haiti as a modern nation after the end of the U.S. American occupation. It focuses on the tensions evolving around the role of Haitian literature in French in relation to Creole as an oral language appearing in the folklore movement. These tensions were visible in the works of Jean Price-Mars, the founder of the Haitian folklore movement in the 1920s, but also in two literary groups centered around the *Revue Indigène* and the *Revue Griots,* and in the literary and anthropological works of Jacques Roumain, Haiti's outstanding writer and ethnologist in the 1930s and early 1940s. While Ortiz's linguistic strategy in Cuba was to claim African and other influences in Cuban Spanish, in Haiti, writers and anthropologists recognized Haiti's diglossia, as linguists call the existence of two differently marked languages in one community, only to ultimately endorse the hegemony of French as Haiti's national language. In this way social and racial rifts within the nationalist movement were reinforced, contributing to the rise of François Duvalier and the imposition of *noirisme* in the 1950s.

As a result of the often circumstantial confluence of interests in Haiti's popular arts and folklore, Haiti became for a brief period a destination for Latin American intellectuals eager to know its unique history and people. Instead of being on the margins, it was, as the country of an acculturated population with a strong literary, arts, and folklore movement, at the center of the broader conversation about Latin America.

Jean Price-Mars: Anthropology, an Avatar of Patriotism

The beginning of anthropology in Haiti is not associated with a learned society, a museum, or a professorship, but rather with the response of Haitian diplomats, doctors, and educators to foreign assumptions about Haiti's cultural inferiority. Anténor Firmin was for several years the Haitian emissary in Paris and one of three Haitians to become members of the Société d'anthropologie in the nineteenth century. There Firmin was asked whether his intellectual ability was not due to a white ancestor in his family. He wrote his book *L'égalité des races humaines* (1885; *The Equality of the Human Races,* 2000) in response to that question and to the Count of Gobineau's *Essai sur l'inégalite des races humaines* (1853–55; *The Inequality of Human Races,* 1915) (Fluehr-Lobban 95). While still acknowledging the idea of African cultures being inferior to European cultures because of their fetishistic religious practices, Firmin argued that this had nothing to do with differences between the races.[4] Similarly, the Haitian authors Hannibal Price, in his *De la réhabilitation de la race noire par la République d'Haiti* (1900; On the rehabilitation of the black race by the Haitian Republic), and Louis Janvier, in his "L'égalité des races" (The equality of races), attempted to project Haiti's unique identity without challenging European perceptions of African backwardness.[5]

A number of Haitian authors wrote at the beginning of the twentieth century on issues of race or religion in Haiti, from a more or less erudite perspective. Among them are included Duverneau Trouillot's *Le vaudou* (1893; Vodou); F. D. Légitime's brochure *La vérité sur le vaudoux* (1892; The truth about vodou); and J. C. Dorsainvil's publications in the journal *Haitai médicale* in the 1910s, recollected later in his books *Vodou et névrose* (1913; Vodou and neurosis), *Une explication philologique du vodou* (1924; A philological explanation of vodou), and *Vodou et magie* (1937; Vodou and magic). The political motivation and strategic value of these publications were clear from their titles and the background of their authors, most of them politicians and educators, with Légitime even being a one-time general and president of his country. They wanted to see vodou separated from the question of race and, more important, see Haiti accepted as an equal nation among others.

Price-Mars, a doctor trained in Paris, began to study the stories and beliefs of his Haitian rural patients from the 1910s on, using the theories of Émile Durkheim, Sigmund Freud, and others whose works he had encountered in Paris. In the 1920s, he gave a series of lectures on the topic of Haitian ethnography, which formed the basis of his *Ainsi parla l'oncle* (1928; *So Spoke the Uncle,* 1983), a book that became greatly influential in Haiti and beyond.

Price-Mars himself had not been untouched by racial prejudice against his person, first in Paris, where he had been deeply disappointed by reading Gustave Le Bon's work, and also as a Haitian delegate at the Louisiana Purchase Exhibition in 1904 (Antoine 34–37). There, Price-Mars had been shocked by the racial segregation in the city and at the exhibition, where a large number of "living exhibits" were shown as part of the campaign of several U.S. American anthropologists to gain recognition for their field.[6] Being at the Haitian stand as a delegate, he observed that a group of black Filipinos, who were being led to their location as living exhibits, started pointing when they saw him. He suddenly felt like a living exhibit himself:

> All of them were shouting, making contortions, pointing at me and laughing. When I decided to go on, all of them made a gesture, as if to reject me. I confess that the most miserable participant in that strange scene was neither a black Filipino nor an onlooker. What was going on in the mind of those primitive people? Maybe they considered me as one of their own who had rejected

> the faith of the ancestors, since I was dressed like the white people and gave the impression that I understood the white man's language and seemed to be on good terms with them, the masters. (In: Antoine 44)

In this postcolonial spectacle of two groups of blacks opposing each other, refusing to acknowledge that they were the object of a spectacle, not its audience, one may think of Fanon's point that the black man is always the object of the gaze of the white man, as a fundamental scene not only of racism but of colonial domination. Yet Price-Mars does not couch the conflict in racial terms but in performative ones, since the Filipinos are dressed as "primitives," which he associates with beliefs that he himself, dressed as a "white man," would have cast aside. While they can claim to have direct access to their culture despite being a colonized country, he as a Haitian finds that he has adopted uncritically the former colonizer's culture in order to be less "primitive." The scene may be read as a moment of recognition in the drama of Price-Mars's life, eventually turning him into an anthropologist: the "others" are not different because of their skin color, origin, or "degree of development," as nineteenth-century evolutionist theories would have it, but because of owning something he felt he didn't own in his country.

Like other Haitian intellectuals before him, Price-Mars came to identify cultural anthropology, or in French, ethnology, as the human science par excellence, allowing him to reject racial prejudice and better understand Haitian culture in all its facets.[7] As he put it in his *Bilan des études ethnologiques en Haiti* (1954; Summary of anthropological studies in Haiti), his vocation as an anthropologist was an "avatar of his patriotism" (4). Yet Price-Mars also saw that in his own country there were racial barriers, reinforced by the U.S. American occupation in 1915, between the Haitian *milat* elite and the rural population.[8] In his early publication *La vocation de l'élite* (1919; The mission of the elite), he accused many Haitians of racism and critiqued the "Bovarism" of the Haitian elite, that is, their submission to French culture and language. *So Spoke the Uncle* finally argued for the first time that Haitian society was uniquely characterized by its African syncretic religion and folklore.

The eight chapters of *So Spoke the Uncle* are directed at a general audience, explaining the fundamentals of the new ethnography that Price-Mars introduces to his audience: folklore, popular beliefs, African cultures and their relations with other continents, animistic African practices, the religious beliefs of Haitians, and finally literature and its relation to folklore. Price-Mars explains why vodou is a religion and not a superstition, and he introduces his readers to the theories of the French sociological school on animism, as well as those of Lucien Lévy-Bruhl on primitive mentality. For the first time he presents Haitians with a comprehensive picture of Haitian religious practices, putting them in relation to African practices, as well as to contemporary sociological studies, and presenting them as signs not of Haiti's backwardness but of the richness of its popular culture. In the appendix to his book, Price-Mars also tells stories and experiences coming out of his practice as a country doctor. He compares Haitian marriage customs to those of Greco-Roman antiquity and those in Africa, here again making it clear to his readers that Haiti's native peasant culture is nothing to be ashamed of but rather rich and unique.

Price-Mars differed from his Haitian predecessors in anthropology in several ways. He deliberately chose not to focus on questions of biological race and miscegenation but instead on the study of the social functions and practices of a given society. In the tradition of Rivet's school of ethnology Price-Mars chose "comparative ethnography" as his method, placing his argument for Haiti's unique popular culture in the context of other African or western societies, as, for example, in a remarkable passage where he compares vodou to Catholicism, arguing that the spirit possession of a vodou practitioner may be compared to the mystic ecstasy of the Catholic and belonged to the elementary forms of religious life (*So Spoke the Uncle* 124–32). Another element that separated him from previous Haitian anthropologists is the fact that next to religion, folklore was at the heart of Price-Mars's ethnology, and he dedicated the first and the last chapters of his book to it. Folklore represented to him the secular, lived, oral culture of Haiti, which until then had not received enough attention. He writes: "We have nourished for a long time the ambition of restoring the value of Haitian folk-lore in the eyes of the people. This entire book is an endeavor to integrate the popular Haitian thought into the discipline of traditional ethnography" (7). Not unlike Ortiz, Boas, or Price-Mars's own models, the French folklorist Paul Sébillot and James Frazer, Price-Mars thought that folklore supplemented the elite culture and also the religious practices of a people, including everything that appeared to be bizarre or superstitious.[9] At the same time, folklore seemed to tie the different realms of human experience together and therefore to circumscribe a popular culture that for Price-Mars represented what was most "authentic," most truly "civilized" about Haiti: "It can be said that folk-lore encompasses all the 'culture' of the people concerning strange and unrefined customs, superstitious associations with animals, flowers, birds, trees, local objects, and with events of human life which have not been employed in the official religion or history of the civilization; it includes the belief in sorcery, in fairies and spirits, the ballads and proverbial sayings that apply to particular localities, the popular names of hills, of streams, of lairs, of burial mounds, of fields, of trees, and so forth" (11–12). The "culture" represented by folklore, while defined in the Cuban *Archivos del Folklore Cubano,* for example, in neutral terms as the act of collecting popular expressions from the past, is here seen by Price-Mars emphatically as that which seems to resist rationality and, by doing so, destabilizes history and religion as sanctioned, rational practices.[10]

Given the subversive quality lent by Price-Mars to folklore, it is not surprising that folklore became immensely popular after the withdrawal of the U.S. American Marines from Haiti in 1934 with intellectuals seeking to capture the national *Volksgeist.* It was a mainstay of the journal *Les Griots,* formed by students of Price-Mars; after 1935 folklore even came to be somewhat perversely promoted by a new law, decreed by Sténiot Vincent's government, prohibiting "superstitious practices" but allowing citizens, "particularly country-dwellers, to enjoy themselves and organize dances according to local customs" (Ramsey, *Spirits and the Law* 187). Folklore slowly morphed in this way in the 1930s into a spectacle of Haitian nationalist discourse. While Price-Mars had understood folklore to include literature and oral Creole expressions, as a secular, politically permitted performance, it began to include music and dance performances that were progressively polished and even exported in one instance to a folklore festival in Washington, D.C. (Ramsey, *Spirits and the Law*). As a reservoir of popular traditions and "strange customs," it finally also became associated by members of the Griots group with vodou as a religion.

Creole, the language of the rural population of Haiti, was for Price-Mars intimately tied to folklore, and it is in his folklore chapters that the concern with the translation from Creole into French became a major concern. The Haitian linguistic situation was entirely different from that of Spanish Caribbean countries. While Ortiz, for example, had noted the work of translation poured into Lydia Cabrera's and Rómulo Lachatañeré's renderings of Afro-Cuban tales, both anthropologists had been dealing with Afro-Cubans whose language was Spanish, even though they were using African words or formulas. In Haiti, in contrast, the majority of the population spoke Creole as their primary language, even though they also might have understood French. Yet, while adamantly advocating the equality of all races and a properly Haitian folklore, even

Price-Mars seems to have been conflicted about the equality of Creole and French as languages expressing Haitian culture. Faced with the task of translation in his own popular tales in *So Spoke the Uncle,* Price-Mars betrayed his undecidedness as to whether Creole was a fully formed language or whether it should be confined to oral expression only.

While Price-Mars proposed that Creole was an oral register and French a written one, he was unsure as to whether Creole should become a national language just like French. Nevertheless, Price-Mars characterized Creole as a subtle and penetrating language that was truly Haitian:

> Tales and legends have found in the Creole language an entirely unexpected manner of expression, subtle and penetratingly acute. And it is here that our capacity for assimilation and our adaptive ability are transformed into the power of creation. Is Creole a language which can produce an original literature which will establish the genius of our race? Ought Creole to become some day the Haitian language just as there is a French language, an Italian language, or a Russian language? Can Creole be used henceforth in such pedagogical applications where in the solution of a problem we use known terms in order to arrive at the discovery of other potential terms? These are difficult and interesting questions that we will inevitably encounter in the course of this study without ever having the leisure to discuss them in depth. (*So Spoke the Uncle* 24)

But a language with potential is not the same as a national language. In the legends told in the first chapter of *So Spoke the Uncle,* for example, the underprivileged black Haitians speak Creole and are at times depicted as incomprehensible or mumbling, whereas the French-speaking whites and mulattoes, even though pretentious and pompous, are always understandable. Indeed, Price-Mars again and again characterizes Creole as essentially different from other written languages, a language of gesture incapable of being translated directly into writing:

> Creole, for those who comprehend it, is a language of great subtlety. Virtue or fault, this characteristic derives less from the clearness of the sounds it expresses than from the unsuspected depth of the ambiguities that it insinuates by its innuendoes, by the inflection of the voice itself, and especially by the mimetic face of the speaker. Perhaps this is why the written Creole loses half the flavor of the spoken language; perhaps this is why the Haitian folk-lore has not blossomed as a written literature. (25)

Creole for Price-Mars was in this way more evocative, more musical and poetic than the French language and its ideal of linguistic clarity; as a consequence, it also ended up being a diminished language. But perhaps because of that, and because French was a "borrowed language" from the colonizer, Price-Mars saw a general lag between "the soul" and language:

> Certainly, whether the language is the vehicle of thought and the winged messenger that supports the principal attribute of social life—intercommunication between the members of the same group—it does not create the thought itself and it is not its exclusive mode of expression at all. It is only an artifice to translate emotions, sensations, all of inner life. Yet in its many modalities it is often subordinate and always subsequent to the gesture [*geste*] which is itself the most elementary expression of the needs of the soul [*l'âme*]. (175; translation modified, A.B.)

Ultimately, language was for Price-Mars a limited vehicle of thought and in particular of the national "soul". This was so because it was a power instrument, imposed by colonizers or created as a form of resistance, ever changing. Language reflected the separation of classes and that of nations; it could not heal them. For the folkloric movement and for Price-Mars, Creole in turn was a "gestural" language, a register of cultural expression that, together with dance and performance, compensated for the expressive deficiencies of the French language but could never replace French.

Throughout the many texts published in the 1920s through the 1950s on Haitian folklore, the linguistic strategy of presenting French as the language able to capture almost all of Haitian culture, with Creole confined to the affective gesture or the religious chant, was consistent. Michelson Paul Hyppolite in his *A Study of Haitian Folklore,* for example, cited to his Jamaican audience several French songs with a few verses added in Creole as his only examples of Haitian folk music. His samples of vodou songs in turn were rendered directly in English, without reference to the Creole original. Louis Maximilien in his *Le vodou haitien* (1945; Haitian vodou), an anthropological treatise and description of vodou rituals, wrote in French, with pages of untranslated vodou prayers in Creole, marking in this way the author's distance from vodou as formulaic. Milo Marcelin's *Mythologie vodou* (1954; Vodou mythology), in turn, gave much space to Creole chants and prayers to individual gods, which then were translated into French. In this case, the book served as a manual for vodou practitioners of the Arada rite. In contrast, in Philippe Toby-Marcelin's later *Contes et légendes d'Haiti* (1967; Stories and legends from Haiti), a volume of Haitian secular legends published in France, French was again dominant, and Creole appeared only in the occasional nickname.

In neither of those texts, however, was there a reflection on the status of Creole as a spoken language, as we have seen in Price-Mars. The only place left for Creole in these publications was in vodou rituals, chants, and prayers, implying that these ceremonies were usually not meant for the French-language reader of the book in question. All other types of folklore studies studiously translated from Creole into French (or in some cases English), without mentioning the difficulties, imprecisions, or gestural qualities that Price-Mars attributed to Creole. There was no open discussion about Creole as a viable written language for folklore studies or in literature.

Literature, indeed, was the natural culmination of folklore for Price-Mars, about which he wrote in the last chapter of *So Spoke the Uncle.* As he saw it, literature served as a conduit toward a successful translation of the Haitian folklore and popular spirit into a universal idiom. He therefore wanted to see a Haitian literature that was French but sounded Haitian, a "folkloric literature" able to evoke Haitian life, incorporating its oral peasant customs, tales, and songs into the French literate culture of the Haitian elite. As Price-Mars saw it, this was the task of future Haitian writers. Georges Sylvain's *Cric-Crac* (1901), a collection of the French writer La Fontaine's fables rendered in Creole verse, had chosen the wrong linguistic strategy in translating La Fontaine instead of collecting properly Haitian fables and translating those into French (Price-Mars, *So Spoke the Uncle* 179).

To write in French about Haiti was indeed the strategy used in the footsteps of Price-Mars by an emerging generation of Haitian writers, who began to produce novels and poetry that sounded different from anything else done in Haitian literature before. It was, in Dash's words, a "violent burst of literary activity," beginning in the 1920s, including René Maran's *Batouala* and poetry by Jacques Roumain, Philippe Toby-Marcelin, and Emile Roumer that was characterized by the single intention to find something like the expression of a Haitian soul (*Literature and Ideology in Haiti* 66–67). This, however, did not lead them as far as probing into Creole. While there had been some realist novels written in Creole by the novelists of the so-called Génération de la Ronde, this trend was not taken up by the Indigenists or the Griots, who wanted to be understood by a larger audience. Put another way, while anthropology and its sister science folklore were to establish Haitian culture as authentic and popular, using Creole as a register of its authenticity, literature was to promote Haitian culture internationally and at home, but in French.

Price-Mars was also less specific than Ortiz with regard to cultural contact. For him, this was a universal trait of human civilizations that was not really specific to the Caribbean or Haiti. In his chapter "African Societies and the External World," he drew a grandiose panorama of the prehistory and early history of the African continent and its rich natural environment, pointing out contacts between Egyptians and Abyssinians and concluding:

> Through these synthetical terms it has seemed possible to recall the life of the black peoples of Africa. This is how we thought we could schematize their efforts to create societies, the organization of their political communities, their utilization of raw materials appropriate to the industrial or artistic needs of their milieu, and especially their power of assimilation to all that the external world could offer them and which was consistent with the fundamental qualities of their genius. What is all of this, if it is not an ideal of collective life realized in a corner of the habitable area of the globe, the testimony of a unique conception of civilization. (*So Spoke the Uncle* 82)

Price-Mars was more interested in the results of such cultural contact and in its authentically Haitian quality. He pointed out, however, that vodou was one more instance of this continued cultural contact between peoples that was common in Africa as well as in the Americas. The colonial slave trade and the forced conversion to Christianity had created bonds and secret associations among the slaves, and so grew the cult of "*our* Voodoo. It is pre-eminently a syncretism of beliefs, a compromise of the animism of the Dahomeans, the Congolese, the Sudanese, and others" (*So Spoke the Uncle* 50). Vodou as a syncretic practice was one element of that Haitian "soul" Price-Mars wished to know and define, evolving just like the languages that eventually combined into Creole.

Price-Mars envisioned Haitian society consequently as marked by assimilation, inevitably driving in the direction of western modern societies. This implication was most noticeable in his side comments on language, where it was clear that French was the universal language, in relation to which Creole posed a problem, a nonassimilated remainder of that Haitian spirit or mentality that otherwise could be rendered in French.

Creole became recognized only in 1987 as the second official language spoken in Haiti and is still considered by many a second-class language (Zéphir). As recently as 2014, the controversy in Haiti flared up again about whether French or Creole should be taught in schools, indicating that the two languages still divide Haiti's population into a majority of poor dark-skinned Creole speakers and a minority of elite light-skinned

French speakers, a matter that speaks to the inner divisions of Haitian society even today (DeGraff and Ruggles).

From Literature to Folklore: *Revue Indigène* and *Les Griots*

The generation of writers coming of age with Price-Mars's book made literature and anthropology their main forms of expression. This can be seen in two literary magazines that frame the period in a peculiar way, the *Revue Indigène* (1927–28), and *Les Griots* (1938–40). Haitian indigenism was, in the words of Michael Dash, "more than an infusion of local colour into Haitian writing, an obsession by the need for cultural wholeness, for the artist to be the voice of a community. . . . Poetry was seen as an *instrument de connaissance* which could retrieve this vital contact with a collective authentic culture by using elements of Haitian folk culture" (*Literature and Ideology in Haiti* 79–80). Ten years later, the Griots group also called for a distinctly Haitian culture, but with an emphasis on science and a racialist view of Haiti, shifting toward opinion articles and the incorporation of the literary into the "scientific." According to René Depestre, the two groups were divided by racial and class lines, the *Revue Indigene* members—among them Roumain—being part of the Haitian mulatto elite, whereas the members of *Les Griots* were without access to the upper-class social circles and salons in Port-au-Prince (37–38). The two groups overlapped, of course, and worked together later on at the Institut d'ethnologie.

The context of the *Revue Indigène* was, of course, the resistance against Haiti's ongoing military occupation, since 1915, by the United States. Its writers emphasized Haiti's legacy as a slave culture, all the while publishing poetry, literature, and the arts to give an intellectual, nonmaterialist expression to their culture. The Indigenists also claimed a place for Haiti within the hemisphere and emphasized their interest in "Latin America." Normil Sylvain wrote in the opening "Chronique Programme" of the journal:

> In this Spanish and English America we have the glorious destiny to maintain, together with Canada and the French Antilles, the traditions and the French language. This is a dark and dangerous honor, since it has cost us one century of isolation. . . . The Dominican Republic, which shares our territory, does not have that unfortunate lot, it belongs to a Latin America of eighteen republics. Writers speak to an audience of ninety million people, one recognizes their joys and troubles. We have to know the literature and the soul of

> Latin America. The people have lived just as difficult a life as ours, they have known the same tentative steps, similar vicissitudes, the era of caudillos and pronunciamientos, the period when the forces of anarchy and the forces of cohesion and order confronted each other, the hard times of the adolescence of young nationalities.[11]

While the Indigenist writers sought to forge ties with the Spanish American essayists José Enrique Rodó, Ventura García Calderón, Manuel Ugarte, and José Vasconcelos, mentioned in Normil Sylvain's programmatic essay ("Chronique—Programme" 8), unlike Rodó, Ugarte, and Vasconcelos, they did not mention race as a uniting force but instead reached back to history to argue that North and South had a shared postcolonial condition. The French language had isolated them from the rest of Latin America, but given the prestige of French, it would only help to add it to the luster of languages spoken in the Americas. Like Rodó, they addressed young readers in their magazine, hoping to inaugurate a Haitian culture that was truly independent from France. This spirit of national innovation was especially inspired by Manuel Ugarte, the Argentine socialist intellectual and writer, who had become known for his antiimperialist rhetoric and writings in favor of a Latin American union comparable to the United States.[12] Sylvain wrote in the second issue of *Revue Indigène:*

> And here is . . . with regard to "nationalism in South American literature" the advice given by Manuel Ugarte, the Uruguayan [*sic*] thinker and critic. "European criticism and the public that follows the world evolution can, from an artistic point of view, only take Latin America into consideration as a new force, if it contributes a special nuance, something original. . . . What Latin America hopes for—what one hopes for—is an art that comes out of its own conscience, violent, unexperimented, naïve, with novelistic tastes for adventure that are full of a certain delicate perceptiveness, full of youth and of confidence in its future. After having been a spectator, it must become an actor in the works that come out of its spirit; it must see itself in the creations coming out of its own milieu and produce a personal art that abandons all colonialisms, even the flattering ones." This advice comprehends the entire problem of our autochthonous and autonomous literature, the true spiritual emancipation.[13]

"True spiritual emancipation," Sylvain suggested, lies in an art that is a direct expression of its milieu, similar to what Latin American regionalist authors in other countries were seeking as well. The taste of the

Indigenists was eclectic—they published avant-garde poets like the Mexicans Manuel Maples Arce and Carlos Pellicer, the Cuban philosopher Rafael García Bárcena, and several poems by Countee Cullen, the African American writer of the Harlem Renaissance. They also showed a distinct taste for symbolist and Modernist writers such as Georges Duhamel, Rainer María Rilke, Valéry Larbaud, Raymond Radiguet, and Francis de Miomandre, as well as featuring several articles on oriental literature. As a rule, however, Normil Sylvain wrote that the Indigenists were convinced that formal experimentation was a luxury Haitian literature could not afford ("Jeune" 42). In this and other aspects they differed from the Peruvian Indigenist poets described by José Carlos Mariátegui, who aimed in their literature at "repairing the injustices done to the Indian," using local themes as well as a formal language inspired by European avant-garde movements (268–72).

Creole made its appearance at several moments, but often in veiled form and never with the pretention to use it as a written language. In the already cited essay by Sylvain on Haiti's young literature, for instance, his example for the best expression of the "Haitian soul" were the Creole songs sung by black nannies. French in contrast expressed this vernacular sensibility insufficiently, and Haitians therefore used it in a "barbarian way":

> If we write in French we are, let's not forget, strangers, perhaps even barbarians; we don't have to follow the refinements of sensitiveness or try to imitate it, but we should render our sensations and express our feelings. Our poems are translated from Haitian; that is, they are the translation of states of the soul that are our own. The great rule is not to please no matter what the mysterious formula is through which the transmutation is achieved; the honest man inhales the perfume, is enchanted by the music, if it moves him. The rest is literature.[14]

For Sylvain, too, Haitians had a special relationship with French, mediated through their very own "Haitian" language (that is, Creole). Like Price-Mars, Sylvain identified "Haitian" with an inner state of mind and French with its transformation into language proper. One might suspect that this is also why many Indigenist poets felt particularly close to symbolist poetry, with its emphasis on the irregular and uneven rhyme, color, and music, to which Sylvain alluded by citing the last verse of Verlaine's famous "Art poétique," "tout le reste est littérature."

Emile Marcelin, in his "Essai sur le langage créole" (Essay on Creole language), the only article addressing Creole directly, made reference to a discussion in Haitian newspapers about teaching Creole as an official language next to French. For him, however, as for Sylvain, Creole was a Haitian "accent," not a language capable of expressing abstract subjects. The term Marcelin preferred to use in French was *langage,* as opposed to *langue,* a way of speaking or expressing oneself rather than a communication system used by a group or nation. Creole in this sense was close to what Herder, in his *Treatise on the Origin of Language,* called an "inner language," or the language of the soul. In this way, the Indigenists, even though challenging stylistically and thematically the limitations of a Haitian literature locked into the French tradition, remained trapped linguistically, like the Spanish and Latin American Hispanists of the time, in the post-Romantic idea of seeking a national language as the expression of a collective soul. This language remained French, Creole being reduced to an oral register used by the uneducated masses.

The Griots, a group formed after the withdrawal of the U.S. American occupying forces, consisted at its core of three black intellectuals who had studied under Price-Mars at the Lycée Pétion, Louis Diaquoi, Lorimer Denis, and François Duvalier. Like the Indigenists, they argued that Haitian identity had to be found through a rearticulation of Haitian folk practices. In contrast to them, however, they used science as a veneer to insist on the "racial authenticity" of Haitians. Their idol Price-Mars, in his preface to their book *Les tendances d'une generation* (1934; The tendencies of a generation), criticized their interpretation of Haitianism and especially the importance they lent to race, making it clear that he did not see how the survival of racial characteristics in the individual psyche—as Denis had claimed for the Haitian indigenous population—was possible over several hundred years (Price-Mars, "Préface" X).

The journal founded by the group, *Les Griots* (1938–40), was subtitled "Revue de science et littérature," and they claimed that through history, anthropology, and ethnography they addressed what they considered the fundamental problem of Haitianness: its racial inferiority complex (L. Denis and Duvalier, "Déclaration no. 2" 152). The table of contents was quite varied, especially in the categories of scientific inquiry that they proposed.[15]

Much of the rhetoric still sounded similar to that of the *Revue Indigène,* and in their opening declaration, Brouard, Denis, and Duvalier, as members of the editing council, committed to continue the work of the *Revue Indigène* and to offer a platform for the integration of Haiti's national literature (Brouard et al.). They also included a statement about the fortification of intellectual ties with Latin America, adding to it their declared attempt to avoid "politics." Yet, their politics shone through most clearly in their commitment to the values they attached to the black race.[16] For example, the first "Doctrine" article of the journal, signed by Brouard, made it clear that Haitians' "Latin" influences were posterior and secondary to their African origins: "To the oriental splendors of the old Saba we dreamed of adding Latin reason, so that an entirely Haitian civilization may be born of this mélange, conforming to the genius of our race."[17]

Their desire for a Haitian nationhood based on African heritage was reiterated on several occasions by the editors, as, for example, when Denis and Duvalier spoke of the "ethnic consciousness" of all Haitians, who were too often ashamed of their African origins (L. Denis and Duvalier, "Le Noir d'Afrique" 12). Following the theory of "ethno-racism" by French anthropologist George Montandon, the Griots located the problem of Haitian identity in what they called their "sang-mêlés," their mixed blood. In his book *La race, les races* (1933; The race, races), Montandon had proposed a racial taxonomy of five "grand races" that were then subdivided into smaller races. According to this book and Montandon's following *L'ethnie française* (1935; The French ethnicity), France was a multiracial country united by its language and culture yet with the French *variété alpe-arménienne* (Alpine-Armenian variety) being more properly French than others.[18] Following his lead, Denis and Duvalier judged the mixing of Africans and the French to be presently characteristic of Haiti. They argued that Haitians had to "balance" their disparate biological heritage and reshape the Haitian "mentality," appreciating properly the "racial factor" that, according to them, had been repressed in Haitian literature and politics (L. Denis and Duvalier, "Déclaration no. 2" 153). For Kléber Georges-Jacob, even the efforts of the Indigenists and of Jean Price-Mars had not been sufficient. Haiti did not have a common culture yet, because its two ethnicities, the "europoid and the soudanoid," had not properly mixed. Therefore, while European culture had found its expression in literature, African culture needed to express itself more properly in rites, drums, and popular songs.

What became clear in such articles was that Haitian intellectuals could not agree on how to explain the traditionally tense relations between light-skinned and dark-skinned, upper-class and lower-class Haitians and resorted to opposing scientific theories to cement their arguments. Whereas *Les Griots* members explained social and class differences by a racial imbalance and by a lack of cultural awareness on the part of dark-skinned Haitians, Price-Mars and others considered the prolonged contact and racial mixing between Europeans and Africans as part of the cultural process of many societies.

Yet, in spite of the polemic racialist views of the magazine, and even though it was critiqued in the prestigious French magazine *Le Mercure de France,* many respected writers continued to publish in it, among them Price-Mars himself.[19] As Dash points out, this was probably because the Griots shared the same general nationalist spirit as the Indigenists, coming out of the Occupation period: "The tendency to see radical left and extreme right in Haiti as diametrically opposed can easily obscure the fact that both these positions share the same ideological beginnings in Haiti. In fact, there is little to distinguish Roumain from his contemporaries in the Occupation period in that they all shared the same anti-establishment sentiments, aggressive populism and fierce nationalism that characterized the late twenties and early thirties" (*Literature and Ideology in Haiti* 230). Indeed, beyond Haiti, racial determinism in the 1920s and 1930s was a temptation for francophone and African American writers, even though it was less so for Afro-Hispanic movements in the Caribbean.[20] As Christopher Miller has discussed, the radical African groups in Paris preceding Léopold Senghor and Aimé Césaire's Negritude movement also voiced essentialist ideas about race in several journals and publications, and at least one of them openly admired Hitler for his racialist policies (30–46). Even pan-African movements in the United States often did not question the underlying racialist assumptions of their identification with ancestral African "roots."[21]

In contrast to the French pan-African movements and even the Harlem Renaissance writers, anthropology became for Haitian intellectuals and writers the principal discourse of authority, evident not least in how Duvalier and Denis listed a host of institutions to which they belonged as "members of the Societé d'Histoire et de Géographie d'Haïti; permanent members of the Institut International d'Anthropologie de Paris; and permanent members of the Société d'Ethnographie de Paris" (L. Denis and Duvalier, "Le noir d'Afrique").

One of the hotly discussed topics in the 1930s therefore became the vodou religion and the popular ritual practices associated with it.[22] Heavily regulated since 1835 by laws prohibiting "spells" and "superstitious practices," and an object of fascination for foreign anthropologists and film audiences, but absent from the *Revue Indigène,* vodou was in *Les Griots* a topic on which authors had vastly diverging perspectives. Louis Mars, an ethnopsychiatrist, qualified vodou in his article as an "antiquated and ridiculous belief" in Haiti and presented an interesting reading of Lucien Lévy-Bruhl's *La mentalité primitive* (1922; *Primitive mentality,* 1923) where he claimed that there was no general evolution from "primitive" to "civilized" societies, but rather that some societies remained the same whereas others progressed. Haiti, he stated, had had only one century of "civilization," and its scientists needed to study more closely Haitian collective psychology with the help of the studies of Paul Rivet, Franz Boas, and others in order to know how to advance the country. Vodou, Mars concluded, had contributed greatly to the Haitian Revolution but also had created a host of pathological phenomena that continued in the present ("La mentalité haitienne et la psychiatrie"). Carl Brouard, on the contrary, presented vodou as a practice that could be compared to the pagan customs of the ancient Greeks and Romans yet was about to disappear and should therefore be studied as a vanishing culture ("Question a l'ordre du jour"). In turn, Denis and Duvalier, joined by Athanase and Louis Duplessis-Louverture, suggested in their essays a cultural identification with vodou rituals, seeking to represent it as a folk practice.[23] This folklore interpretation of vodou was certainly a hallmark of the journal, which included a number of Haitian tales and vodou rituals. The word *griots* itself, as Carl Brouard explained, was taken from the African term for a sorcerer or singer who, similar to the Provencal troubadour, conjured up tales and myths communicated directly to their audience. The task of the Haitian *griot* was for Brouard that of a folklorist, dedicated to the "passionate study of our folklore," that is, an insider and outsider at the same time, a translator of his own culture for his own people ("Déclaration").[24]

Perhaps because of its investment in folklore, *Les Griots* was the only journal valuing Creole as a language, even though it did not print poems or essays in Creole. But in a programmatic essay, Philippe Toby-Marcelin made a strong statement in favor of its establishment as a literary language, a possibility that he compared to the Belgians' return to the use of Dutch as a written language or the German Swiss people's use of their dialect instead of High German ("Problèmes à l'ordre du jour" 383). In another article on Creole, Christian Beaulieu even drafted a number of orthographic rules for writing Creole and recommended that readers should begin writing it without delay. Yet another article lauded the beauty of African-derived onomatopoeia in Creole (H. Denis).

The Griots pushed in this way a strong identification of Haitians with vodou and with folklore. Indeed, in their article "Pour un humanisme totalitaire" (For a humanitarian totalitarianism), Denis and Duvalier emphasized that to become "authentically Haitian" it was necessary to arrive at a "scientific humanism" able to include the "material and the spiritual," that is, secular and religious practices.

It was after Jacques Roumain's return to Haiti, when the Bureau d'ethnologie haitienne was founded, that Haitian anthropology became a contested ground among different groups of Haitian intellectuals. The tensions between former Griot members and the new institutional structure that was being created for Haitian ethnology had to do not only with differences in attitude toward the African heritage in Haiti but also with the adherence to different French schools of anthropology. The Griots were influenced by George Montandon's conservative anthropology, as we have seen, whereas Roumain as the director of the bureau and Price-Mars as the director of the new museum followed Paul Rivet and the Institut d'ethnologie of the Sorbonne.[25]

Haiti's Bureau of Ethnology, Comparative Ethnography, and the Scientific Study of Vodou

Jacques Roumain's short life was certainly remarkable. Born in Haiti, sent to boarding school in Switzerland, and after his return a cofounder of the *Revue Indigène,* Roumain was a poet, journalist, writer, and committed Communist. As the founder of the Haitian Communist Party, he spent almost two years in prison for Communist conspiracy and then lived for several years in exile in Brussels, Paris, New York, and Havana before returning to Haiti in 1941, only to die in 1944 at the age of thirty-seven. His incessant journalistic and literary activities, culminating in his late novel *Gouverneurs de la rosée* (1944; *Masters of the Dew,* 1947), made him famous in Haiti and beyond. But Roumain was also an anthropologist, trained in Paris under Paul Rivet between 1937 and 1939 and with some studies both at Columbia University in New York and in Havana, where he met Fernando Ortiz and did research at the National Library. Roumain arrived in Paris just when Rivet's Musée de l'Homme was being readied for its opening. He worked as one of its many volunteers in the Department of American Archaeology, while also taking classes at the Institut d'ethnologie, at the Institut de paléontologie humaine, and at the Ecole Pratique des Hautes Etudes of the Sorbonne. On his return to Haiti he did not hesitate to create institutions of anthropology similar to those he had seen in Paris.

The founding of the Institut d'ethnologie, the Bureau d'ethnologie, and the Musée d'Ethnologie in Haiti was, however, not simply an attempt to mimic a structure seen first in the former colonizing country. Rather, it used Rivet's model, turning ethnology into an instrument of documenting Haiti's own past and present culture. This was not unlike what had happened in the neighboring Dominican Republic, which in 1930 had opened its first "national museum," the Museo del hombre dominicano, an anthropological museum that emphasized the autochthonous past of the island over Spanish, African, or Haitian heritage.[26] The three Haitian anthropological institutions began as a government response to the so-called "antisuperstition campaign" of the Catholic Church, started in 1940, initially with President Elie Lescot's support, to eradicate the so-called *mélange*, that is, the practice of both Christian- and African-derived beliefs by the peasant population. By 1941, however, the confiscation of objects and the coercion of larger numbers of the Haitian rural population into publicly abdicating vodou had caused much harm.[27] Roumain was moved to write a series of articles and became one of the most outspoken opponents of the antisuperstition campaign. He convinced President Lescot, weary by then of the bad publicity created by the Catholic Church through the campaign, to create the Bureau d'ethnologie and the Musée d'Ethnologie (under Roumain's directorship) and the Institut d'ethnologie (under the directorship of Jean Price-Mars), where many objects were safeguarded from the antisuperstition campaign and became exhibits. The Institut d'ethnologie originated in a law signed on March 10, 1941, by President Lescot, followed by the creation of the Bureau d'ethnologie, also by governmental mandate, on October 31, 1941.[28]

Although vodou was a way for Roumain and his friends to turn attention to the common people, its inclusion in their Museum of Ethnology was also a way of confining it to the past and turning it into an object of analysis next to the other archaeological and prehistorical objects collected in the museum.[29] Even in his articles written against the antisuperstition campaign, Roumain's defense of vodou was not about the religion and the culture attached to it but about the individual rights of Haitians to religious freedom. Suspecting that behind the religious arguments waged by the Catholic Church were its pro-Vichy sympathies, Roumain considered it a national necessity to end the antisuperstition campaign, not because he identified vodou with Haitian national values but because he thought that the Catholic clergy were attempting to polarize Haitian society and move its government away from its American allies, toward collaborating with Vichy France (*Oeuvres complètes* 752).

Similar to Rivet's Institut d'ethnologie and Bureau d'ethnologie, the Haitian institute and bureau were meant to complement each other in the creation of the Musée d'Ethnologie in Port-au-Prince. The institute taught staff members the principles of ethnography and archaeology, while at the bureau they applied their newly acquired knowledge to the classification and preparation of objects and collections for the museum. The bureau also launched a journal, the *Bulletin du Bureau d'ethnologie haitienne,* where it published findings in Haitian anthropology, not unlike the *Revista de etnología* in Tucumán, founded by Métraux when he was the director of the Instituto de etnología there. In contrast to Métraux's Argentinian enterprise, the Haitian institute and bureau included everyone able and interested to work on Haitian anthropology and folklore, among them Denis and Duvalier. Roumain also opened a library and an archive, intending to establish a classification system with cards for each object. The resulting institutional structure was well poised to promote research as well as educational outreach, and it was up to the standards of anthropological research "in Europe, the Americas and even, in our Antillean archiple, in Cuba," as Price-Mars duly noted (*Le bilan des études ethnologiques en Haiti* 20).

The museum initially had two sections, the section of archaeology and the section of Afro-Haitian ethnology, one being dedicated to the exploration and protection of excavation sites, the other to the history of Africa and its contribution to Haitian contemporary culture, especially vodou (Roumain, *Oeuvres complètes* 1159–60).[30] Faithful to Rivet's method, l*ongue durée* history complemented the study of Haiti's contemporary culture and put it into perspective, emphasizing especially those areas of Haitian history that had not been dominated by colonization. Also, as Charlier-Doucet suggests, the study of Haitian archaeology counterbalanced the preconception that Haiti was simply a cultural province of Africa or France (111). The activities of each section were reported in the *Bulletin du Bureau d'ethnologie.*[31]

Already in the 1930s, some Haitian scholars had engaged with comparative approaches to Haitian folklore and ethnography. In 1936, Suzanne Comhaire-Sylvain, having written her doctoral thesis in literature at the Ecole Pratique des Hautes Etudes in Paris, had published in Belgium and Port-au-Prince the first linguistic study of Creole (Comhaire-Sylvain) and her *Contes Haitiens* (1937, Haitian stories) in Paris. The latter was a collection of short Haitian legends in which Comhaire-Sylvain looked at parallel motifs in the Amerindian world, in Europe, and in Africa. Also in 1936, an exhibit in Port-au-Prince on Haitian pre-Columbian art had been organized by Edmond Mangonès and Louis Maximilien on the occasion of the Third Caribbean Congress, which for the first time exhibited objects of Haiti's indigenous cultures, ranging from cave art to pottery from before the Spanish conquest, and produced a splendid catalog published in 1941. In their introduction the authors presented their work as the first contribution to an "American ethnography," emphasizing that America had been settled by peoples coming from Asia and Oceania and that there was evidence of early relations with Africa. They also argued that race prejudice and economic theories of power and weakness had to be left behind to arrive at a more idealist notion of pan-Americanism (3–4).

The three institutions—the institute, the bureau, and the museum—were similarly dedicated to establishing basic anthropological collections of objects and knowledge of folklore practices that would help researchers gain a broader knowledge of the Caribbean in its relation to other areas of the Americas. Archaeological excavations at different sites in Haiti, helped by donations from private collectors, resulted in a fast-growing collection—already in October 1943 the *Bulletin* reported that the archeological section held 8,312 objects in its possession. Roumain and Métraux studied and classified objects found at La Tortue and a few other excavation sites (Source Matelas, Trou-Forban, Débé, Gateau, and Merger) and worked to explore and protect those sites (Métraux, "Jacques Roumain" 1634). On the other hand, researchers also continued to work on Haitian folklore, inserting it into a larger than national context. Rémy Bastien published his *Anthologie du folklore Haitien* (1946; Anthology of Haitian folklore) in Mexico, dedicated to the memory of Roumain, based on stories that he had collected between 1941 and 1944 in Haiti, which he translated from Creole into French, arriving at a classification of folktales according to their situation and paying attention to elements taken from African story-lore. Bastien, who had left Haiti in the early 1940s to study anthropology at the Mexican Escuela Nacional de Antropología, even engaged, albeit timidly, with ideas of acculturation (*Anthologie du folklore haitien*).

The former members of the Griot group became active especially in the section of Afro-Haitian Ethnography, which had secured a large number of vodou-related objects by 1943.[32] They published several important book-length studies, including Lorimer Denis and Francois Duvalier's *Evolution Stadiale du Vodou* (1944), Louis Maximilien's *Le vodou haitien* (1945) with a preface by Pierre Mabille, and Paul Emmanuel's *Essai d'Organographie Haitienne* (1948).

During the early 1940s, the Institut d'ethnologie made itself known as a social hub for all classes in Haiti. Similar to Rivet's popular Musée de l'Homme, Roumain encouraged the museum's involvement in community activities, writing in a didactic tone that "a museum is above all a social and pedagogical organism. It is essentially destined for the teaching of the biggest sectors of society. It must be similar to an open and well-explained book. Its mission is not to seduce a leisurely curiosity but to instruct and stimulate study."[33] Indeed, the museum became a center for the Haitian folklore movement, which included elite folk-song collectors and performers (Ramsey, *Spirits and the Law* 216–17). Its comparative outlook on anthropology was also clear from the number of invited writers and anthropologists who gave lectures and taught workshops in anthropology, among them Aimé Césaire and his wife, Suzanne, from Martinique; the French critic Pierre Mabille; and the French Catholic philosopher Jacques Maritain. Roumain worked to connect Haitians to other institutes of anthropology in Latin America, writing soon after the creation of the bureau and the museum to Rivet, by then exiled in Colombia, exploring possibilities of collaboration with Colombian anthropologists (Laurière, "Jacques Roumain" 194).

After Roumain's departure for Mexico in 1943, however, the bureau began to transition toward a new profile, more tuned to the Griot group's ideas. While promoting folklore even more than it had before, the institute turned more toward physical anthropology, away from the archaeological and broadly cultural sections that Roumain had laid out. Mangonès, the bureau's new director, created a third section in the bureau, of Haitian Anthropometrics, at its head Louis Maximilien, who subsequently donated his collection of skulls and skeletons to the bureau (Bastien, *Rapport annuel*). The funding of the three institutes also seemed to become more erratic. At Métraux's visit in September 1944, he noted in his journal that the institute lacked funds; that most of its distinguished professors, among them Mabille and Comhaire-Sylvain, had left; and that Price-Mars therefore wanted to close the institute.[34] A definite change in the policies of the bureau and the museum was announced in the fourth issue of the *Bulletin* in 1946, when Lorimer Denis became the new director of the bureau after the interim directorship of Mangonès. In his introduction, Denis wrote of the necessity of a racial awakening and announced more changes to come.[35] In the following years, research in archaeology, and even vodou and physical anthropology, seems to have come to a standstill, with no more publications in those areas and the *Bulletin* ceasing to appear regularly. Still, the museum had a large and well-presented collection of objects. Métraux himself wrote in praise of the museum in 1945, calling it "the museum of the world where the survivals of African cults are illustrated by the richest collections" ("Le Bureau d'ethnologie" 82). Price-Mars wrote in 1951, too, that the bureau and the institute did admirable work, in spite of financial and other limitations (*Le bilan des études ethnologiques en Haiti* 22–26). The institute clearly took on a more active role as a cultural promoter: performances of vodou chants and dances took place, and the bureau even had a choir. Many studies of contemporary Haitian folklore continued to be published, such as Lorimer's *Folklore enfantin* (1949; Folklore for children), *Quelques aspects de notre folklore musical* (1950; Some aspects of our musical folklore), *Le musée du Bureau d'Ethnologie d'Haiti* (1953; The Museum of the Bureau of Ethnology in Haiti), Michel Aubourg and Jacques Oriol's *Le mouvement folklorique en Haiti* (1952; The folklore movement in Haiti), and Lamartinière Honorat's *Les danses folkloriques haitiennes* (1955; Haitian folklore dances).[36] In the late 1950s, however, the activities of the institute and the museum seem to have come to a slow halt, and no more book publications or bulletin issues were produced. At Denis's death in 1957, Emmanuel Paul became the head of the bureau; he directly collaborated with the then newly elected president of Haiti, François Duvalier.

The International Institute of Afro-American Studies: Americanist Collaborations

While the institute, the bureau, and the museum included members of both the Griots and the Indigenist group, with Duvalier's allies only slowly gaining influence from the mid-1940s on, the International Institute of Afro-American Studies (IIAAS), an initiative started by Fernando Ortiz in 1942, included Roumain and Price-Mars but not Duvalier, Denis, or Paul, indicating the divide in international recognition between the two groups. A typical product of the internationalist humanist fervor of the interwar years, the IIAAS was devoted to a scientific cause and an antiracist policy. It was also the only institution that was founded together by anthropologists from several Latin American countries and the United States. Even though Roumain unexpectedly died when the IIAAS was still in its planning stages, his participation was noticeable in the institute's journal, *Afroamérica,* which published three issues in 1945 and 1946. The second issue of the journal contained an homage to Roumain, including his late treatise "L'outillage lithique des Ciboney d'Haiti" (The stone tools of the Ciboney people in Haiti), as well as contributions by Ludwig Renn, Camille Roussan, Lorimer Denis, Rémy Bastien, and others.

The IIAAS managed to exist for only about two years, from 1943 to 1945, until it floundered at the end of World War II, probably for lack of funding.[37] Founded at the suggestion of Fernando Ortiz at the first Interamerican Congress of Demography in Mexico from October 12 to 21, 1943, the same congress at which Ortiz proposed to have the word *race* banned from official communications, the institute was led by an executive board whose membership was a who's-who of scholars in Afro-American studies: Ortiz as chair; the Mexican anthropologist Gonzalo Aguirre Beltrán as vice director; Roumain as secretary; and as advisors the Mexicans Alfonso Caso and Miguel Covarrubias, the U.S. Americans Melville Herskovits and Alain Locke, the Brazilians Arthur Ramos and Renato F. M. de Mendonça, and the Cuban Julio Le Riverend. It officially proposed to study the "Negro populations of America in their biological and cultural aspects, and in their influences on the American peoples."[38]

The institute received funds from the Carnegie Foundation, which, having earlier sponsored research on eugenics in the United States, had decided in the 1930s, under its president Frederick Paul Keppel, to sponsor more scientific pursuits (Lagemann). Especially in the third and last issue of *Afroamérica,* the Carnegie's influence can be seen clearly. As the journal's editors explain, Mexico's Escuela Nacional de Antropología e Historia had held a "Seminario sobre Problemas de las Poblaciones Indígena y Negra de América," where Gunnar Myrdal's book *An American Dilemma: The Negro Problem and Modern Democracy* (1944) was discussed, next to works by Herskovits, Charles S. Johnson, Richard Sterner, Otto Klineberg, and their students. A summary of Myrdal's book was included in the issue, as well as a selection of presentation abstracts.

The main focus of the first two issues of *Afroamérica,* however, equally concerned all of the anthropologists represented: the question of cultures in contact and studies of acculturation. Articles by and book reviews on Herskovits, Aguirre Beltrán, Ortiz, Le Riverend, and Price-Mars offered a unique window into the dialogue between North and South on Afro-American studies and cultural contact.

In his programmatic article "Problem, Method and Theory in Afroamerican Studies," Herskovits described the new field of Afro-American studies as remarkable for its interdisciplinary nature, reaching from the social sciences to the humanities. He emphasized the necessity not to limit Afro-American studies to the study of African heritage but also to consider the cultural exchanges that occurred in the New World:

> Just as race-crossing invariably follows on contact between peoples of different physical types, so cultural borrowing—two-way borrowing—also ensues. The theoretical importance of this fact is clear. Here the problem is stated to emphasize the necessity of including, in the repertory of Afro-American research, investigation not only into the maintenance of African tradition in the New World, but also into how, and to what extent African custom was diffused to the aboriginal Indian peoples and to those of European derivation who experienced prolonged contact with Africans and their descendants. (10)

Herskovits suggested the combination of what he called "applied sciences and long-term research" in Afro-American studies, including both fieldwork and the study of historic sources and documentation. In contrast, Aguirre Beltrán in his reply was less interested in the distinction between theoretical and applied anthropology but marked the aspects of Herskovits's definition of culture that stood out for him:

> The hypothesis that underlies the study of African cultural survivals in the New World derives from a conception of human civilization that affirms social conduct as something learned, not inherited or instinctive. Which means that, even though there may be as many cultures—that is, accepted modes of conduct, configurations of institutions, value systems, and goals—as societies, each culture or any of its elements may be learned by any individual, no matter to what race it belongs, or by any group that has the will and the opportunity to learn. From our concept of culture as something learned it follows that the borrowing of traditions taken by one people from another is an easy thing; research has shown indeed that cultural borrowing is universal in the social human experience. . . . The concept of culture on which our hypothesis is based includes then the operation of the principle of constant change—but at the same time it supposes a high degree of the stability of each culture, which is secured through the transmission from one generation to the next of habits, customs, beliefs, and institutions.[39]

While agreeing with Herskovits, Aguirre Beltrán placed the accent elsewhere: an open concept of culture as changing constantly through cultural borrowing yet remaining stable thanks to inherited traditions and customs was crucial to him, whereas Herskovits was more interested in setting out an institutional and methodical framework of anthropological studies.

Afroamérica included anthropological essays next to linguistic analyses and literary reviews. For example, Fernando Ortiz published an essay titled "Algunos afronegrismos en la toponimía cubana" (Some Afronegrisms in Cuban toponomy), analyzing African place names in Cuba, and Ildefonso Valdés Pereira published an essay on Afro-Cuban poetry. Book reviews included pieces on the translation of Richard Wright's *Native Son* into Spanish and on Rómulo Gallego's *Pobre negro* (Poor black man), next to reviews of books by Alain Locke, the Brazilian Arthur Ramos, José Antonio Saco, Ruth Benedict, and Lorimer Denis and François Duvalier. These different publications coexisted in a thematic continuum, whereby literary works, works of linguistic analysis, and more strictly anthropological works were considered equally relevant in the analysis of Afro-American cultures. Denis and Duvalier's book *Evolution stadiale du vodou* (The evolution by stages of vodou), to be sure, was not well received by its reviewer, who remarked that Denis and Duvalier's interpretation of the historical importance of vodou for the Haitian Revolution went too far in claiming that the instauration of vodou had been the final goal of the revolution, more so than the liberation from colonialism (Anonymous).

Unfortunately, the dialogue between Latin American and North American anthropologists and writers did not continue after the end of World War II, whether because of a lack of financial and institutional support or because anthropologists returned to their own national context after the war. The most notable publication by any of the members of the IIAAS, Aguirre Beltrán's path-breaking 1946 book *La población negra de México (1519–1810)* (The black population of Mexico), in any case, was not translated into English, nor did joint initiatives between Latin American and North American anthropologists continue to evolve.

Roumain's Scientific Essays

Roumain's anthropological research was less remarkable than his literary production, but as hurried as it was, and as limited in its achievements, it is nevertheless telling of the ways in which his method and outlook on local and international anthropology were connected to Ortiz and Rivet but disconnected from the local concerns of Haitian *noiriste* intellectuals.

Contribution à l'Etude de l'Ethnobotanique Précolombienne des Grandes Antilles (1942; Contribution to the study of pre-Columbian ethno-botanics of the Greater Antilles) consists of lists of plants, divided by Roumain into seven thematic sections (plants playing a role in myths, in relation to religious beliefs, in making garments and body painting, in construction, in food, in making fabrics, and in other miscellaneous uses), with a total of fifty-five numbered entries. Composing a glossary more than an essay, Roumain classified each entry by the Latin name, family, and species of the plant; the current Haitian name was indicated in comparison to other Spanish Caribbean islands or Latin American countries, and quotes from colonial chronicles by Bartolomé de las Casas, Oviedo, Francisco de Gómara, and others were provided. Roumain wanted to render "through the analysis of the vegetative world of the Indians, a general idea of their myths, religious beliefs, material culture and social organization" (*Contribution à l'Etude* 7–8). Like Ortiz, Roumain in this way used a metonymic principle, focusing on a class of natural objects that had been in the vicinity of humans for a long time and reconstructing from the ways in which they were described the changing shape of the society that was the real object of his analysis.[40]

Roumain's list of plant names was, of course, far from complete, and even individual entries were quite elliptical at times. His entry 32, on "Anana" or "Pineapple," for example, mentions accounts by Christopher Columbus and the conquistador Grijalva, as well as the historian Oviedo. It does not mention, however, Oviedos's famous story that Charles V at his court in Seville refused to eat the pineapple that he was shown. Roumain is clearly more interested in accounts of the pineapple's "diffusion" all over the Caribbean and in Mexico than in the anecdotes attached to the pineapple that would not have been lost on Ortiz.

Ultimately, Roumain's analysis suggested two things about the Taino indigenous: first, their utilization, before the Spanish colonization, of plants unique to the Americas; and second, the insertion of Haiti into a universal taxonomy of knowledge, the *sistema naturae* of plants first developed by the Swedish botanist Carl von Linné. In these comparative translations, Creole also appeared, even though not in a systematic way. For *guayaba,* for example, Roumain gives references in Quechua, Arawak, Calinago, and Taíno, but not in Creole or French. *Caimito* is referenced as *ti-caimite* in Haitian Creole and as *caimito blanco cimarrón* in Santo Domingo; *guanábana* in turn is rendered in French as *corossol* but has no separate translation into Creole. In some cases, the word seems to be the same in French and Spanish, as with *mamey.* With *mahiz* (corn), in turn, Roumain used an antiquated spelling of the word in both Spanish and French.

The principle of selection of terms seems to have been their cultural relevance. The longest entries in Roumain's study are devoted to plants like *tabac* (tobacco), *coton* (cotton), *mahiz* (corn), *ají* (chili), and *yuca* (manioc). In his entry on corn, for example, Roumain argues that the plant was at the economic foundation of all American civilizations and suggested their common origin and evolution in Mexico and North America, spreading from there to Ecuador, Bolivia, Peru, and the Tainos.[41] But there are also shorter entries, more specifically relevant to Haitian culture. The entry on *guayacan,* indeed, allowed Roumain to speculate about the origins of syphilis in Haiti, a disease that the indigenous, according to Roumain, knew how to treat with this particular plant (*Contribution à l'Etude* 16–18).

As unsystematic and preliminary as it was, Roumain's *Contribution* had a line of interpretation that was clearly different from Ortiz's, being less interested in etymologies and in refuting other authorities, as Ortiz had been in his argument against the dictionary of the Real Academia Española. Instead, Roumain studied plant names to uncover their early uses by the pre-Hispanic Taino people in Haiti and to uncover the connections or at least the common cultural traits that existed between them and other populations in the Americas. The glossary therefore allowed him to think of the Americas as one large botanical zone, which, if analyzed properly, could yield information about some of the elements that had created a common regional culture.

Roumain's essay "L'outillage lithique des ciboney d'Haiti" (1943; The stone tools of the Ciboney people of Haiti) appeared posthumously in the *Bulletin du Bureau d'ethnologie.*[42] Here again, Roumain's method was the study of historical texts, in combination with recent studies in archaeology. He used the Spanish chroniclers Oviedo, Pedro Mártir, and Las Casas, as well as the nineteenth-century Cuban historian Antonio Bachiller y Morales, as sources of information for his analysis of Ciboney tools found during his own excavations in Haiti, arguing against the perception that the Ciboney were a primitive tribe of cave dwellers and fishers. Roumain cited contemporary publications by Sven Loven and the results of an expedition of the U.S. National Museum to Samaná, in the Dominican Republic, also showing that the Ciboney of Santo Domingo practiced agriculture but had been invaded by the Taínos and almost eliminated when the Spaniards arrived.[43] As he stated in the introduction, he wanted to study the "still little known chapter of the prehistory of the Greater Antilles," establishing through the study of their tools a map of the Ciboney culture (*Oeuvres complètes* 1154). Unfortunately this study breaks off after ten pages. It is clear, however, that Roumain again proceeded deductively, from the observation of a group of similar tools to conclusions about how they helped understanding the activities of the Ciboney Indians, and keeping in mind the larger Caribbean context. Whereas his botanical study had clearly taken its cue from Ortiz's method of textual analysis, this study was closer to the methods used by Rivet. Similar to Rivet in *Los orígenes del hombre americano* (1943), Roumain was attempting to reconstruct the earliest beginnings of human culture in the Caribbean, using empirical evidence.

The only work in which he focused on contemporary Haitian culture and specifically vodou was Roumain's *Le sacrifice du tambour-Assotô(r)* (1943; The sacrifice of the Assoto(r) drum). In this most systematic and eloquent essay, Roumain used his comparative ethnographic approach to the greatest effect, commended especially by Métraux, who found that Roumain's sensitivity to the parallels between vodou and the classic "oriental cults" made his descriptions stand out ("Jacques Roumain" 1636).[44] Sustained by a substantial bibliography of contemporary international anthropologists, among them Herskovits, Curt Sachs, Pierre Schaeffner, Mauss, and Frazer, Roumain introduced vodou to readers without prior knowledge. He began by explaining the principles of song, dance, and music in their relation to religion and from there moved on to explain the particularity of the Rada rite, dedicated to the blessing of the Assotor drum, suggesting that the sacred nature of musical instruments was not particular to vodou but that it was here staged through a hierarchy among three basic drums, the Asson, the Ogan, and finally the Assotor as the principal protagonist, carrying the skin of a sacrificed animal representing the powerful Afro-Haitian god Assoto Micho Tokodun Vodoun (*Le sacrifice du tambour-Assôtô(r)* 11). The text used the Durkheimian distinction between realms of the profane (at the beginning of the ritual) and the sacred (marked by the consecration of a place, the sacrifice of a series of roosters and finally a bull or a goat, the baptizing of the drum). Roumain also emphasized the Catholic subtext of the ritual and suggested that the idea of reincarnation, for example, was common to both religions, as well as prayers such as the Ave Maria and the Our Father, present in the last phase of the Assotor ritual. Vodou emerged in his account as a religion that was anything but primitive, containing many elements of western religions—singing and dancing, a purification rite, a sacred meal with the *loas* (the spirits of the gods), a symbolic sacrifice, the reincarnation of the god, and then departure. It was also a ritual that shared *loas* with other neighboring cults such as Cuban santería, due to their common roots in the African Yoruba culture.

This was indeed not a participant observation study, like Herskovits's *Life in a Haitian Valley* (1938) or even Seabrook's *The Magic Island* (1929) had been. Roumain's own voice in this text was in fact more that of a narrator than of an anthropologist, confined to an impersonal third-person account, describing the typical sequence of ceremonies associated with the Assotor drum and reproducing and translating into French the Creole chants that accompanied it.[45] The strength of Roumain's rendering instead was precisely his distance toward the ritual and his ability to interpret, using etymologies to explain the ancestral connections in Hebrew and Arabic cultures, as well as in vodou, among feast, dance, and ritual: "The Hebrew word for the feast, *hag,* meant exactly dance. It is the same word as Arabic *hadj,* which in pre-Islamic times designated the processional circle around the Ka'aba; the term was applied by extension to the entire pilgrimage."[46] To Roumain, the symbolic value of the Assotor drum lay in the threefold displacement whereby God was identified with an object, the Assotor drum, which in turn was replaced with a sacrificed animal, so that then God could return to Africa. The readability of this ritual as a narrative scenario of the return of the gods to a mythical Guinea and of the return of the humans with them, reuniting with their ancestors, seemed to interest Roumain more for its poetic associations than as a Haitian religious ritual.[47]

The ultimate lesson of the Assotor ritual was for Roumain that the community of worshippers became aware of their diasporic condition and separation from the gods of Dahomey, and he emphasized, especially toward the end, the separation between the "Creoles" and the gods, as well as the multiple origins of "Creole" worshippers: "The Houngan traces a last veve. He plants a lit candle in the middle. The expulsion ceremony is finished. The divinity has been sent back forever to Africa, to that ancestral Guinea that still survives, enveloped in a mythological fog, with an extraordinary tenacity in the faithful memory of these descendants of slaves. Everyone retreats singing in the same desolate tone: The family is over / Assotor has left / He has left nothing behind / It is sad / Amen."[48] Roumain as the narrator clearly distanced himself from "these descendants of slaves," yet empathized with them as a community marked less by a sense of common origin than by dispersal.

The only reviewer who did not appreciate Roumain's essay was, tellingly, François Duvalier. In a review-article he lamented Roumain's lack of a "mythic" perspective, stating that he would have preferred a work closer to Leo Frobenius's storytelling (in: Dayan 125–26). In 1931 Duvalier had written a quite positive review of Roumain's early novel *Les fantoches* (The puppets), where he remembered their high school days together and called the novel a "happy accident in the history of a young literature" (in: Roumain, *Oeuvres complètes* 1474). However, by 1943, Roumain was not an aspiring writer anymore but had after his return to Haiti become a dominant figure in the burgeoning folklore and anthropology movement. Even though Roumain had defended vodou in this essay and in his journalistic writings against the antisuperstition campaign, his clear disassociation in this book from the local context and his representation of vodou in a comparative instead of a sociological, psychological, or historical perspective must have given pause to other Haitian anthropologists, who shortly afterward published a number of texts on vodou, identifying more closely with vodou as a practice.[49] Roumain had attempted to present his audience with a Haitian culture that was not defined by its mythic connections to Africa or collective psychology but that had a past that extended far beyond the colonization of Hispaniola, back to the Pre-Columbian past and to other Caribbean and Latin American countries.

Masters of the Dew: Ritual and the Literature of Engagement

Roumain's novel *Gouverneurs de la rosée* (1944; *Masters of the Dew*) continued in a literary register Roumain's reflection on Haitian national identity and the role of vodou in it. Whereas in *Le sacrifice* Roumain described vodou as belonging to universal religious practices, in *Masters of the Dew* he suggested that vodou, if interpreted the wrong way, was holding back the rural population from taking action to improve their lives. *Masters of the Dew* treated Creole with similar distance; it had been present in Roumain's *Le sacrifice,* next to French, as part of the rituals described there, but now it had disappeared, with all the characters speaking French. Creole, vodou, and other traditional customs such as the *coumbite* appeared as markers of Haitian identity, but they were inserted in a universal tale of death and redemption that told of the necessity of change and reinterpretation instead of repetition and diglossia.

The novel is about a drought in a Haitian valley caused by deforestation. All the wells have dried up, and more and more of the younger peasants decide to leave for the Dominican Republic, or at least for the city—Port-au-Prince—where the women inevitably prostitute themselves. The older generation who stays back cannot but wait and pray for rain. Something changes, though, when one of the younger generation, Manuel, returns from Cuba, where he has learned about the mobilizing of workers, strikes, and rebellion: "Experience is the staff of the blind, and I learned that what counts, since you're asking me, is rebellion, and the knowledge that man is the baker of life" (*Masters of the Dew* 88). This is a version of the tale of the prodigal son, who has come back to help the village get on its feet again. Inspired by his Cuban experience, Manuel goes to find a well and then proposes to revive the old Haitian custom of the *coumbite,* the work cooperative (analyzed also by Herskovits), to build a water canal that would allow the villagers to make the dried-out valley productive and rich.[50] However, he is killed by a rival, and the *coumbite* takes place after his death, led by Manuel's beloved Annaise.

As Dash has shown superbly, the novel exemplifies Roumain's will to create a new foundational discourse of the Caribbean's mythic origins in mankind's communion with nature. Roumain's love couple in particular reflects an orphic ideal where the individual and the world come together, whose finding of water symbolizes a return to the origin of history and time (Dash, *Other America* 61–81).

For all the beauty of the novel's evocations of nature, however, humankind's union with nature cannot provide relief from the dire social conditions in which the peasants live. What the *coumbite,* the vodou ritual, and the recollection of Creole chants ultimately show is not a celebration of community and culturally essential values, as a naïve anthropological perspective would suggest, but rather the ways in which rituals can make social problems invisible.[51] Most strikingly, the vodou ceremony celebrated by Manuel's parents and the village to honor his return has an ambiguous role in the novel, as it brings into the open Manuel's divide between his instinctive loyalty and his critique of the villagers' all too passive assuming of traditions that precisely had caused the drought in the valley. During the ceremony two *loas* (spirits), Legba, the *loa* of crossroads, and Ogoun, the *loa* of war, are in dispute. Ogoun at first prevails and demands to speak to Manuel, in order to reprimand him and announce that the canal will be made and that blood will flow. Only then is Legba allowed to make its appearance. Instead of an ethnographic description of a spirit possession, as we saw in *Le sacrifice,* this evocation of a vodou ritual has added allegorical meaning as it accompanies and foreshadows the coming events where Manuel will be killed.[52] Furthermore, Manuel's later opinion about the vodou ritual is openly critical: "No, I respect the customs of the old folks, but the blood of a rooster or a young goat can't make the seasons change, or alter the course of the clouds and fill them with water like bladders. The other night, at the Legba ceremonies, I danced and sang to my heart's content. I'm Negro, no? And I enjoyed myself like a real Negro. When the drums beat, I feel it in the pit of my stomach. I feel an itch in my loins and an electric current in my legs, and I've got to join the dance. But that's all there is to it for me" (*Masters of the Dew* 87–88). The vodou ritual is for

Manuel something purely instinctual, which he enjoys but really considers a distraction from the problems that are plaguing the village. Another problem in the village related to "traditions" is the existence of an old feud between rival families, which has prevented them from acting together. Here also the oral customs—the insistence on honor and loyalty only toward one's camp—are not seen as beneficial for the villagers.

Other scenes in the novel, too, reveal a double meaning, speaking to anthropologists and literary critics alike but suggesting a distanced perspective toward anthropological objectification of knowledge. Toward the end of the novel, for example, the idea is suggested that Manuel has to die so that the villagers can live. Frazer notes that in scapegoat situations, a divine man or animal is often picked as the sacrificial victim and that the custom combines two purposes: the divine life is saved from the degeneracy of old age, and a periodic cleansing is enacted that carries away the entire village's sufferings and sins (689–93). For René Girard, in turn, the "surrogate victim" is at the origin of symbolic thought as such and is a fundamental instance of "arbitration." According to Girard, societies function on the basis of acts of collective violence that institute the calm necessary to the creation of myths, rituals, and kinship systems (235). Roumain had described an instance of the scapegoat motif in *Le sacrifice,* yet the idea of the surrogate victim, after whose death new kinship systems may be created, only comes to life in *Masters of the Dew.* The death of Manuel brings redemption to the other villagers, who adopt his ethic and his goals. This ethic consists of respect for "the old ways" and of staying "close to their dead ones," in contrast to those who "have lost respect for the old customs" or who leave. But the old ways need to be actively reinterpreted: one has to strengthen human interaction with the earth—the finding and using of water, the planting and harvesting of crops—in order to bring or keep Haitian culture alive and prevent peasants from leaving. This message is cast in ritual terms.

The funeral rites of Manuel are another instance of the active reinterpretation of customs suggested in the novel. In an ironic twist, an inexpensive fellow ex-sacristan, a *pere-savane* and not a church priest, is hired for Manuel's funerals. The replacement of the consecrated priest by someone who is described as "dishonest" indicates both disdain for the church and the resourcefulness of the peasants, whose dignity is not diminished by their poverty.

The songs of the *simidor,* the singer of the *coumbite,* function like the comments of the choir in Greek tragedy after Manuel's death, with Roumain emphasizing the close relationship between music and ritual, repetition and song. Here again, Roumain combines "anthropological" knowledge with literary form. *Simidors*, as Herskovits tells us, have a vital function in a *coumbite*. Playing a drum, they lead the singing and help keep everyone in rhythm while working. They also transmit town gossip and provide entertainment to the workers. The story ends thus not only with the *coumbite,* the renewed ritual that promises to bring wealth to the village again, but also with a new collective narrative, whose bard, Antoine, announces the passing of the king and the arrival of a new regime.

The novel suggests then that the traditional, rural life of Haitians is not to be denied its rites and religious beliefs. The life of the villagers is described as ruled and structured by these rites in all-important moments. But they need to be constantly challenged and reinterpreted in order to work for the benefit of the population. Most emphatically, religion itself is at the end of the novel replaced by the secular community of the *coumbite,* led by its singer, the *simidor*.

In this more free-ranging, novelistic evocation of traditional peasant life, Roumain has moved closer than in his scientific essays to Melville Herskovits's classic study *Life in a Haitian Valley* (1937). Both describe picturesque scenes of communal labor, of vodou ceremonies and customs of old. Yet, Roumain provides a reading of Haitian society that is markedly different from that of Herskovits in that it puts the accent on the present time and the need for modernization. Herskovits's *Life in a Haitian Valley* points systematically back to the past, claiming that Haiti can only be understood by taking into account the provenience of black Haitians from different African cultures and similarly that of the French and colonizers from different areas in France. It is a fascinating study of Haiti that argues for its mixed heritage and defines Haiti as an "amalgam" or mosaic, with pointed reference, notably in the last chapter, to blacks living in the United States, suggesting the need to undertake similar studies on Afro-American communities (292–305). Herskovits sees Haiti as a case in point for the phenomenon of "cultures in contact," where it is important first to focus on the continuity with the past in order to find a strong voice in the present.

Roumain's idea of politically engaged writing and comparative focus is different. In his novel he paints a society that suffers from the exploitation of the poor and from a corrupt church and government. His interest is not in depicting religious practice as essential to maintaining a sense of identity. Roumain's Haitian society is falling apart, in spite and perhaps even because of some of its local customs. Roumain's idea of committed writing also differs from Price-Mars and from most of his Haitian colleagues. While they make the study of Haitian folklore the center of their search for an authentic Haitian cultural identity, Roumain in this novel moves away from a strictly classifying anthropological approach toward a universalizing argument about human suffering and solidarity, even though acknowledging local customs and characters.

While his anthropological works are studies in cultural comparison, Roumain's last novel is a call to arms for all in defense of the workers' rights.[53] That call, however, implies that the Creole-speaking peasants will need to change, casting aside vodou and possibly other customs. Roumain evokes Haitian peasant life not for its bucolic origins but to point to a shared future that will be more just and modern but also less bilingual and less bent on traditions.

4 Gilberto Freyre and the Science of Culture

More explicitly than Ortiz or Roumain, Gilberto Freyre was emphatically not a social scientist in the quantitative and empirical sense that came to dominate Latin American studies after 1945, but a writer-scholar and defender of the broadly interdisciplinary and interpretive analysis of Brazilian society. Trained in Franz Boas's school of thought yet idiosyncratic in his own method, Freyre established, through his book *Casa-grande & Senzala* (1933; *The Masters and the Slaves,* 1946), as well as through a number of lectures and conferences collected in book publications, a reputation as an intellectual, known for his ideas and style of thought rather than for his academic authority or institutional innovations, in Brazil and abroad. This chapter traces Freyre's impact and evolution in the 1930s and 1940s in the context of the Brazilian social sciences, on the one hand, and his contemporary milieu of literature and the arts, on the other. It also reconstructs Freyre's international contacts and places him in relation to the discussion of an antiracist, humanist science of Latin American culture.

The Brazilian Science of Race

From the 1920s on, Freyre's career speaks to the ambiguous status that the social sciences had in Brazil in the 1920s. Even though he received undergraduate and master's degrees in the United States at Baylor University and Columbia University respectively, Freyre chose a life independent from any single institution, partly following the advice of his mentor Manuel de Oliveira Lima, then the Brazilian ambassador in Washington, D.C., but mostly because of his own inclination toward literature and journalism (Skidmore, "Raízes de Gilberto Freyre" 6). During his formative years Freyre read a host of literary, philosophical, and anthropological texts of the western tradition.[1] He later collected his reflections on

Brazilian literature and social science in a book of intellectual portraits, *Perfil de Euclydes e outros perfis* (Portrait of Euclydes da Cunha and others), where his reading of Euclides da Cunha's *Os Sertões* (1900; *Rebellion in the Backlands,* 1944) stands out for the fascination it shows with da Cunha as something of a poet and a prophet yet also a social scientist and geographer ("Euclydes da Cunha" 26).[2] And for many, Freyre himself would turn out to be just that, a "public intellectual" and a "renaissance man," apt in public dialogue as well as in social theory (Burke and Pallares-Burke 99–131), and a writer, too, later in his life, as Jossianna Arroyo has shown in her analysis of Freyre's "seminovels" *Dona Sinhá e o Filho Padre* (1967; Doña Sinhá and the son who was a father) and *O Outro Amor de D. Paulo* (1977; The other love of don Paulo) (140–58). Already his shift, in the 1920s, from journalism to the brilliant work of scholarship *The Masters and the Slaves*, however, leaves no doubt that Freyre felt he had above all a scientific calling to rewrite and refute earlier theories about Brazilian culture.

The notion that race—and in particular racial mixing—alongside Brazil's climate was responsible for its difficulties in becoming a modern nation had been supported in the nineteenth century by European evolutionary scientists such as Arthur de Gobineau and Louis Agassiz, who after visiting Brazil had concluded that the country was "weakened" by its *mestiço* population. The Brazilian scientists coming out of medical schools were clearly influenced by these racialist views, as well as by the local network of knowledge forming in three newly founded museums where Brazilian physical anthropologists worked to document the country's racial and cultural evolution: the Museo Paraense (later the Museu Paraense Emílio Goeldi) in Belem, the Museu Nacional do Rio de Janeiro, and the Museu Paulista.[3] Not unlike what happened in other Spanish American countries, it became generally accepted in Brazil that "racial whitening" presented a solution to the country's problems (Skidmore, *Black into White* 64–69). Toward the end of the century, a doctor from Marañao, Nina Rodrigues, began to gather data on the origin and number of Brazil's Afro-descended population, as well as their syncretic religious practices, coinciding with Sílvio Romero's research on the oral traditions of Afro-Brazilians, amounting effectively to what Octavio di Leo has called a moment of "vernacular anthropology" (29–41) that included authors such as da Cunha and also the Afro-Brazilian writer Machado de Assis. Even though these writers still subscribed to the whitening ideal of Brazilian society and did not attempt to challenge theories of race, they also paid attention to Afro-Brazilian and Afro-Cuban traditions and customs.[4] In the first decades of the twentieth century, more and more disagreements on the role of race in Brazilian society arose. The eugenicist movement developed policies of "racial hygiene" that were implemented until well into the 1920s.[5] The positivist politician Alberto Torres in turn proposed in his work *A organização nacional* (1914; The national organization) that Brazil's problem was its decentralization, not its racial composition (Henrique Cardoso 103). Edgard Roquette-Pinto himself, the president of the Museum of Anthropology in Rio de Janeiro and the organizer of a eugenicist congress in 1929, declared that none of Brazil's racial types presented traits of degeneration (Ventura Santos S17–S18).

The government's creation in the early 1930s of anthropology and sociology departments in Brazil's newly founded universities in São Paulo and Rio de Janeiro acknowledged the need for more sophisticated methods of analyzing Brazil's social composition. In São Paulo, there were two social science institutions, the Escola livre de sociología e política, founded in 1933 as an independent institution with a strong empirical bent meant to train civil servants, and the Facultade de ciencia, filosofia e letras at the University of São Paulo, which combined the study of literature and the social sciences and was more indebted to the Durkheimian sociological tradition.[6] Eager to establish international contacts, both institutions famously invited foreign scientists to help them establish a teaching curriculum. The Escola livre hired the Chicago School American anthropologist Donald Pierson in 1939 to create an ambitious postgraduate program, training teachers and academics in the social sciences and the humanities (Limongi in: Miceli 217–34). The Universidade de São Paulo invited a large contingent of French social scientists (Lévi-Strauss, Roger Bastide, Georges Gurvitch, and Gilles Gaston Granger, among others).[7] In Rio de Janeiro, too, the Universidade do Distrito Federal, under the direction of Anísio Teixeira, created a social sciences department in the 1930s in which Freyre served as director for three years. It was dissolved in 1938, when the new Universidade do Brasil was founded, with its own social sciences department.

The tasks for Brazilian scientists in the 1930s were twofold: on the one hand to establish social science departments with a focus on the study of *mestiçagem,* considered fundamental when thinking about Brazil's unique potential as a modern nation; on the other hand to connect Brazilian science with the anthropological discussion that was happening in France and the United States. A third, perhaps unintended outcome was the empowering of Afro-Brazilian culture in particular, which for the first time, in the aftermath of Freyre's publications and those of other Brazilian anthropologists such as Arthur Ramos, gained a voice and representation.

Freyre's *The Masters and the Slaves:* The Anthropologist-Author and His Interlocutors

Freyre's *The Masters and the Slaves* was the single most important work written in the 1930s to reorient the scientific and intellectual discussion on Brazilian culture, departing from previous ethnocentric or culture-area methods of analysis. It was, as Fernand Braudel saw it, the most documented of all Brazilian essays, yet it was also an intellectual exercise, an essay in understanding Brazil, that mobilized the available archive of anthropological knowledge and opened it up to speculative reflections as well (Braudel, Bassols Batalla, and Aguirre Rojas). Freyre's modernity was precisely in his emphasis on interpretation and on the subject position of the author, not far from what Clifford Geertz would later consider the dilemma of the "anthropologist-author," identifying with a culture yet having to translate it for readers foreign to the subject.[8] His Brazilian colleague Darcy Ribeiro would characterize Freyre's particularly empathetic style of argumentation as a performance, akin to a rite of possession. For Ribeiro, Freyre had an almost uncanny ability to transform himself into his subject—the inhabitant of the nineteenth-century Brazilian mansion or the slave quarters—and then turn around to write about it, bringing alive and illuminating the past for the reader ("Prólogo" xii).

The notion of becoming another and also remaining oneself was at the heart of the participant-observation approach that became established with Malinowski from the 1920s on, in the Anglophone world but also in France and Latin America. As Vincent Debaene has argued, fieldwork became, at least for French ethnographers like Marcel Griaule, Michel Leiris, and Claude Lévi-Strauss, not only a place to do work but a personal experience, a defining moment for the anthropologist that shaped his text, lending it at times a confessional quality. However, Freyre, like other Latin Americans, did not use the fieldwork technique typical of the community studies done by U.S. anthropologists. Rather, he investigated a particular social complex of the past by reading archival sources, using methods that were more typical of an "essay in genetic sociology and social history" (Freyre, *Masters and the Slaves* lxi), terms he made up to circumscribe his study of family life from the sixteenth through the nineteenth centuries. His claim to "authorship" relied therefore on several types of inspiration: that of the historian and sociologist but also that of the literary author, in this case Proust. As Freyre writes in his preface of 1933:

> The study of the intimate history of a people has in it something of Proustian introspection—the Goncourts called it "ce roman vrai." The architect Lúcio Costa has given us his impression in the presence of the old mansions of Sabará, São João d'El Rei, Ouro Preto, and Mariana, the old Big Houses of Minas: "How one meets oneself here. . . . And one remembers things one never knew but which were there inside all the while; I do not know how to put it—it would take a Proust to explain it. (*Masters and the Slaves* xliii)

Introspection refers here both to the author Freyre's method of attempting to access something like the inner history of Brazilian social life and to his interlocutors in the course of his research, who in response to his questions remembered things from their past lives.

The novelty of Freyre's approach lay therefore not so much in the adoption of a participant-observation and fieldwork ethics, but rather in his claim that an intuitive approach, valuing associations and metaphor, in combination with his detailed study of the archive, produced his authority as a writer. As Fernando Henrique Cardoso has written, Freyre's enormous capacity for dominating the sociological literature of his time was impressive, and it was certainly not out of a lack of knowledge that he pointed to an obscure historical essay when speaking of "imaginative sympathy." Freyre's way of legitimating himself through references simply was eclectic and purposefully heterodox, including, in his preface to the second English-language edition of *The Masters and the Slaves* (1955), references to the *Spiritual Exercises* of the Jesuit founder Ignatius of Loyola and also to Oswald Spengler and to Picasso. He deliberately turned away from the quantitative, objective tone of social science research and sought out a voice for himself inspired by religious leaders, philosophers, and artists, rather than social scientists.

The way in which he used literary technique in his own writing was therefore not rooted in pure intuition or fictionalization. In his 1955 preface, he justified what he called the literary language of his essay by arguing that in the field of social history and anthropology, material facts were not enough and that the field had become increasingly "humanized" and close to literature: "The sociological, anthropological, and historical-social essay has a language of its own; it is not obliged to limit itself to an exact terminology as conceived by other sciences that are not concerned with human values. Its language may at times resemble the language of the novel or the literary essay" (*Masters and the Slaves* lxi). And indeed, both Freyre and Ortiz had a sense of the detail, the richness of everyday life on the plantation, which characterized so many nineteenth-century realist novels and in Freyre's case included aspects of daily life that did not commonly figure in scientific studies: cooking and eating habits, sexual mores, sense of fashion, linguistic expressions, and even shoe stores and hat makers were described in his works, painting the life of an entire society in ways similar to a novel indeed. His critics admiringly called this Freyre's "lack of method" (Ribeiro, "Prólogo" xxvi). Frank Tannenbaum wrote of Freyre's work as having "something of the Bergsonian intuition, of the poet's insight and the artist's vision" (in: Freyre, *Mansions and the Shanties* x). For Alfredo César Melo, too, it was Freyre's preference for antinomies, for revealing contradictions and adversary terms, that made Freyre stand out as a literary as well as a scientific writer ("A face de Janus no ensaísmo latino-americano"). Indeed, Freyre's contract with his reader was that he himself as the anthropologist-author preserved the identification with his subject by describing it in the greatest detail possible to his readers. This triangular empathy between the author and his subject, and the subject and the reader, characterized both the author of novels and the author of scientific essays. Both types of discourse, the scientific and the literary, however, remained distinct, and there is no attempt on Freyre's part to go "beyond" science, as would have been the case with Sarmiento or Euclides da Cunha in the nineteenth century, as analyzed by González Echevarría (110–41).

Freyre's style of argumentation was certainly unusual for a work of history, nonchronological, jumping across centuries and circulating around his topics rather than advancing from one to the next. Yet, in its spatial rather than historical focus, it alluded to other contemporary ways of approaching history, coming closer to the French *histoire intime,* or the Spanish *intra-historia,* as Freyre himself didn't neglect to point out (*Masters and the Slaves* lxix–lxx). It also spoke to the *longue durée* method of the French Annales school, without having been influenced by it. Of the book's five chapters, the first and the third explore the Portuguese colonization, and the fourth and the fifth explore the African slave, while chapter 2 is about Brazilian indigenous peoples. This seemingly repetitive proceeding allowed Freyre to go back and forth between the present and the past, demonstrating in ever-renewed analyses of individual regions, families, and plantations the complexity of adaptation processes among the Portuguese, African slaves, and the Amerindians. As he explained: "A psychological time is sometimes to be made the predominant one for the more vivid presentation of relations among events and among human beings artificially separated by conventional historical time" (*Masters and the Slaves* lxix).

If less common in the Brazilian and Anglo-American social sciences, Freyre's use of images and his argumentative style were not untypical of the German tradition of cultural philosophy, promoted widely in Latin America through the Spanish *Revista de Occidente*. Freyre referred prominently to Spengler's attention to architecture and in particular to the house as a way of determining the character of a given society (*Masters and the Slaves* xli). From Spengler Freyre also might have taken the idea that an analysis of space and of the interaction of the group with a given environment was more fruitful for the analysis of culture than a chronometrical historicizing effort. Spengler's "historical morphology" emphasized this point of view by assuming regular cycles of rising and falling cultures, different only in their spatial, climactic, and other individual characteristics, but not in their relative historical existence.[9]

Freyre's focus on the family as the core of society was, of course, reminiscent of realist family dramas but also not far from Sigmund Freud's psychoanalytical method. Freud had coined the concept of the "family romance" as central for a child's psychic life in an article published in 1909. As Burke and Pallares-Burke argue, Freyre was indebted to Freud and his disciples in other central aspects of his argument as well, especially in the attention he paid to the sexual symbolism of food and swear words and overall to the importance of childhood in the formation of adult relations (69). Nietzsche was another formative influence on Freyre in the early 1920s, when Freyre published several articles in the *Diario de Pernambuco* on his readings (in French translation) of the German philosopher. Pallares-Burke considers that it was probably Nietzsche's "perspectivism" that attracted Freyre (107). More generally, Nietzsche's polemic style of writing, his preference for aphorisms, and his radical questioning of previous philosophical and hermeneutic tradition also must have interested Freyre. While being unconventional in the Brazilian and U.S. American anthropological context, *The Masters and the Slaves* did speak to a learned but not necessarily scientific audience of readers familiar with writers such as Spengler, Freud, and Nietzsche, who were for much of their lifetimes outsiders in their respective fields of philosophy and psychology.

Yet Freyre's main interlocutors, as presented in the first chapter of *The Masters and the Slaves*, were predominantly historians, anthropologists, and sociologists, and even though Freyre wrote in a more colorful manner, he deeply engaged with them in order to propose that Brazilian colonial society was based not so much on the imposition of Portuguese mores and knowledge on Brazilian territory, or on racial mixing, but on a number of economic and social factors:

> In tropical America there was formed a society agrarian in structure, slave-holding in its technique of economic exploitation, and hybrid in composition, with an admixture of the Indian and later of the Negro. This was a society that in its evolution was protected less by a consciousness of race, which was practically non-existent in the cosmopolitan and plastic-minded Portuguese, than it was by a religious exclusiveness given expression in a system of social and political prophylaxis. (*Masters and the Slaves* 3)

He called Portuguese culture characteristically elastic ("plastic"), because the Portuguese, through their commercial empire, had come in contact with other tropical countries such as India and Africa. Race played a role in his argument, but only in so far as Freyre denied its role for the Portuguese, who in his view had been intent on imposing a particular economy and religion.

In his programmatic preface to the first edition of the book, in 1933, the refutation of racial determinism had been important, and Freyre had displayed a host of readings of travelogues and other older sources, as well as the theses of prior Brazilian scientists including Nina Rodrigues and Edgard Roquette-Pinto, pointing out their good intuitions as well as criticizing their shortcomings. In this preface Freyre also placed himself in contrast to, on the one hand, the racial segregation of the U.S. American South, which he had visited in the 1920s, and, on the other, the "Germanic *Weltanschauung*" of the time, by which he alluded to the Nazi doctrine of racial purity that had begun to dominate Germany and Italy from the late 1920s on. Against these, Freyre argued that the close domestic contacts between slave workers and masters, legitimate and illegitimate, white and colored, created a practice of day-to-day interactions that resulted in a characteristic *plasticidade:* the flexibility of its people to integrate and adapt to the most diverse cultures and climates.[10]

Overall, however, Freyre was less interested in discussing anthropological concepts of race and culture and instead presented a long list of environmental and social factors that had given shape to Brazil's colonial society. Emphasizing always the unique over the general law, Freyre discussed the influences of climate, nature, the economic system, the Jesuits, the diets of individual groups, and sexual practices in shaping Brazil. He displayed a distinct taste for inverting arguments, arguing, for example, that against the opinion that the tropical climate did not encourage agriculture and hard work, the Portuguese in fact had to work especially hard to make a living. As a result, they introduced the plantation economy, shifting from a colonialism of mere extraction to permanent settlement (*Masters and the Slaves* 23–24). In another instance of an argument turned upside down, Freyre wrote that the fact that the Portuguese kings did not impose a strong administrative system on Portugal's colonies, as the Spaniards had, was an advantage instead of a disadvantage, producing not a traumatized, oppressive society but instead one of private interactions that were quasi-democratic, from the bottom up.[11] Playing with stereotypes, Freyre even wrote that the social composition of the settlers—adventurers, new Christians, exiles, all of them rumored to be sexually voracious—was not an ethnic flaw but a sign of physical health. Similarly, he considered the geographic extension of the land and the varied economies it had produced—sugar, mining, and coffee—not a disadvantage but an advantage, producing strong regional cultures within the country. Freyre thus represented the relation of humans with each other, with the climate, or with nature as an adaptation process, whereby individuals inscribed their culture into the landscape and the climate as much as they were imprinted with it.

Thus Freyre's general argument, namely that Brazil was a "hybrid society," implied, more so than Ortiz, a tension between opposites, or, as Freyre called it, a "balance of antagonisms":

> The formation of Brazilian society . . . has been in reality a process of balancing antagonisms. Economic and cultural antagonisms. Atagonisms between European culture and native culture. Between the African and the native. Between an agrarian and a pastoral economy, between that of the agrarian and that of the mining regions. Between Catholic and heretic. Jesuit and *fazendeiro*. The *bandeirante* and the plantation-owner. The Paulista and the *emboaba*. The Pernambucan and the *mascate*. The landed proprietor and the pariah. The university graduate and the illiterate. But predominant over all these antagonisms was the more general and the deeper one: that between master and slave. (*Masters and the Slaves* 79–80)

This tension was not predominantly racial but social, a tension between people of different origins, economies, and religions, occupying different social positions in the colonial hierarchy. It produced a fabric of social relations so complex that Freyre's "balance of antagonisms" resulted, impossible to argue with or simplify, in a challenge to any social historian taking up the study of Brazil or any other country for that matter. Freyre's reticence toward branding concepts and thus simplifying the argument about Brazilian culture was noticeable everywhere in his text. Even though Freyre generalized in his chapter titles when speaking of "the indigenous," "the Portuguese colonizer," or "the black slave," he tended to categorize people by their regional origin or their occupation. Also, in his use of certain heavily connoted terms, such as *mulatto,* Freyre made sure to apply them in unexpected ways, for example, by calling "mulattoes" the Portuguese colonizers who had been in contact with African populations before coming to Brazil. Freyre's concern for emphasizing the gradual process of Portuguese adaptation in Brazil was so great that at times he minted new language. In his revision of early Portuguese history, for example, Freyre spoke of three formative elements: *mobilidade, miscibilidade,* and *aclimatabilidade* (*Casa-grande* 72): mobility, brought to Portugal by Jewish immigrants; "miscibility"—white men having intercourse with women of color, a tendency Freyre attributes to an Arabic influence on the Portuguese; and third, "acclimatibility" to the Brazilian tropical climate, due to Portugal's geographic proximity to Africa.

Not unlike Paul Rivet, Freyre used *longue durée* history, referring to the Paleolithic to explain that the Portuguese colonizers of the sixteenth century could not be understood by looking at contemporary Portuguese society only; rather, they had to be seen as a product of thousands of years of ethnic and cultural heterogeneity on the Iberian Peninsula. This then allowed him to claim that the Portuguese were the most "cosmopolitan" of the modern colonizers, more so than the Spaniards, accepting Europeans of all nations as part of the colonial enterprise in Brazil, as long as they professed to be Catholic (*Masters and the Slaves* 197). The survival of traces, among the Portuguese, of the Roman conquest, the Nordic invaders, and the contact with African peoples at the time of the colonization of Brazil showed, according to Freyre, the complex intermingling of cultures among the Portuguese and the rise of an aristocratic class that then sailed out to colonize America. In this way, he suggested that cultural hybridity was a continuous trait of culture, whereby the modern cosmopolitan experience became comparable to encounters from thousands of years ago.

While racial mingling was always implied in his argument about hybridity, the emphasis lay for Freyre on the always evolving process of culture, effectively contradicting eugenicist beliefs. For example, alcoholism, believed by eugenicists to be typical of the often mixed-race poor and the working class, with hereditary defects in offspring (Stepan 63–102), was recontextualized as a social ill by Freyre, who discussed streaks of alcoholism in Brazil's richest families of the nineteenth century, some of them proud of their Nordic heritage. As he pointed out, the phenomenon of degeneration associated with these families was social and economic, having to do with the instability of rural wealth in the nineteenth century, especially in the Northeast (*Masters and the Slaves* 270). Only at one point did Freyre address eugenics openly, in his chapter "The Negro Slave in the Sexual and Family Life of the Brazilian," arguing that Africans didn't respond better to the tropical climate than the Portuguese because of their genetic makeup, as the German eugenicist August Weismann had suggested, but instead because of the similarity of the climates of Africa and Brazil. He pointed to the revival of "neo-Lamarckian" theories about acquired characteristics becoming hereditary, citing Pavlov's experiments in the Soviet Union on automatic responses of mice to stimuli before receiving food and finally Boas's research on changes in the physical shape of immigrants to the United States. Freyre concluded that the factors typically cited by eugenicists and neo-Lamarckian scholars—climate and race—were less important than the demands placed on human beings by the economic system of the plantation in which the slaves had to function: "If we compare the moral or, better, the social effects of monoculture and the system of slave labor upon the Brazilian people with those produced by the same system upon peoples of a different race and under diverse conditions of climate and physical environment—in the Antilles and in the Southern U.S., for example—the preponderance of economic and social causes (the slave-holding technique of production and the patriarchal type of family) over the influence of race or that of climate is verified" (401).

While taking seriously these theories about the relation between climate and race, Freyre marked his distance from them and emphasized the importance of the colonial economic system in combination with the social structure of the patriarchal family for the evolution of Brazilian society. Similar to Ortiz, Rivet, and Roumain, Freyre responded to earlier theories about race and racial mixing by turning to history, looking at those factors of culture that had been disregarded by earlier anthropologists. In Freyre's case, these factors were not so much archaeology and the study of material artifacts, as with Rivet and Roumain, nor language or colonial literature, as with Ortiz. Freyre, rather, studied aspects of the everyday culture and life of Brazilians, such as their working conditions, economic systems, food habits, and dwellings, gleaning information from archival records and drawings, as well as from personal interviews. Characteristically, Fernand Braudel, who lived and taught at the Escola

Livre in São Paulo from 1935 to 1937, greatly appreciated Freyre's work, which indeed had much in common with his own approach to history, developed in publications after 1945.

Freyre's innovative approach to Brazilian culture coincided at many points with that of his today lesser-known contemporary the Brazilian anthropologist Arthur Ramos. Yet Ramos and Freyre exemplify in a way the two possible trajectories for the study of culture in Brazil in the 1930s and 1940s, Ramos representing the emphasis on method and institution building, continuing in the nineteenth-century positivist tradition; Freyre placing an intentionally unsystematic emphasis on history and interpretation in the study of Brazilian and Latin American culture.

Ramos and Freyre: The New Cultural Anthropology

Ramos received a doctorate in medicine from the Universidade Federal da Bahía, after which he worked at the Nina Rodrigues Institute in Bahía, where he also began to study physical anthropology.[12] A follower of Sigmund Freud's psychoanalysis, he was called in 1933 to Rio de Janeiro, to become the chief of Mental Hygiene Service, with unlimited access to Rio's schoolchildren to conduct research on educational reform, resulting in instructional brochures for the betterment of the poor population of Rio.[13] The following year his first and perhaps most important book, *O negro Brasileiro (The Negro in Brazil),* appeared; Ramos also became the director of a special series at Editora Civilização Brasileira. He received a chair in social psychology at the Federal University of Rio de Janeiro, where he met Freyre, then the director of the Department of Social Sciences. However, when the University of Brazil in Rio de Janeiro was created by decree in 1937, as part of an effort to concentrate the education of teachers in one national model, Ramos ended up being favored over Freyre by the government's minister, Gustavo Capanema.[14] He was the first acting chair of anthropology at the newly founded Facultade Nacional de Filosofia (a position that was permanent from 1946 on) and got to establish its first regular teaching curriculum, a position that granted him visibility as an anthropologist, in Brazil and abroad. It was from this point that his international career took off. Between 1939 and 1941 he held several visiting positions at universities in the United States. At his return in 1941, Ramos founded the Sociedade Brasileira de Antropologia e Etnologia (SBAE), the first scientific anthropological society in the country. Between 1943 and 1947, he published an important textbook, *Introdução à antropologia brasileira* (An introduction to Brazilian anthropology), which for the first time described the diverse populations of Brazil according to their African, indigenous, or European origin, building on the research of Nina Rodrigues, whose work Ramos had reedited in the 1930s.[15] Having the same medical background as Rodrigues, with added expertise in psychoanalytical theory, Ramos combined the physical and psychological classification of Brazilian ethnic groups typical of Rodrigues's research with the methods of cultural anthropology and acculturation studies, with which he had become familiar in the United States. After his return, Ramos also set out to publish *A aculturação negra no Brasil* (1942; The acculturation of blacks in Brazil) and *Guerra e relações de raça* (1943; War and race relations). Ramos's thus established research reputation, his international contacts, and his administrative experience in Brazil made him an ideal candidate for UNESCO, where in 1949 he became the chair of the Department of Social Sciences, working alongside Jean Piaget, Julien Huxley, Otto Klineberg, Bertrand Russell, and Maria Montessori. Ramos was able to initiate UNESCO's Project on Race Relations in Brazil before dying prematurely in 1949.

Freyre in contrast had been propelled to stardom in Brazil with his two books *The Masters and the Slaves* and *The Mansions and the Shanties,* published in the 1930s in Brazil, both of which decisively broke with nineteenth- and early-twentieth-century ideas on race and miscegenation and received instant acclaim from both a scientific and a nonscientific readership. Having returned to Recife in 1923, after his university education and some travels in Europe, he had in the meantime helped found a cultural center, the Centro Regional do Nordeste, and organized a Regionalist Congress in 1926. He published *The Masters and the Slaves* after two years of exile, following the Vargas revolution of 1930, during which he had been to Portugal and Stanford University. After the publication of *The Masters and the Slaves,* Freyre had a brief academic career, becoming in 1935 a professor of sociology at the Law Faculty of Recife as well as a professor and chair of the Department of Social Sciences at the Universidad do Distrito Federal (UDF) in Rio de Janeiro, teaching sociology, social anthropology, and social investigation. He was also the director of the Social Sciences Department at the UDF during that time. After the contentious dissolution of the school by the Vargas regime and Freyre's resignation from the UDF, however, Freyre rejected offers for chairs in sociology at the University of Brazil, in social philosophy at Yale University, and in social Brazilian studies at Harvard University. At that point, Freyre clearly did not want to have academic constraints any longer, allowing him to continuously defy academic boundaries among anthropology, sociology, history, and literary criticism.[16] While he was well connected among social scientists internationally and in Brazil, Freyre, it seems, preferred not to play a role in any international organizations either—it was Ramos who became a member of the editorial board of *Afroamérica,* the journal founded by Ortiz, and it was Ramos who worked for UNESCO in 1949, after Freyre rejected the offer (Burke and Pallares-Burke 114). Freyre's influence was more diffuse, generating new ways of studying culture that clearly had an impact on Ortiz's thought, for example, yet with little institutional consequence.[17]

Ramos and Freyre both promoted Brazil as a culture of mixed ethnicities at a time when such views were gaining currency in Brazil under Getulio Vargas's regime. It is true that Vargas imprisoned both Ramos and Freyre for short intervals, suspecting them of communist activities; yet he seems to have appreciated Freyre's as well as Ramos's works for their generally popular message. Freyre himself even admitted to having been impressed with Vargas's charismatic personality (Burke and Pallares-Burke 127–28). Ramos, too, worked closely with Vargas government officials, and his notion of Brazil as a *cultura de compromisso* (culture of compromise) was interpreted even more so than Freyre's thought as an ideology of the Estado Novo.[18] But as Lucia Campos writes: "The search for 'solutions of compromise' seems to have spanned the entire thought system of that period's government and the elite."[19] The general zeitgeist was such that visions of racial or cultural mixing permeated the Brazilian elite to which Freyre and Ramos belonged, as well as Vargas's government.

The passage from an anthropological "scientific" concept to a political ideology also meant that race became emphasized yet again over the idea of culture. The term *racial democracy,* referring to the perception that Brazil had always had harmonious relations among its different ethnic constituencies, was first used by Arthur Ramos in his *Guerra e relaçoes de raça* (1943; War and race relations) and then picked up in the journalistic publications of Roger Bastide, who associated it with Freyre, who had indeed presented many of the basic ideas undergirding the concept in *The Masters and the Slaves* but never used the term itself.[20] Abdias do Nascimento's Black Movement, with its Teatro Experimental Nacional (TEN), used the concept of racial democracy in turn to reclaim a black voice in Brazil, with a column titled "Democracia racial" in its journal *Quilombo.* According to Idelber Avelar, the notion of racial democracy also influenced the U.S. American reception of Freyre's work greatly, as U.S. American black activists cited Freyre to critique racial segregation in their own country.[21]

Ramos himself, in the 1940s, began to speak more and more of *mestiçagem* as the unique "advantage" of Brazilian society, promoting the idea of racial democracy as a model of peaceful race relations (Campos 205; Barros 219–20).[22] In particular, *Guerra e relações de raça,* destined for a wider readership, was meant to dispel prejudices about racial differences. Similar to Benedict's *Race: Science and Politics* and Fernando Ortiz's *El engaño de las razas* (The deception of the races), it was a work of politically committed scholarship in which Ramos presented World War II as a war of conquest, with Germany and Italy attempting to impose ideologies of racial superiority over the rest of the world. Anthropology was called to arms in order to dispel such notions: "One thing is certain: This War is being conducted under the mark of Mankind. Protected by the lessons of Anthropology—considered in its ample sense as the science of Mankind and of Culture—let us fight, on an ideological level, the maleficent attempts by those who have constructed myths of racial superiority/inferiority that may have served their agenda of conquest and spoil."[23] He called for an "applied anthropology" to be established, that is, for accumulating empirical data about Brazilian racial mixing. Once these data were at hand, the good anthropologist would become a *vidente,* a fortune-teller capable "not of divining events, but in a certain sense of foretelling them within the laws of empirical observation" (27).[24]

Freyre was supportive of the antiracist cause too, of course, but he advocated, in his lecture "A propósito da política cultural do Brasil na América" (1942; On the cultural politics of Brazil in America), a generalized "'scientific humanism' more interested . . . in interhuman relational and interregional contact problems without this interest impairing the science or sacrificing the intellectual dignity of the new humanists."[25]

It was in the end Freyre's focus on "interregional contact" that won over Ramos's empiricism, to the point that today, ironically, many critics of the concept of racial democracy do not mention Ramos as the one who coined the concept.[26] Clearly, Ramos had a fairly mechanical view of race and culture, whereby he saw the anthropologist's task as studying, in the line of Nina Rodrigues, the origins of black and indigenous populations in Brazil and the survival of their customs and practices. His methods quickly became obsolete, as Florestan Fernandes noted in his book *A Etnologia e a Sociologia no Brasil* (1958; Ethnology and sociology in Brazil). Freyre's notion of cultural hybridity in turn became problematic for those who accused him of simply inverting racial hierarchies, being himself in the privileged position of a white scientist. But perhaps precisely because of their ambiguity and despite his later reactionary "Luso-Tropicalist" views on the benefits of Portuguese colonialism, Freyre continued to be read, even in other Portuguese colonies such as Cape Verde, where intellectuals of the 1950s read hybridity and the "social engineering" initiated by the Portuguese colonizers as a process leading to Cape Verdean autonomy (Melo, "Hibridismos (in) domáveis").[27]

The differences between Freyre and Ramos, however, were not only due to Ramos's local training in the line of Nina Rodrigues's physical anthropology and Freyre's training with Boas; rather, they corresponded to two larger schools of thought within anthropology that were still very much alive at the time. Ramos's more empirical orientation was indebted to the diffusionist school, represented by Fritz Graebner and Leo Frobenius, with Paul Rivet as a late follower. Meanwhile, Freyre's more pliable, interpretive approach came, as we know, from Franz Boas's school, with Clark Wissler as an important point of reference.[28] Both schools theorized cultural contact in fundamentally opposing ways. Diffusionists such as Graebner assumed that cultures evolved not through spontaneous invention, but rather through the material transmission of traits and knowledge. A "culture area" was a geographic area where a relatively homogeneous society had continuously lived, adopting traits that included religion, social organization, habitat, weapons, and tools (Graebner 132–34). Cultural contact for Graebner could only be thought of in terms of conquest, when thinking, for example, of empires such as the Greek or the Roman empires, which had extended their domain and imposed a series of principles, forming in this way new culture areas. When looking at other less explored areas, however, Graebner found that it was difficult to determine the borders between distinct culture areas, and he insisted on the importance of historically reconstructing the arrival of individual groups and their dominance over others. Graebner's notion of culture area was quoted by Ramos in several publications and used, for example, in his *O folclore negro do Brasil* (1937; Black folklore in Brazil), where Ramos classified Brazil's African populations by area of origin and then studied the processes of acculturation that had occurred after their arrival in Brazil. Franz Boas's newer school of thought, however, took its distance from such comparative approaches and insisted on the importance of analyzing individual "psychological" responses to a given environment next to physical ones. Boas had already, in his 1911 review of Graebner's *Methode der Ethnologie* (Method of ethnology,) contested the "mechanical" claims of Graebner, finding it problematic to assume that individual creativity and interpretation did not have any role in the development of societies. Boas especially protested against the assumption that cultural groups exhibiting the same traits had been in contact earlier on or even descended from each other. Ramos, however, continued to hold on to the idea that the survival of practices particular to a given culture area could be traced through an analysis of the ethnic provenience of subgroups and their practices, even though he cited Boas's works.

Freyre's approach to the idea of distinct cultural areas, on the contrary, followed Boas's school in focusing on a combination of factors. In one of the few methodological books that he wrote, *Problemas brasileiros de antropologia* (Problems in Brazilian anthropology), he argued, with Clark Wissler, that it was insufficient to determine culture areas based on race or origin only, but that a complex pattern of traits had to be taken into consideration.[29] Freyre was adamant that social psychology did not play a role in the definition of such areas, nor did geographic or political frontiers by themselves (*Problemas brasileiros de antropologia* 51–61). For Freyre it was less the study of history itself that was important, but rather the study of the many practices and habits, including agriculture and food, that had allowed for the forming of a culture.

These differences in method also had reverberations in how Freyre and Ramos viewed the cultural impact of slavery in Brazil, for example. For Ramos, "psycho-social" factors like the separation of the individual from his or her group and the "contact between cultures and races" were decisive elements (*Las culturas negras en el Nuevo Mundo* 318). For Freyre, in turn, the daily interaction between slaves and masters, as well as their response to new environments, defined that particular culture area, or culture "complex."

Ramos's more traditional approach and Freyre's adoption of Boas's cultural anthropology also led to major differences between the two in regard to their understanding of the branches of anthropology. Whereas for Freyre race, language, and culture were the three most basic categories necessary to analyze the "complex whole" that was the object of anthropology (*Problemas brasileiros de antropologia* 61–76), for Ramos, the psychological analysis of a culture's *paideuma* was decisive: "Culture is not just language. It is something more, which transcends the mere political injunctions of a given moment. It is a determinism of the people. In this sense, we can speak of a culture of the New World, characterized by their different spirit, by their 'direction,' using Keyserling's expression, or by their 'Paideuma,' employing an expression dear to Frobenius."[30] On the one hand then Ramos depicted Brazilian society as racially mixed yet not predetermined biologically, a society having the same problems as others. On the other hand, he considered that if only one knew the origins of Brazil's different ethnic groups, one would be able to determine its particular "spirit." Freyre instead generally emphasized the changing nature of cultures and the importance of studying them in the present time. Against the diffusionist idea that culture areas were determined by the transmission of specific cultural traits toward subsequent generations, Freyre took a long view of locally specific social groups, discarding all prior assumptions and reading and observing individual behavior.

Degradação da raça: Fissures in Freyre's and the Brazilian Modernists' Racial Discourse

Vicente de Rego Monteiro's artist book published in France, *Quelques visages de Paris* (1925, Some faces of Paris), presents a parody of a European tourist trip, with drawings of Paris combined with short comments by a "savage chief, who one day came incognito to visit Paris." In this irreverent inversion, each tourist site of Parisian monuments becomes the occasion of a humorous, defamiliarizing observation—the Eiffel Tower, the Place de la Concorde, the Louvre acquire functions for an imaginary "primitive" society that are far removed from their historical purpose. Also included is a drawing of the Trocadero palace, the site of the Musée d'Ethnographie at the time, demolished and transformed in the 1930s by Paul Rivet into the Musée de l'Homme (fig. 2). The site is depicted in schematic brushes, with the building itself looming dark in the upper margin of the drawing and the center taken up by a fish pond, surrounded by the contours of flower beds and water basins. The stylized character of the drawing and the clearly symbolic meaning of some of its motifs, like a single leaf and the water lines, almost suggest a hieroglyph, half image and half sign, enclosing a secret meaning that we have to extract.[31] The brief comment of Rego Monteiro's savage chief interprets part of the drawing for us: "House of a great warrior, to judge from its trophies; he seems to be very good at the art of embalming and stuffing the heads and bodies of his enemies. It was with the greatest pang of the heart that I saw my ancestors in such funny postures."

Rego Monteiro exposes in this drawing the colonial implications of French and Brazilian anthropology, whose practitioners appropriate indigenous authority to represent that culture as they wish. The anthropologists and artists "investigate" cultural contact between western and indigenous cultures yet rarely give those indigenous peoples an opportunity

Fig. 2. Vicente de Rego Monteiro, "Trocadero." *Quelques visages de Paris* (Paris: Juan Dura, 1925; facsim. ed. Jorge Schwartz, ed. São Paulo: EDUSP, Imprensaoficial, 2005. N.pag.). (Galeria Ranulpho, Pernambuco, Brazil)

to reply. Even Rego Monteiro, while mocking the historicizing efforts of anthropologists, also caricaturizes, unwillingly perhaps, the indigenous point of view as that which is marginalized, enigmatic, and somewhat closer to nature—hence the fish pond and the park as counterpoints to the contents of the Trocadero palace itself, turned into a European graveyard for primitives.

Freyre's own argument about cultural contact was clearly stronger with respect to African slaves and Portuguese colonizers than in what he had to say about Brazilian indigenous cultures.[32] His chapter structure in *The Masters and the Slaves* indicated as much, since he devoted two chapters each to the Portuguese colonizer and the African slave culture but only one to "The Native in the Brazilian Family." In this one chapter, Freyre's perspective on cultural contact seems to be strikingly different from his previous chapters. If he had been speaking until then of a hybrid culture that was created through mutual contacts, Freyre now became more gloomy, speaking of a "degradation of the backward race" that had occurred with the European intrusion and of the subsequent end of the "balance in the relations of man to his physical environment (*Masters and the Slaves* 81). He contrasted the degradation of indigenous peoples with the technical and cultural "superiority" of Africans, noting especially their biological and psychological strength.

His chapter on the Brazilian "natives" exposes more than any of the others Freyre's complicated negotiations between past and present paradigms of race and culture and the fissures, in *The Masters and the Slaves,* of the new discourse on culture as it was being established in the 1930s. In Freyre's discourse on the indigenous peoples we can see echoes of nineteenth-century theories of racial degradation. But because so much of it had to do with a properly humanistic inquiry into questions of human dignity, Freyre probed a variety of answers. In one instance, he argued that the indigenous communities of the rain forest retreated into themselves when faced with Europeans: "The reaction to European rule in that area of Amerindian culture which was invaded by the Portuguese was almost one of pure vegetable sensitivity and contractility, with the Indian withdrawing or shrinking back at civilizing contact with the European, out of an incapacity to accommodate himself to the new economic technique and the new social and moral regime. Even when he became an enemy, the native was still vegetable in his mode of aggression, little more than an auxiliary of the forest" (*Masters and the Slaves* 82). Different from the "bronze-like" high cultures of the Incas, the Aztecs, and the Mayas (82), Brazilian Amerindians had a "vegetation-like sensibility." To speak of cultures as plants implied that they went through organic stages of growth—youth, adolescence (or semicivilization), maturity—and that they were able to die by themselves. Freyre made this organicist view on culture clear at several points of the chapter: the Portuguese civilization was in a state of "maturity," whereas the Incas, Mayas, and Aztecs had reached a degree that was close to "adolescence" or "semi-civilization" (*Masters and the Slaves* 82). The Brazilian indigenous populations, however, were among the most *rasteiras* or "backward" populations of the continent. For Freyre's theory of the "harmonious amalgamation" of cultures in Brazil this meant that only if the indigenous were depicted as somehow naturally adopting western culture or else disappearing could they be integrated into Brazilian society. Even though Freyre rejected race as a determining factor in the development of cultures across time and space, he was not ready to give up on the properly romantic idea that some cultures, like the Brazilian indigenous cultures, were "younger" and closer to nature than others and therefore were not able to adapt but were rather destroyed by the more "advanced" cultures. This was the inherently violent background to Freyre's thesis that cultures had blended more easily in Brazil than elsewhere. Freyre claimed that in comparison to the difficulty that other colonial powers encountered, the Portuguese colonizer had still assimilated indigenous cultures better than the English or Spanish colonizers: "The truth is that in Brazil, contrary to what is to be observed in other American countries and in those parts of Africa that have been recently colonized by Europeans, the primitive culture—the Amerindian as well as the African—has not been isolated into hard, dry, indigestible lumps incapable of being assimilated by the European social system" (181). Still, Freyre himself deplored the havoc that had been wreaked on indigenous cultures in Brazil, particularly by the religious orders, which had forcefully converted and educated the indigenous cultures, leaving them disoriented and torn from their world.

In his evolutionist ideas about the superiority of European civilizations over primitive cultures, Freyre referred in particular to the German anthropologist Rüdiger Bilden to discuss types of colonization in relation to the "civilizational stage" of the culture encountered. Using Frobenius's classification of African culture areas, aided by Wissler and Kroeber, he argued that the African slaves transplanted to Brazil had come from areas that were "superior" to Brazilian indigenous cultures (*Masters and the Slaves* 88–89).[33] More important, in analyzing the "clash of the two cultures," the Europeans and the Amerindians, Freyre pointed to studies by Augustus Pitt-Rivers, in *The Clash of Cultures and the Contact of Races* (1927), and Edward B. Tylor, in *Primitive Culture,* then in its fifth edition of 1929. The two British scientists had written about the notion of the "degeneration" of certain cultures due to the clash with other superior ones. Freyre agreed with them in concluding that in America, "the domination of the native populations by the colonizer or the missionary had caused a complete moral degradation" (*Masters and the Slaves* 106–7). It was here that Freyre showed a certain conflictedness. He cited Pitt

Rivers's argument about the loss of a culture's "potential" or rhythm under the influence of imperialist domination but then distanced himself from the notion of a culture's inherent superiority:

> The history of the contact of the so-called "superior" races with those looked upon as "inferior" is always the same. Extermination or degradation. Chiefly because the conqueror means to impose upon the subject people the whole of his own culture, in one piece, without any compromise to soften the imposition. From the sixteenth century to the present day the missionary has been the great destroyer of non-European cultures, his activities in this respect having been more dissolvent than those of the layman. (107)

Whereas Pitt-Rivers had assumed that there were laws inherent to the relation between superior and inferior "races," for Freyre the matter was a question of upon whom the victorious invader could impose himself. Leaving open to interpretation the idea of cultural superiority, Freyre noted that the political fact of colonization determined the imposition of religious and moral norms, putting the conquered culture at a disadvantage. Here, all of a sudden, he thus implied that it was not a lack of cultural "matureness" or persistence that caused the disintegration of indigenous cultures in Brazil, but the more mechanical fact of the ability of the Portuguese to impose themselves, through their weapons, agriculture, and political and religious institutions.

Overall, his argument in this chapter wavered between evocative descriptions of indigenous sexuality, gender relations, clothing, child rearing, hygiene, color preference, games, and beliefs, as found in travel accounts and anthropological studies, on the one hand, and, on the other, accounts of the disastrous influence particularly of the Jesuits on Brazilian indigenous populations, criticizing Jesuits' educational efforts and what Freyre called the "segregation" of indigenous people in the so-called Jesuit missions, which had prevented indigenous groups from engaging on a daily basis with colonial Brazilian culture. Yet all the while emphasizing the social and economic constraints in which they had been placed, Freyre called the indigenous "primitives," in the sense conferred to the term by Lévy-Bruhl, of a "prelogical" mentality tied to mystical, totemic, and animist beliefs. Freyre accused the Jesuits of having "broken" this primitive indigenous mentality by removing indigenous peoples from their territories and segregating them in missions (*Masters and the Slaves* 172–73). He thus admitted the political and religious oppression they suffered and the unfavorable conditions under which they experienced cultural contact with Europeans, but he was unable to integrate them into his larger picture of Brazilian society. While Afro-descendant Brazilians represented to him an example of strength and flexibility at the same time, Freyre was at a loss to include significant indigenous traits and characteristics in his portrait.

In his rather conflicted interest in indigenous cultures Freyre was not so different from the Brazilian Modernist artists. Already in the 1920s, the "Anthropophagist Manifesto" of Oswald de Andrade had famously proposed that Brazilians had to return to the fierceness of the indigenous Tupi, an indigenous population that had famously attacked and eaten Portuguese settlers in the sixteenth century, and had to reclaim a uniquely Brazilian cultural identity able to "digest" both European and indigenous heritage. Another member of the group, Mario de Andrade, had traveled together with a few others to Minas Gerais to collect traditional lore and legends from the backland. Ultimately, however, Andrade and his group, while reading widely about Amazon indigenous peoples, did not identify with indigenous tropical culture. As Lúcia Sá writes in her study *Rain Forest Literatures,* "Despite the decisive impact that indigenous texts had on their works, *modernistas* of all ideological colors showed no more concern than most of their Romantic predecessors for the survival of the indigenous cultures, for the place actually occupied by Indians and their descendants in Brazilian society" (144). Fernando Rosenberg, too, argues regarding Mario de Andrade's works *The Apprentice Tourist* and *Macunaíma* that indigenous characters and communities were depicted from an outsider's perspective, without further reflection on preserving traditional indigenous cultures.

In contrast, the Modernists' depiction of mixed-race people was more dynamic and forward looking. Figures such as Emiliano di Cavalcanti's *Mulata* (1938), Cândido Portinari's *Mestiça* (1934), and Bruno Giorgi's *Mulata* (1944) (figs. 3, 4, and 5) represent women who are modern, because they are characterized by their skin color as well as by class markers. Portinari's *Mestiça* is a stout working-class woman, who looks at the observer, expressionless and straightforward, as if she were being photographed. Giorgi's *Mulata* in turn is depicted as a classical beauty with long hair held back and fine features, only the title indicating that she is a mixed-race woman. Only Cavalcanti's *Mulata* displays a tension between different human types, a dressed mulata woman in the front and a naked white woman in the back. Two men in the background are watching the two women, who seem deliberately ignorant of each other.[34] All these artworks represented a modern Brazilian society made of different shades of ethnicities and classes.

Fig. 3. Emiliano di Cavalcanti, *Mulata,* 1938. Oil on canvas, 93 × 74 cm. (© Elisabeth di Cavalcanti. Museu de Arte Brasileira da FAAP, São Paulo, Brazil)

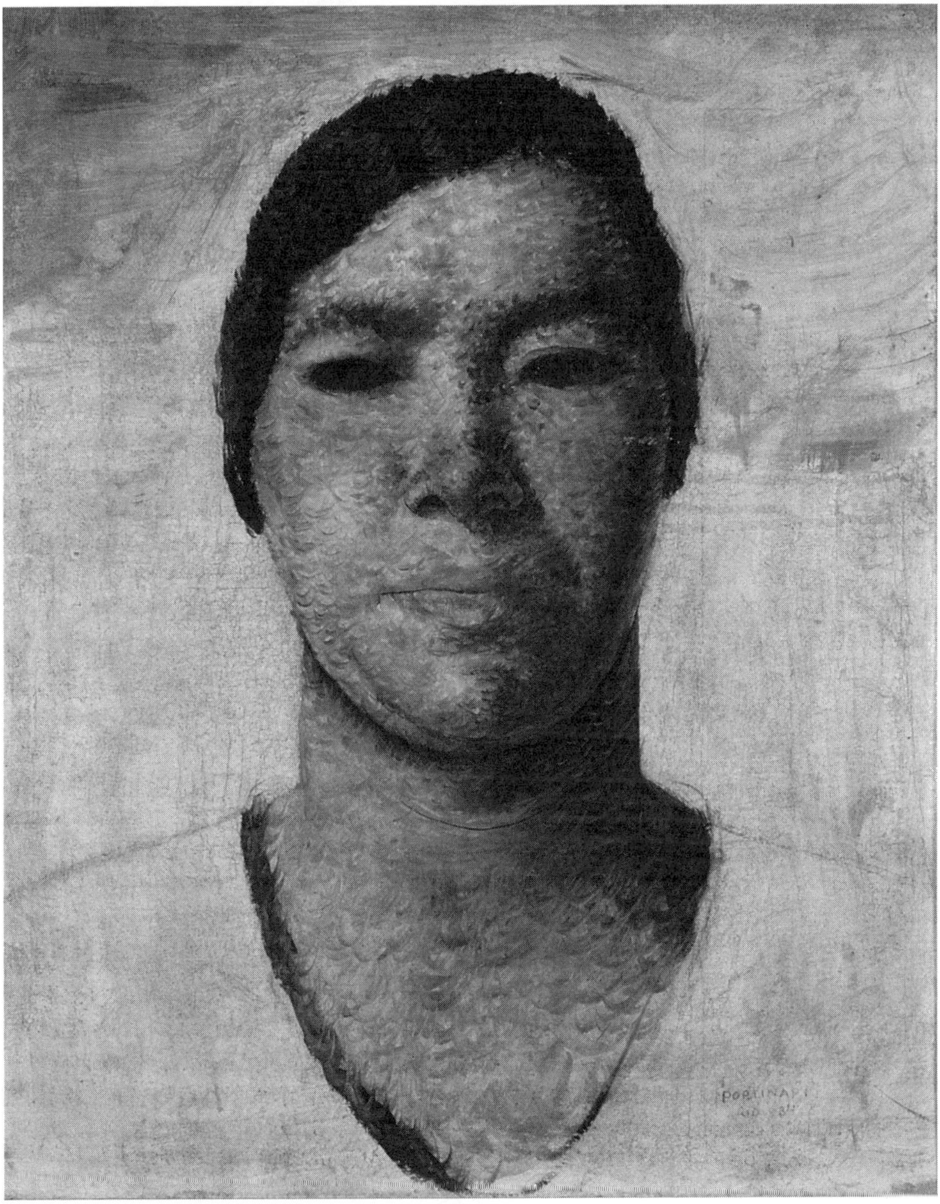

Fig. 4. Cándido Portinari, *Mestiça,* 1934. Oil on canvas, 46.5 × 38 cm. (Museu de Arte Brasileira de FAAP, São Paulo, Brazil)

Fig. 5. Bruno Giorgi, *Mulata,* 1944. Terracotta, 55 × 39 × 30 cm. (Collection Marta y Paulo Kuczynski)

While it turned out to be compelling to artists and anthropologists alike to depict Brazil as a racially mixed society, modern precisely because it had profited from its diverse cultures, Freyre and his contemporaries struggled to understand radical cultural otherness—what Alfred Métraux termed "inadaptation," referring to the Chaco indigenous peoples of Argentina. Since 1910 Brazil had had a federal agency for indigenous communities, the Serviço de Proteção aos Índios (SPI), with the declared aim to protect the indigenous populations of the lower Amazon from outside contact yet give them all the possibilities of development that were compatible with their prior lives.[35] In addition, several anthropologists in the first half of the twentieth century had studied Brazilian indigenous populations of the present, most important among them Curt Nimuendaju, Karl von den Steinen, Fritz Krause, Edgard Roquette-Pinto, and Max Schmidt. In the 1930s, however, these studies of indigenous life were less understood. Freyre, in focusing his analysis on Brazilian domestic life on the plantation, turned away from scenarios of primal Brazilian cultures, focusing instead on the plantation house as the locus of Brazilian culture and cultural contact, thus sharing important characteristics with the Modernist painters, none of whom was able to consider indigenous communities' unwillingness to become assimilated.[36]

Freyre's Reflection on "Science"

Freyre's general ideas on the function of the social sciences in contemporary society evolved decisively during the 1930s and the 1940s, following invitations and diverse university appointments that gave Freyre the occasion to compare national traditions of scientific and intellectual production. His 1934 lecture "O estudo das ciencias sociais nas universidades americanas" (The study of social sciences in American universities) was the first published instance where he compared his experience as a student and teacher of the social sciences in the United States to the Brazilian situation. For Freyre there was a "revolution" going on in the United States, with respect to both its governing ideas and its politics. He noticed among scientists as well as writers and poets that they were turning away from Anglo-Saxon colonial and puritan traditions and looking with fresh eyes at contemporary reality. This spirit was exemplified in the interdisciplinary way in which the social sciences were taught at the universities he had come to know:

> I believe, for that matter, that in light of the conflicts regarding frontiers and zones of influence among social studies, it is best for students to flee from the

> excess of specializations in a specific social science to acquire, through contact with other social studies, a richer body of observations and a greater variety of points of view. If university organization in the U.S. favors and encourages, on one hand, specialization, on the other hand it allows the student greater flexibility in his/her program of study. . . . It is up to scientists in general, and social scientists in particular, to acquire a minimum amount of generalized culture that is indispensable for their specializations. Without this minimum, perhaps a great physicist or a great chemist can be made, but not a great sociologist or economist.[37]

As Freyre emphasized, the social sciences were not exact sciences but obeyed laws of "perpetual tentativeness," having moved beyond the dogmatism of nineteenth-century scientists such as Comte, Tarde, Spencer, and others. The need for interpretation in the social sciences was precisely the trait he most appreciated and called part of the "humanization of knowledge" at U.S. American universities. It included for him the avoidance of scientific jargon and the attempt to communicate with general readers and scientists (*O, estudo das ciencias sociais* 50). It also included the rigorous study of all available literature with an emphasis on primary sources and fieldwork or sociological surveys.

By emphasizing the need for interpretation in the social sciences, Freyre was following, of course, in the steps of Franz Boas. But his emphasis on the interdisciplinary outlook of social science research shifted the perspective somewhat toward the more essayistic approach followed by only a few of Boas's students, such as Ruth Benedict and Robert Lowie.

His three years of teaching at the Universidade do Distrito Federal in Rio de Janeiro brought with them an increased focus on the limits and the classification of anthropology and sociology. Based on the experience, Freyre published two textbook-style works on anthropology and sociology. *Problemas brasileiros de antropologia* (1943; Problems in Brazilian anthropology), dedicated to Fernando Ortiz and four other Latin American intellectuals and scientists, argued for the practical applicability of anthropology in all areas of public life, concerning Brazil's regions, ecology, and history. His two-volume work *Sociologia* (1945), in turn, was based on his lecture notes for the courses on sociology and social anthropology he taught at the Universidade do Distrito Federal between 1935 and 1938. Here too Freyre argued that there was much sociology in some texts that were not sociological, as, for example, in Walter Pater, Aldous Huxley, George Santayana, Gilberto Amado, Angel Ganivet, Unamuno,

Ortega y Gasset, Joaquim Nabuco, Euclides da Cunha, José Verissimo, and Nina Rodrigues (15–16).

In Freyre's view, the complexity of the material or the "social situation" itself had to dictate which reading or method should be chosen for investigation. Freyre emphatically called himself a dilettante or, even better, an *amador:* "If we are considered amateurs, let us be consoled by Havelock Ellis, the greatest apologist of the English amateurs and their 'unsystematic method of thinking'"[38] All the while claiming not to write as an academic, he was nevertheless acutely aware of the disciplinary divisions surrounding the fields of sociology and anthropology. Despite his constant emphasis on the uses of literature in particular for the social sciences, he also insisted on having both anthropology and sociology recognized as social sciences. He reminded his readers in the preface that he had taught both sociology and anthropology and had also insisted on having the sociology class shifted from the Facultade de Filosofia e Letras and into the Faculdade de Economia e Direito (*Sociologia* 67–68).

During his time at the university in Rio de Janeiro, Freyre seems to have been relatively untouched by the two schools of sociology that had been established in São Paulo under the guidance of Donald Pierson, on the one hand, and, on the other, the French school of sociology, with Bastide, Braudel, Pierre Verger, and Claude Lévi-Strauss among the visiting French scientists. From the 1940s on, he developed his controversial theory of Luso-Tropicalism, developing ideas on the special Portuguese skills in the tropics, a theory that was used by the Portuguese dictator Salazar to justify Portugal's colonial empire in Africa. Luso-Tropicalism, as well as Freyre's support of Brazil's military coup in 1964, contributed to his increasing isolation in the Brazilian social science milieu of the 1950s and 1960s (Burke and Pallares-Burke 119–29).

His institutional independence allowed Freyre to continue to argue for an interdisciplinary approach to the social sciences, separate but not distinct from the humanities. After World War II, Freyre was unabashedly in favor of the rise of U.S. American "area studies" as integrating the humanities with the social sciences. In his 1955 "Preface" he wrote:

> Changes in attitude in the relations between the social sciences and the humanities have been such in the U.S. and Europe during the past decade that university teachers of sociology, psychology, and other social sciences frankly admit that the social problems confronting the modern world challenge everyone to seek greater social insight. . . . This . . . integrative point of view dominates

> the area studies that have been introduced in a number of Anglo-American universities since the Second World War. . . . The value of literary and folkloric approaches should not be disregarded or thought unworthy of contributing, alongside scientific analysis of their inter-relationships, to a deeper, more comprehensive interpretation of such regional complexes. (*Masters and the Slaves* xxi).

As is well known, however, area studies institutes in the United States typically do not include literary studies, which have come to live in foreign language departments.[39] Freyre's vision for the integrated study of culture in the social sciences and the humanities remained a shared project of some social scientists and cultural critics, but one condemned to exist on the side, next to the separate institutionalization of the social sciences and literary studies after 1945.

After 1945

Freyre had produced with *The Masters and the Slaves* an epic portrait of Brazilian colonial society, tempting in its optimism about Brazil and strikingly modern in its ideas about cultural contact, similar to Ortiz's later concept of transculturation. Even though his vision of cultural contact in Brazil was a strikingly conflictive one, in particular in relation to indigenous peoples, it had given rise to the concept of racial democracy that had been eagerly appropriated by Vargas's Estado Novo but also by the Afro-Brazilian movement of Abdias do Nascimento. Partly in response to this new conciliatory discourse on race in Brazil, the postwar project on race relations of the newly founded UNESCO centered on Brazil. This program was the last and most comprehensive scientific project that, in response to the genocides of World War II, attempted to draw definitive conclusions about the scientific definition of race and racism, pointing to ways to end racism.

While in the 1930s and during the war, as we have seen, international collaboration between anthropologists had mainly consisted of appeals and declarations signed jointly against scientific racism, after the war, the recently founded UNESCO took a novel approach. A Department of Social Sciences was created, of which Arthur Ramos and later Alfred Métraux became the presidents. Several projects were brought together, consisting of the International Institute of the Hylean Amazon, in which Rivet became involved; the Fundação para o Desenvolvimento da Ciência na Bahia, a collaboration between the State of Bahia and the Anthropology Department at Columbia University; and finally UNESCO's Program for the Study of Race Relations in Brazil. The outcomes were important studies such as Charles's Wagley's edited volume *Race and Class in Rural Brazil* (1952), L. A. Costa Pinto's *O Negro en Rio de Janeiro* (1953; The black man in Rio de Janeiro), Thales de Azevedo's *Les élites de couleur dans une ville brésilienne* (1953; The elites of color in a Brazilian town), Roger Bastide and Florestan Fernandes's *Relações Raciais entre Pretos e Brancos em São Paulo* (1955; Racial relations between blacks and whites in São Paulo), and several more. The UNESCO project, in the view of Marcos Chor Maio, "played a catalytic role in the consolidation of Brazilian academic intelligentsia" and laid the groundwork for later studies on the existence of racial prejudice in Brazil ("UNESCO's Anti-Racist Agenda").[40] However, as Thomas Skidmore writes, in the 1960s it became increasingly clear that the new studies on race relations did not fulfill the expectations of many UNESCO officials.[41] Several of those studies in fact revealed that there was persistent racism in Brazil and that skin color in Brazil, too, was closely related to class divisions (Skidmore, *Black into White*).

Next to these programs, the Department of Social Sciences at UNESCO also attempted to come to a conclusive declaration on race and racism and to this effect organized two meetings in 1949 and in 1951, in which a number of physical and cultural anthropologists participated, among them Otto Klineberg, Ashley Montagu, and Claude Lévi-Strauss. The results, however, were not satisfactory, since physical and cultural anthropologists could not agree on a minimal common definition of race. For Chor Maio and Ventura Santos, this had to do with the uneven goals set by UNESCO, which were on the one hand political, meant to cement an antiracist consensus, and on the other too much set on "scientific" proof. To reduce the question of race and racism to a matter of scientific agreement on humanistic grounds did not produce good results.

Freyre had introduced with *The Masters and the Slaves* a major shift in the study of race and culture in Brazil, away from racial determinism toward the *longue durée* focus on cultural contact and the human capacity to adapt to new environments, climates, and social hierarchies. Still, it is telling that after all of Freyre's, Ramos's, and others' efforts, the UNESCO project on race still found that the "specter of the races" continued to exist in Brazil just as it did in other countries.

Epilogue

When entering the old Seminary Co-op Bookstore in the basement of the Chicago Theological Seminary, readers were led into uncharted intellectual territory via colored paths. Following a blue line, etched on the floor, one arrived in the "blue history room"; on the way, one might have wanted to dwell in the "literary criticism hallway" or else turn and walk along a yellow line into the "yellow philosophy room." The division was partly due to the location—the Theological Seminary's basement consisted of small rooms that had not been meant to be turned into the repositories of a bookstore. Yet, as every bibliophile knows, the expediency of place can make for inspiring rearrangements. As for books by Fernando Ortiz, Alfred Métraux, Gilberto Freyre, or Pedro Henríquez Ureña, the Seminary Co-op held them neither in the impressive literary criticism section, nor in anthropology, but mostly in the "blue history room." In it, there was a section on "Latin America," with the classics of Latin American anthropology standing next to literary criticism and history books.

The arrangement—if uniquely that of the Seminary Co-op—is not surprising. The grouping of works on Latin American history, literature, anthropology, and cultural studies follows conventions that have long been established for those "areas" that during the Cold War became politically relevant subjects of interest taught and researched in an interdisciplinary setup of "area studies" institutes that combined humanistic and social scientist approaches.[1] Cold War politics, together with the international publishing boom of Latin American literature in the 1960s, led to an unprecedented rise of Latin American studies at U.S. American universities, also in foreign languages departments, where Latin American literature began to supersede peninsular Spanish literature (Adorno, "Havana and Macondo"). Indeed, the success of the so-called Latin American boom literature of the 1960s, as Deborah Cohn has shown, was crucially helped by U.S. American cultural politics in regard to Latin America in the 1960s and 1970s, with funding given for translations, magazines, and journals.

Library bookshelves are still dominated by this "culturalist" approach to Latin America, whereby literary critics and philologists are often grouped together with historians and anthropologists and where "history" has become a repository, at least in bookstores, for those who look to read about the larger region of Latin America, without much reflection on which common approaches and concerns might offer insight into the field of Latin American studies, apart from geopolitics. On the other hand, from the 1990s onward there have been new assessments and proposals challenging this earlier Cold War configuration and questioning the divide between the humanities and the social sciences that had opened up in the meantime. The canon wars of the 1990s and the rise of cultural studies, together with postcolonial studies and newer trends such as Global South studies and "glotopolitics" (within Hispanic studies), all have attempted to do away with post-1945 divisions between humanities-based foreign language and literature departments and social science–oriented area studies programs.[2]

It has been the tenet of this book to locate the synergy among literature, linguistics, the visual arts, anthropology, and history in regard to Latin America not in Cold War area studies but in the period preceding it, the time between the two World Wars. While at this moment anthropology became definitively established as a social science central to the study of Latin America, its most important representatives in Latin America, analyzed here (Ortiz, Roumain, Rivet, and Freyre), turned away from a merely classifying study of race toward the humanist study of culture, responding to more and more pressing questions about cultural contact and acculturation. The interwar period was a crucial moment for the interconnected, humanistic, and social scientist reflection on the political, economic, and broadly cultural and political implications of such processes of cultural contact.

The works produced in this period straddled the pamphlet and the scientific essay, the novel and the political speech, as forms of committed writing, whereby different audiences could be touched and science legitimately stray out of the ivory tower. This specifically Latin American tradition of intellectual thought produced during the interwar period was located at universities and conferences but also in cultural journals, essays, and novels. It took on the critical task of reflecting on processes of making culture, as well as processes of transculturation, and of political activism against the scientific racism that had been pervasive up to then.

Jorge Luis Borges once wrote that there was no such thing as Americanism; there were just Americans. For him, the sense of what was "American" was sporadic, tied to moments of crisis, like the Spanish Civil War or the dictatorships of the twentieth century, which brought people together in solidarity (viii–ix). Indeed, I have argued that it was ironically a period of prolonged political crises that made possible the interdisciplinary study of Latin America as an area united by common concerns. But as contingent as it was on the exiles and encounters of the interwar years, Latin American culture began to be understood in new ways by those intellectuals, philologists, and anthropologists, who, all the while working in specific national contexts, found ways to dialogue and devise new ways of approaching Latin America as a unified object of study.

The Seminary Co-op Bookstore moved in 2012 to its new, larger location, giving up the old divisions into colored rooms. Similarly, our ways of thinking about Latin American studies are changing, with Departments of "Spanish and Portuguese" calling themselves Departments of "Hispanic Studies," "Iberian and Latin American Cultures," or "Latin American and Latino Cultures." Other "areas" such as Latino and Chicana studies, American studies, inter-American studies, trans-Atlantic studies, and more are increasingly competing with the older disciplinary divisions. As we are learning to envision the global and the local from ever-changing angles, we inevitably ask ourselves about the continuous objects that we study, the methods that we use, and the ways in which any division of Latin American culture studies might be justified beyond pragmatic institutional decisions. My answer has been a historicizing one, as I have argued that there has been a continuous intellectual reflection on Latin American cultural production, well worth taking into account.

Notes

Introduction

1. The description that accompanies the installation characterizes Freyre as someone who "identified the origins of the country's cultural miscegenation in its indigenous peoples' encounters with European colonizers and imported African slaves." See Andrade, *Posters for the Museum of the Man of the Northeast* at the Guggenheim's "Collections Online" website, http://www.guggenheim.org/new-york/collections/collection-online/artwork/33078, accessed Dec. 22, 2014.

2. Gabriella Nouzeilles discusses in detail the positivist Latin American essays by Sarmiento, Bunge, and others. For Nouzeilles, science was the "language authorized to talk about the body" in the period between 1870 and 1940, giving prestige to scientific racism, with a major change in attitude occurring only later on, with Ortiz's concept of transculturation (284).

3. See Skidmore's classic *Black into White* for a comprehensive analysis of the whitening ideology in Brazil in the nineteenth and twentieth centuries. In my view Helg is compelling in her comparative analysis of Argentina and Cuba but too harsh in her view of scientific racism in Cuba. Alejandro de la Fuente's more recent study *A Nation for All: Race, Inequality, and Politics in Twentieth-Century Cuba* has since provided some nuance: "Neither unqualified racial integration nor linear exclusion characterizes the history of Cuba as an independent nation. Theories about the institutionalization of racial orders provide important analytical insights, but they study precisely what Cuba lacked: a social order based on rigid, codified distinctions of race. . . . Ambiguity is what best defines the evolution of race relations in twentieth-century Cuba" (11).

4. As Nancy Stepan tells it, eugenics was enhanced by the growing economic competition among nations at the end of the nineteenth century, whereby previously marginalized groups such as industrial workers and women became a major part of the workforce and the question of hereditary diseases and infirmities turned into a collective obsession. Eugenicist programs of involuntary

sterilization were implemented in several U.S. American states and in Latin American and European countries long before they became infamous through the German racial laws of the 1930s.

5. On European imperialist anthropology for twentieth-century France, see Lebovics; de L'Estoile, "Rationalizing Colonial Domination"; and de L'Estoile, *Le goût des autres*. For Germany, see H. Glenn Penny's book *Objects of Culture*. For the history of British anthropology, see Henrika Kuklick's *The Savage Within,* and for a critique of British colonialist theories of culture, see Robert J. C. Young's *Colonial Desire.*

6. Spengler himself in *The Decline of the West* (1918–22) refers only in a few passages to Spanish American countries like Mexico and Peru, even though he, too, became more interested in Latin America in the 1920s, after meeting the Argentine sociologist and diplomat Ernesto Quesada (Birkenmaier, "Scenarios").

7. "Ciertamente, en más de un sentido, puede hablarse de 'el espectro racial.' Las 'razas' son como espectros; irreales, pero inspiradores de muy fuertes emociones. Por eso son más temibles los racismos" (Ortiz, *El engaño de las razas* 420–21). (All translations from Spanish are mine, if not indicated otherwise. A.B.)

8. "Es ahora y no antes cuando el hombre americano, el hombre inserto en la situación llamada América, se ha hecho esta pregunta: ¿existe una cultura americana? Y, si existe ¿qué clase de cultura es ésta?" (Zea 15).

9. Frank Andre Guridy's *Forging Diaspora* discusses encounters between Afro-Cubans and Afro-Americans from 1898 through the end of the early Cold War era and speaks of a transcultural African diaspora that was created in this way. Antonio López's *Unbecoming Blackness* in turn looks at the works of Afro-Cuban writers and performers in the United States, among them Rómulo Lachatañeré, an anthropologist close to Ortiz, analyzing the transformations in the Cuban racial identity they experienced when living in the United States. Finally, the edited collection *Anywhere but Here* presents essays in the wake of Paul Gilroy's *Black Atlantic* that discuss notions of hybridity among the transnational networks between African and Afro-American intellectuals since the nineteenth century (Radcliffe, Scott, and Werner).

10. In 1910 Boas founded an International School of American Archaeology and Ethnology in Mexico that never opened because of the Mexican Revolution. He also participated in the Britten Survey of Puerto Rico (1913–16) (Duany 74–78).

11. Boas's research was published first in 1911 ("Changes in the Bodily Form"). For a more detailed account, see Barkan (81–85). For a contemporary perspective on how revolutionary Boas's war against racism was, see Roth Pierpont.

12. There are a number of excellent studies on Mexico's European exile communities, including Sebastiaan Faber's study of the Mexican Spanish exile community; see also Yankelevich; Cate-Arries and Arries; and Corral, Souto Alabarce, and James.

13. Scholars have often spoken of *mestizaje* as the prevailing discourse of identity in Cuba since the nineteenth century, an "invented tradition," in the words of Luis Duno Gottberg, that established continuity with the past by virtue of repetition instead of discussion. Vera Kutzinski locates this discourse of *mestizaje* in Cuba in José Martí's term *América mestiza*, mentioned in his essay "Nuestra América." Duno Gottberg analyzes earlier writings by José Antonio Saco and Domingo del Monte, as well as Gertrudis Gómez de Avellaneda's *Sab* (25). Both Estelle Tarica and Marilyn Miller have further shown how the idea of *mestizaje* was exploited, usually to the detriment of indigenous communities and other racial minorities, to create nationalist ideologies in Mexico, as well as in the Andes and Brazil. While these scholars focus on the popular and literary discourse of *mestizaje*, Deborah Poole in turn discusses the importance of the idea of *mestizaje* and also of left-wing political movements for the development of Latin American anthropology.

14. For an insightful comparison of Freyre's *plasticidade* and Ortiz's transculturation, see Alfredo Cesar Melo's article "A face de Janus no ensaísmo latinoamericano," where he claims that both terms are fundamental to understanding the Latin American postcolonial experience.

15. For an analysis of the trajectory of transculturation in cultural studies, see Liliana Weinberg's entry in *Diccionario de estudios culturales latinoamericanos*.

16. For Szurmuk and McKee Irwin, Latin American essayists, just like later cultural studies scholars, practiced political intervention through their writings by raising questions of ethnic relations, emergent national identities, and modernity (13). Similarly, the *Latin American Cultural Studies Reader* (Del Sarto, Ríos, and Trigo) argues that Latin American cultural studies build on the tradition of the Latin American essay, including some of the authors that I study, such as José Martí, Fernando Ortiz, Pedro Henríquez Ureña, Alfonso Reyes, and Gilberto Freyre.

17. Helen Delpar also notes in her book *Looking South* that the emergence of Latin American studies in the United States was not only due to the hegemonic ambitions of the United States but also had to do with an international shift in the configuration of anthropology, from a broadly defined unsystematic field of knowledge to a key social science. Where Delpar analyzes Latin American studies in the United States, I focus on the development in Latin America of an interdisciplinary Latin Americanist discourse.

18. Indeed, Mercedes López-Baralt has read the work of these colonial historians as "anthropology *avant la lettre*." She notes especially the fact that the authors describe themselves as witnesses to the culture that they depict and that Sahagún used methods akin to those of modern anthropologists, such as questionnaires given to carefully selected informants (26–29).

19. Regina Horta Duarte discusses the organization of congresses and the foundation of museums of natural history in Latin America after independence as part of the natural history scientific network that existed in the nineteenth and

twentieth centuries. She also mentions the difficulties in some cases of obtaining and retaining materials carried away by European expeditions (785–86).

20. Humboldt's travels in Spanish America have been extensively researched by Ottmar Ette. See his two recent publications in English, coedited with Vera Kutzinski, *Views of the Cordilleras and Monuments of the Indigenous Peoples of the Americas: A Critical Edition* (2011) and *Alexander von Humboldt and the Americas* (2012), an edited volume that includes translations of correspondences and diary entries by Humboldt. R. Tripp Evans, in his *Romancing the Maya,* analyzes several works with highly speculative ideas about Mayan culture, such as John L. Stephens's *Incidents of Travel in Central America, Chiapas and Yucatán,* Désiré Charnay's *Cités et ruines américaines,* and Charles Étienne Brasseur de Bourboug's *Recherches sur les ruines de Palenqué.* Humboldt, too, had speculated about a possible connection between Mayan and Egyptian hieroglyphs, and the idea was widely discussed, as Wauchope shows as well (*Lost Tribes* 7–28).

21. For an excellent analysis of the competing discourses of travel narrative, realist novel, and anthropological treatise in the Spanish Caribbean, see Daylet Domínguez's dissertation "Etnografía, literatura y proyectos nacionales en el Caribe insular hispánico" (Princeton University, 2014).

22. As Belfored Moré has argued, however, even Bello's textual examples in his *Gramática* were taken from canonical Spanish works ranging from *El Cid,* to Golden Age theater, to Cervantes, to Bello's own contemporaries in Spain, with the exception of one Venezuelan author.

23. Hatzfeld's article "Hispanic Philology in Latin America" offers a comprehensive survey of nineteenth-century philology in Latin America. For a discussion of early tensions between Spanish and Spanish American philologists, see also del Valle's analysis of the controversy between the Spanish Juan Valera and the Colombian Rufino Cuervo (del Valle and Gabriel-Stheeman 93–109).

24. R. Howard Bloch has pointed out the impact of positivism on philologists in Germany and France. For Bloch the philology of the Romantic founders Wilhelm von Humboldt, Friedrich Schlegel, and Franz Bopp already appropriated models taken from the natural sciences, with the positivist tendency of philology reaching its high point later on: "But nothing in the early 'Romantic' era can match, beginning in the 1860s, the reduction of medieval literary study to the level of a technique, the containment of philology within the limits of method for an establishment, dating, identification, and localization of texts. To the extent that this evolution coincides with a belated high moment of positivism and of literary naturalism, it can be seen as the aftereffect of the Enlightenment faith in reason" (39–40).

25. At the beginning of the nineteenth century, the Romantic generation of writers and philologists, including the brothers Grimm, Friedrich Schlegel, Wilhelm Tieck, and others, began to write German dictionaries and collect folktales as part of the nationalist movement to unite Germany politically; in England, France, and the Austro-Hungarian empire too, as Benedict Anderson has argued, there

was a "lexicographic revolution," driven by the English and French colonial conquests of India and Egypt, on the one hand, and, on the other, by groups such as the Magyars of Hungary and the Rumanians, who were seeking independence from Austria (67–82).

26. José Luis Abellán's *La idea de América* speaks of an "anti-positivist" reaction in reference to the Mexican Ateneo group (Alfonso Reyes, Pedro Henríquez Ureña, José Vasconcelos, Antonio Caso) and to José Enrique Rodó as their precursor (87–103).

27. As Robert Conn has argued in *The Politics of Philology,* Alfonso Reyes was uniquely preoccupied with building through his literary essays and classical philological scholarship an "aesthetic state" that centered around the writer as humanist. Similarly, Henríquez Ureña, as Juan Valdez has shown, produced an important body of writings on linguistics, unfortunately at times with racist implications.

28. This is not to say that "Indianness" did not play a role in the national imagination of Caribbean nations. Most notably in the Dominican Republic, to be racially "Indian" and culturally "Hispanic" was promoted especially under the Dominican dictator Leonidas Trujillo and became a commonly accepted idea until today, in contrast to neighboring Haiti (Candelario).

29. For a presentation of Hispanic philology in Argentina, see Helmut Hatzfeld's already mentioned article and also Fernando Degiovanni's excellent *Los textos de la patria,* with a focus on the literary canon established by Ricardo Rojas in the first decades of the twentieth century in Argentina. For more discussion of the history of Mexican anthropology, I refer to Mechthild Rutsch's *Entre el campo y el gabinete. Nacionales y extranjeros en la profesionalización de la antropología mexicana (1877–1920),* which studies Mexico's own cultural exchanges with foreign anthropologists, as well as to Claudio Lomnitz's chapter on anthropology in his *Deep Mexico, Silent Mexico* ("Bordering on Anthropology"). Lomnitz argues that Mexico's strong national anthropology always was situated in relation to U.S. American scientific institutions but also in relation to French missions.

30. After World War II, funding for Americanist institutions from the United States and France dropped drastically. As Jean Franco puts it, the Cold War was also a "culture war" between the United States and the Soviet Union, leading with regard to Latin America to the promotion of literature from Latin America but not to support for its scientists.

1. Fernando Ortiz and the Meanings of *raza*

1. For Michel-Rolph Trouillot in his *Silencing the Past: Power and the Production of History,* the Día de la raza is an "anniversary in the making." Over time, it became a "day for ourselves, however defined, for ethnicity however constructed" (136).

2. Didier T. Jaén writes in his introduction: "What does the 'Cosmic race' mean to Chicanos? In some cases, it appears as a concept vaguely equivalent

to the concept of 'La Raza' but with a sense of the future: It is the triumphant 'raza.' For others, however, 'la raza cósmica' is the universal race, the race of the future, as explained by Vasconcelos: The race in which all other races disappear" (Vasconcelos, *Cosmic Race* xvi).

3. Lomnitz explains: "In northern Mexico and the United States, the word 'raza' . . . is used to mean 'us'—the 'raza' is going to the movies, for example. It parallels the way in which 'a gente' ('the people') is used in Portuguese" ("On the Origin" 208).

4. For more analysis of the origins of Columbus Day and the Día de la Raza in the United States, Spain, and Latin America, see Miguel Rodríguez's book *Celebración de "la raza": una historia comparativa del 12 de octubre,* Ilan Rachum's "Origins and Historical Significance of Día de la Raza," and Trouillot's already mentioned chapter "Good Day, Columbus."

5. See Vasconcelos, "Discurso en la Universidad el Día de la Raza"; Quesada, *El día de la raza;* and Züñiga Montúfar; Rivarola. Aside from Quesada, the Argentine writer Manuel Gálvez also pronounced himself in favor of the idea of a Hispanic race, in solidarity with the writers of the Generation of 1898 (Gálvez, *El espíritu de aristocracia;* Gálvez, *El solar de la raza;* Quesada, *Nuestra raza*).

6. "El vocablo raza, a pesar de su flagrante inexactitud, ha adquirido para nosotros valor convencional, que las festividades del 12 de octubre ayudan a cargar de contenidos de sentimiento y emoción. *El Día de la Raza* bien podría llamarse el Día de la Cultura Hispánica, porque eso es lo que en suma representa; pero sería inútil proponer semejante sustitución, porque el vocablo cultura, en el significado que hoy tiene dentro del lenguaje técnico de la sociología y de la historia, no despierta en el oyente la resonancia afectiva que la costumbre da al vocablo raza" (Henríquez Ureña, "Raza y cultura hispánica" 320).

7. As Noel Salomon writes, in opposing imported scientific ideas, Martí targeted especially the Spencerian positivism that dominated in Latin America in the 1880s and 1890s. Spencer had Latin American adepts such as the Mexican "científicos" and Francisco Bulnes, who mocked Benito Juárez for being a mestizo (Salomon 37–41).

8. In his book of lectures, reports, and homilies from this trip, Altamira was defensive about the purpose and the economic means with which he traveled and emphasized that the trip was financed by the generosity of Latin American universities, governments, and Spanish clubs and not by the Spanish government.

9. The Mexican Hispanist Aurelio Espinosa welcomed the publication of *Archivos del Folklore Cubano* in a review and expressed enthusiasm for the seriousness and broad scope of the journal, stating that *Archivos* "can well serve the scholarly interests of all the Antilles and Central and South America" (416).

10. See Ortiz to Chacón y Calvo, Dec. 27, 1922 (Gutiérrez Vega 30).

11. "La Sociedad del Folklore Cubano tiene por objeto acopiar, clasificar y comparar los elementos tradicionales de nuestra vida popular. Así son materias propias de esta Sociedad la recopilación y estudio de los cuentos, las consejas,

las leyendas conservados por la tradición oral de nuestro pueblo; los romances, las décimas, los cantres, los boleros y otras manifestaciones típicas de nuestra poesía y nuestra música populares; las locuciones, los giros típicos, los trabalenguas, los cubanismos y tantas otras formas de la filología popular; los refranes, proverbios, adivinanzas y otros modos de expresión característicos del ingenio de los pueblos; los conocimientos populares, conservados por la tradición, referentes a los distintos ramos de la ciencia (geografía, botánica, medicina, agricultura); las creencias fantásticas y sobrenaturales" ("Actas de la *Sociedad del folklore cubano*. No. 1" 77).

12. Ortiz, "El lenguaje vernáculo de Cuba"; Marinello, "Un guacalito de cubanismos" (1924); Marinello, "Un guacalito de cubanismos" (1925); Nascentes; Galbis.

13. See Ortiz to Chacón y Calvo, Jan. 25, 1924 (Gutiérrez Vega 34).

14. Ortiz mentions as much to Chacón y Calvo in his letter from Havana dated Jan. 25, 1924 (Gutiérrez Vega 33–35).

15. "Me encanta saber que habrá de contribuir a la académica reivindicación de los plátanos fritos. ¡Lo merecen! He ordenado desde aquí que envíen las capillas de más de 400 páginas ya tiradas de mi próximo *Glosario de afronegrismos* a Menéndez Pidal, en vista de una amabilísima carta, en la que me anuncia su propósito de aprovechar el jugo que logre sacar de los cubanismos del cataurito para la edición 15ª del Diccionario de la Real Academia" (Gutiérrez Vega 36).

16. "Aún no lo he leído, pero ya he notado un mejoramiento en los cubanismos, aunque faltan muchos y aún tiene errors. Tiempo y paciencia y le haremos un trabajo para la 16 edición" (Gutiérrez Vega 42).

17. "Usted, con sorprendente actividad, ha querido que sus investigaciones científicas no se redujesen a lo que la Antropología en su expresión étnica pudiera ofrecer, ha ido más allá, ha espigado con éxito en la esfera del lenguaje dentro de la raza que ha venido analizando con singular cuidado, y no han sido sus deseos referir tan sólo lo que las lenguas de estos pueblos significan, sino ahondar más" (Ortiz, *Glosario de afronegrismos* xi).

18. "Por nuestra parte hemos hallado la palabra MAMBÍ con varios significados en los lenguajes de Africa. *Mamby* es el título de jefe en una región de la Senegambia, *Mambí* es una región del Congo francés, cerca de Mayumba vocablo que en Cuba significa una especie de brujería. *Mambí* en congo significa 'hombre malo,' 'abominable,' 'injurioso,' 'pernicioso,' 'repulsivo,' 'vil,' 'sucio,' 'cruel,' 'dañino,' 'vicioso,' 'malvado,' etc. La última de estas tres palabras parece la más fácil de adoptar como origen de los mambises cimarrones, o rebeldes dominicanos. Los esclavos congos llamaron MAMBI a los rebeldes, en su lengua, con la palabra más despreciativa, traduciendo así el odio de sus amos hacia aquéllos y las palabras injuriosas con que los denominaban. No intentamos esta opinión como segura; pero creemos que de África nos vino la palabreja, que después ha sido título de gloria para nuestros libertadores heroicos" (Ortiz, *Glosario de afronegrismos* 315).

19. "Y filológicamente, aunque no puede apreciarse el valor real de un vocabulario de afronegrismos sin el estudio científico de los dialectos negroafricanos, las papeletas lexicológicas que acaba de ordenar el Dr. O. en reciente glosario de afronegrismos, serán siempre un precioso elemento de consulta, ya que cada vocablo va ilustrado con una autoridad o tiene una concreta indicación e la fuente popular de que procede" (Chacón y Calvo 302).

20. "Es muy verosímil la hipótesis académica, por más que no cabe desconocer que esta voz pertenece radicalmente al grupo onomatopéyico universal, por el fonema *bab*. Entre los negros de Sierra Leona se llama BOBO al 'mudo de nacimiento' (Thomas 16). Igual sucede entre los malinkés (Un Miss. Ob. Cit. p. 110), lo cual puede explicarse por onomatopeya como el de la balbucencia, como el *balbus* latino. Por igual razón llaman al 'mudo' *ebaba* en el Congo (Bentley, 264), *ribubu* en Angola (Cannecattim, p. 11), *bebi* los hausas, *obu* los ibos, *mumo* los fulas, *mumuo* los mandingas, y *bobo* los bambara. Habrá influido el bobo de los negros esclavos, en el castellano? Para determinarlo habría que estudiar la historia del vocablo y la época y zona de su aparición en España. Sin embargo, basta la razón onomatopéyica ya expuesta" (Ortiz, *Glosario de afronegrismos* 58).

21. "Se trata, pues, de un curioso afronegrismo, considerando la etimología en rigor. No es la palabra originaria formada por elementos de la lingüística negra; pero decimos guarapo, porque tomamos la voz tal como fue por los negros africanos corrompida la palabra, que los descubridores les enseñaron, aprendida de los árabes. Es una genealogía etimológica de zigzag: del árabe al español y portugués, de éstos al congo, y del congo otra vez al español y portugués de las colonias" (Ortiz, *Glosario de afronegrismos* 232–33).

22. The Cuban linguist Sergio Valdés Bernal has taken Ortiz's often improvised ideas seriously and established more systematic associations between the linguistic analysis of Cuban Spanish and Ortiz's concept of transculturation in his *Lengua nacional e identidad cultural del cubano*. He corrects several entries of Ortiz's *Glosario* (Valdés Bernal, *Lengua nacional e identidad cultural del cubano* 103).

23. See Ortiz to Chacón y Calvo, July 8, July 30, 1925. Ortiz mentions that someone is trying to create a Cuban Academy of Language by law decree in Congress, expressing his disagreement with such a proceeding. Instead, he mentions that he has contacted Menéndez Pidal and several other academics in Spain. He asks Chacón y Calvo to look after the matter (Gutiérrez Vega 42–43).

24. See Patricia Motorola and Marialys Perdomo's excellent article for a more detailed account of the origins of the academy and its history until today.

25. According to Araceli García-Carranza's *Bio-bibliografía,* Ortiz organized a Cuban Alliance for a Free World that had as its objective to defend the cause of freedom and democracy and combat totalitarian regimes (30). See also Consuelo Naranjo Orovio's article "Las redes de un exilio errante," where she points out that Ortiz was crucial in helping Spanish exiles come to Cuba to give lectures and find work (154–56).

26. The Instituto Panamericano de Geografía e Historia is today an entity belonging to the Organisation of American States (OAS).

27. Ortiz was a member of the Unión Panamericana (succeeded in 1948 by the OEA), the Instituto Indigenista Interamericano (founded in 1940), the International Society of Ethnology and Geography, the Asociación de Escritores y Artistas Americanos, the Hispanic Society of America, and the French Société des Américanistes and the president of the Instituto cultural cubano-soviético (García Carranza, Suárez Suárez, and Quesada Morales).

28. "Una iniciativa académica con ese propósito cultural haría más por los intereses morales de la 'raza,' que esa espumosa declaración patriotera, escanciada a los brindis en todo banquete patriótico. Afortunadamente, los iberoamericanos tenemos tradición filológica que no desmerece en nada de la española y no pocos autorizados maestros" (Ortiz, *Catauro de cubanismos* 15).

29. "Es que debemos convertir estas evocaciones del descubrimiento de América, como hacen algunos, en unas 'fiestas de la raza'? No. Porque no hay tal raza, pues, como dijera el buen maestro Miguel de Unamuno, 'esa raza se inventó al mismo tiempo que la fiesta' y, además, ello no sería sino engañar a las ingenuas emociones colectivas, llevándolas a las mentidas y anticristianas pasiones de los racismos, cuya satánica encarnación, Adolfo Hitler, está ahora ensangrentando los continentes por el imperio de su raza; de esa raza aria tan mitológica como son las otras razas creadas para estímulo de las inculturas agresivas y encubrimiento de las políticas predatorias. No hay raza alguna en el mundo que merezca exaltación especial. La edad de los racismos ya pasó" (Ortiz, "El mutuo descubrimiento de dos mundos" 24).

30. "Reglamento de la Sociedad de Estudios Afrocubanos," Ortiz Archive, Biblioteca Nacional José Martí, Havana, Cuba, folder 383.

31. "Es muy apremiante que sobre las razas, como se hace sobre las enfermedades, los crímenes y los conflictos económicos, se vayan difundiendo los criterios propuestos por la ciencia; única manera de ir afrontando las desventuras sociales y poderlas reducir" (Ortiz, *El engaño de las razas* 13).

32. "Ciertamente, en más de un sentido, puede hablarse de 'el espectro racial.' Las 'razas' son como espectros; irreales, pero inspiradores de muy fuertes emociones. Por eso son más temibles los racismos. . . . Hay que lograr la desracialización de la humanidad. Hay que 'desracificarla.' Hay que exorcizar a ese mal espíritu que es el espectro racial, librándonos de sus pavores. La sociedad humana, que creó las 'razas,' habrá que suprimirlas" (Ortiz, *El engaño de las razas* 420–21).

33. "Los 'problemas de raza' son de gran importancia en América y están llamados a grandes y trágicos episodios. Se ha creado con los siglos un sistema de injusticias sociales encubiertas con los mitos de las sangres diversas, y es muy improbable que los ídolos de las razas y los holocaustos exigidos por sus cultos puedan ser acabados sin más afrenta ni más crueles sacrificios. Toda América está sintiendo estos dolores. Porque en este hemisferio, que fue Nuevo Mundo y que ya exige una total y urgente renovación para seguirlo siendo, son varios los

grupos humanos definidos como 'razas' que están en contraposiciones sociales intensas, agriadas y cada día menos estables" (Ortiz, *El engaño de las razas* 13).

34. "La historia americana no puede ser comprendida sin conocer la de todas las esencias étnicas que en este continente se han fundido y sin apreciar cuál ha sido el verdadero resultado de su recíproca transculturación" (Ortiz, *El engaño de las razas* 14).

35. "El estudio de la brujería y el ñañiguismo desde el punto de vista médico-legal, determina, naturalmente, la reducción del tema en su aspecto sociológico y la amplitud del asunto desde el punto de vista estrictamente científico. Hay, por tal razón, que hacer abstracción de muchas consideraciones sociales, jurídicas e históricas, para conceder preferente atención a todos los factores y caracteres que interesan superlativamente al médico forense" (I. Castellanos 5).

36. Antonio López's excellent chapter on Lachatañeré's life in New York gives a full picture of how Lachatañeré received feedback on his research from Melville Herskovits and Ruth Benedict and argues that his experience as an Afro-Latino in New York marked several of his works published in Cuba (121–42).

37. Maguire's comparative analysis of Cabrera's *Cuentos negros* and *El Monte* together with Ortiz's *Los negros brujos* and *Cuban Counterpoint* shows that while the two privileged different spatial or temporal angles of analysis, both tried to contain Afro-Cuban culture in carefully framed conceptual spaces that were nonthreatening to their own control of Cuban culture at large (29–62).

38. Maguire notes that beyond their familial relationship little is known of shared scholarly projects or institutional activities. Ortiz did, however, claim that he had introduced Cabrera to the study of Afro-Cuban folklore, and Cabrera's masterwork *El Monte* is dedicated to him (Maguire 32, 194 n4).

39. Lachatañeré was referring to Lucien Lévy-Bruhl's work *Primitive Mentality* (1923), published in French as *La mentalité primitive* (1911).

40. Interestingly, as López shows, Lachatañeré himself fell back to using the term *brujo,* or sorcerer, for which he had criticized Ortiz, when applying in New York for a fellowship and having to describe *santería* to U.S. American readers (130–31).

41. Ortiz Archive, folder "Revista de Estudios Afrocubanos."

42. These impressions are based on my consultation of the "Correspondencia" at the Fernando Ortiz archive at the Biblioteca Nacional José Martí, where I was able to see a fraction of the alphabetically ordered letters written to Ortiz, preserved there.

43. Boas's compilations of myths, such as *Tsimshian Mythology* (1916) and *Kwakiutl Culture as Reflected in Mythology* (1935), are products of this attempt to document linguistic as much as cultural change.

44. Enrico Mario Santí has published the correspondence between Ortiz and Malinowski and provided an insightful comparison between Ortiz's concept of transculturation and Malinowski's concept of acculturation.

45. See Fernando Coronil's excellent introduction to *Cuban Counterpoint,* where he surveys the elimination of references to Ortiz in the edited works of Malinowski, his omission in U.S. American textbooks of social sciences, and the lack of references to Ortiz in the works of major anthropologists and critics like Claude Lévi-Strauss and Edward Said. Coronil suggests that in 1942, shortly before his death, Malinowski might have recognized the importance of Ortiz's approach to the transculturation of oppressed people (in: Ortiz, *Cuban Counterpoint* xlvii).

46 As María del Rosario Díaz writes, several of Ortiz's works of that period, among them *El engaño de las razas* and *El huracán,* are byproducts of his university teaching in those years.

47. I will discuss this conference in greater detail in chapter 2, on Paul Rivet.

48. Elazar Barkan's *The Retreat of Scientific Racism* describes the interwar period in Britain and the United States as one where a fundamental change occurred in anthropology. The idea of a paradigmatic change in the configuration of the social sciences also appears in Stocking, "Franz Boas and the Culture Concept."

49. See, for example, chapter 11, on the differences between *cañal* and *cañaveral.* This chapter doesn't appear in the English translation, obviously because the discussion of Spanish terms for "sugarfield," as here, is not relevant to the English reader. In this philological commentary, Ortiz notes that even though the word *cañaveral* is the common term used to talk about a sugarcane field, *cañal,* derived from *caña* (*de azúcar*), is more accurate than *cañaveral,* derived from the native Spanish plant *cañavera* (*Contrapunteo cubano* 273–79). See also chapter 13 on *Cachimbos* and *Cachimbas;* chapter 17 on the meanings of *cañafístola* or *cañandonga;* chapter 19 on the *tabacano;* chapter 21 on the *tubano;* and the final chapter, 25, on *tabaco habano* and the seal of warranty it has received.

50. Ortiz's publications on "mulatto" poetry in *Revista Bimestre Cubana* are the following: "Los últimos versos mulatos" (1934) and "Más acerca de la poesía mulata" (I, II, III, 1936). In *Revista de Estudios Afrocubanos* he finally published "La religión en la poesía mulata" (1936). Kutzinski, in her *Sugar's Secrets,* discusses the wider cultural context of Afro-Cuban poetry.

51. Ortiz republished and reworked this essay several times for separate occasions and venues. He presented a first version of it in 1934 at the Sociedad Cubana de Estudios Históricos e Internacionales. He then delivered a lecture on the same topic in 1941 in the Municipal Palace of Havana, which he published in *Revista Bimestre Cubana* ("Martí y las razas"). In 1942, it was published as a separate book publication with Molina & Compañía in Havana. In 1945 a short version of the essay was published under the title "Martí y las razas de librería" in *Cuadernos Americanos* in Mexico. In his essay "La sinrazón de los racismos," presented in 1949 at the Club Atenas in Havana, Ortiz used passages of from the earlier essay. Finally, in 1953, on the occasion of the celebrations of Martí's

anniversary, the essay was republished in Cuba and its short version again in Chile. Another indication of the importance of the Martí essay for Ortiz is that it was published in English translation by Mercer Cook, which is the version I quote here (Ortiz, "Cuba, Martí and the Race Problem").

52. Julio Ramos reads Martí as a fin-de-siècle writer who asserted the authority of literature and the humanities against the modernization and massification of society and who was reacting, like Alfonso Reyes and Pedro Henríquez Ureña, against the positivist and racist discourse of science that marginalized indigenous populations and Afro-Americans in the name of racial purity (251–68). Ortiz's essay, on the contrary, inscribes Martí into his own anthropological discourse.

53. Ortiz mentions especially Martí's drafts of book projects, among them "Los indios hoy. Estado actual de las razas indias en América"; "Mis negros," which was going to be a series of portraits of local characters; and yet another more scientific one, "La raza negra. Su constitución, corriente y tendencias" ("Martí y las razas" 118–19).

2. Paul Rivet's Museum Matrix and the "Drama of Inadaptation"

1. Paul Rivet appears briefly at the beginning of Mariano Picón Salas's *De la conquista a la independencia* (1944) and in Pedro Henríquez Ureña's *Historia de la cultura en la América hispánica* (1947) but is altogether absent from Alfonso Reyes's, José Vasconcelos's, and José Carlos Mariátegui's works. Picón Salas alludes half mockingly to Rivet's thesis, presented in his *Los orígenes del hombre americano,* that the Americas had received migrations not only over the Bering Strait but also from Melanesia and other Pacific areas but doesn't take it seriously (21). Henríquez Ureña mentions Rivet's name when recounting the great variety of indigenous cultures and the many languages they spoke, giving Rivet's count of 123 language families, and calls him a "philologist" (11).

2. For a general history of anthropology in France in the nineteenth century, see the first two chapters of Nélia Dias's book *Le Musée d'ethnographie du Trocadéro (1878–1908).* Pascale Riviale's article describes French Americanism before the foundation of the Société des Américanistes, and Laurière discusses the transition from the learned society to the academic society (*Paul Rivet* 288–99).

3. Lévy-Bruhl was a French philosopher who, most important, wrote about the "primitive" mentality of indigenous peoples, arguing that they were governed by a prelogical mentality that was fundamentally different from that of western societies but highly complex in its organization. His much-read work *La mentalité primitive* (1922; *Primitive Mentality*) was published in translation in Spain and in Argentina in the 1920s. The French sociologist Marcel Mauss was a nephew of the sociologist Émile Durkheim and together with him developed methods of studying religion and so-called total social facts such as gift-giving in nonliterate societies. Mauss was a charismatic teacher, whose emphasis on point of view and psychology influenced Claude Lévi-Strauss's later structural anthropology.

4. The best source of information about the history of French anthropology is here again Nélia Dias's *Le Musée d'ethnographie du Trocadéro (1878–1908).*

5. "L'Institut d'ethnologie, soutenu exclusivement par des fonds votés sur les budgets de diverses colonies, aura trois buts essentiels: former, par l'utilisation des cours existants ou la création de nouveaux enseignements, des observateurs instruits et avertis pour l'étude des indigènes; fournir aux voyageurs et aux coloniaux, à leur retour dans la métropole, les moyens et les facilités pour la mise en valeur de leurs collections et de leurs notes; publier sous forme de monographies soigneusement éditées et largement illustrées, les études dues à ces collaborateurs. Le nouvel Institut sera, comme il est naturel, plus spécialement orienté vers les colonies françaises, mais cette spécialisation légitime n'exclut nullement la possibilité d'enquêtes ou d'études sortant de ce cadre" (Rivet, "Institut d'ethnologie" 15).

6. This is one of the arguments of Christine Laurière's excellent intellectual biography *Paul Rivet. L'homme politique et le savant,* where Laurière describes Rivet as an intensely polemical figure, both in his shaping of French anthropology and in his politics.

7. The complete curriculum, as Rivet detailed it in his article "L'ethnologie" for *La science française* (1937), was: "1. Ethnographie descriptive: Marcel Mauss; 2. Linguistique descriptive: Marcel Cohen; 3. Anthropologie: Paul Rivet; 4. Préhistoire exotique: Henri Breuil; 5. Ethnographie de l'Afrique: Hanri Labouret; 6. Linguistique de l'Afrique: Mlle Homburger; 7. Linguistique et ethnographie de l'Asie orientale et de l'Océanie: Jean Przyluski; 8. Anthropologie zoologique et biologique: Etienne Rabaud; a Géologie des temps quaternaires et paléontologie humaine: Léonce Joleaud; 10. Psycho-physiologie de l'homme et des anthropoides: Paul Guillaume; 11. Physiologie comparée des races humaines: Jacques Millot" (10–11).

8. Deleporte called the state-sponsored system of museums representing to the French people the entire scope of contemporary and ancient cultures and their arts and crafts the French "museum matrix." I use the term here only in relation to Rivet's organization of ethnology as a discipline in its own right (Deleporte, "Resolutely New Outlook?"). See also Deleporte's "Trocadero Matrix."

9. "Ce qu'il importe de connaître, ce sont tous les aspects, ou tout au moins l'aspect moyen, d'une civilisation, et non l'aspect exceptionnel qu'elle revêt dans les classes privilégiées" (Rivet, *L'espèce humaine* 8–13).

10. "Il faut que les populations régionales de la France continentale et d'outre-mer aient a leur disposition des musées locaux, des musées de plein air dans les régions et les colonies, où elles verront leur histoire et leur art populaire prendre vie dans des expositions concrétes où elles connaîtront à la fois ce qui les lie à l'ensemble du pays et ce qui les en distingue" (Soustelle, "Pour une culture populaire").

11. *L'espèce humaine* was reviewed in Ortiz's journal *Estudios afrocubanos* (Camejo) and also cited by Gilberto Freyre in his *Casa-grande e senzala.*

12. The history of the terms *ethnography* and *ethnology* is long and complicated. They preceded the term *anthropology*, which became dominant in English and French only later in the twentieth century. Thomas Barfield's entry "Ethnography and Ethnology" in his *Dictionary of Anthropology* concludes: "In contemporary usage, ethnology is the attempt to develop rigorous and scientifically grounded explanations of cultural phenomena by comparing and contrasting many human cultures. By contrast, ethnography is the systematic description of a single contemporary culture, often through ethnographic fieldwork" (157).

13. Robert Lowie describes most anthropologists of the first decades of the twentieth century as diffusionists, among them even his teacher Franz Boas. Lowie only mentions as diffusionist excesses the pan-Egyptionist Elliot Smith in England and the Africanist Leo Frobenius in Germany, for attempting to trace the cultures of West Africa and Oceania to one common origin (157).

14. The introduction to *La science française* is explicit in this respect as well (Cavalier in: Rivet "L'ethnologie" i).

15. James Clifford has proposed that the contact between ethnography and the arts, especially Surrealism, led in the 1930s to a creative blurring between the frontiers of science and the arts. As Michel Beaujour argues, the creative contact between Surrealists and anthropologists intensified further during the exile years spent by anthropologists and Surrealists alike in New York, where they collaborated in the acquisition and discussion of anthropological objects.

16. For a study of this traditionalist conservative anthropology in France, see Lebovics's chapter "Louis Marin and the Conservative School" (12–51) and also Conklin's section on George Montandon (91–97).

17. Conklin attributes Rivet's error with respect to linguistics to his insufficient linguistic training. She writes: "Unfortunately Rivet never managed to acquire the basic training in linguistics that might have led him to study various languages' internal structures properly. . . . Much of the linguistic classification he came up with was therefore wrong, undertaken without sufficient method or data" (65).

18. The delayed reception of Guaman Poma's chronicle in the twentieth century and after Rivet's facsimile publication had to do with the way in which the indigenous author Guaman Poma was read in Peru and by the international scientific community. Rolena Adorno, who in 1980 published the definitive critical edition of Guaman Poma's *El primer nueva corónica y buen gobierno,* now available online, wrote in 1974 that what most harmed the reception of Guaman Poma's text was the perception of him as an indigenous author, which led to his being identified with an anticolonialist and pro-Inca agenda. Since the text heavily criticized the Inca Empire yet also targeted Spanish cruelties, critics discredited the work at first as contradictory (Adorno, "Racial Scorn").

19. Several points of contact can be found between Rivet and the Strasburg-based Annales editors and historians Marc Bloch and Lucien Febvre. For example, Fevbre was the principal editor of the *Encyclopédie française*, for which

Rivet edited *L'espèce humaine.* Also, François Chevalier dedicated his later study, published in "Travaux et Mémoires," *La formation des grands domaines au Mexique* (vol. 56, 1952), to both Bloch and Rivet.

20. I am citing from Bloch's posthumously published definitive work, *The Historian's Craft,* first published in French as *Apologie pour l'histoire. Le métier d'historien* (1949).

21. Despite these parallels, the two histories of the Annales school that I have consulted do not mention the contacts between Rivet and the Annales historians. Peter Burke mentions Claude Lévi-Strauss and the English anthropologist Edward E. Evans-Pritchard as anthropologists with an early interest in the Annales school (Burke 104; Burguière).

22. A list of notable students trained by the Institut d'ethnologie from Apr. 1956 cites Jacques Soustelle, André Leroi-Gourhan, Michel Leiris, Jean Pierre Vernant, Georges Devereux, Marcel Reynier, Jean Lefebre-d'Ormesson, Alfred Métraux, Jean Rouch, Leopold Senghor, Marc Hérodin (a professor in Mexico), Gregorio Hernández de Alba (a professor in Bogotá), Pierre Lesoure (a professor in Guatemala), and Henri La Besnerays (at a mission in Venezuela), as well as six anthropologists who died in the French Resistance or otherwise during the war (Paul Rivet Archive, Bibliothèque Centrale du Muséum d'Histoire Naturelle, Paris, Catalogue no. 2AM2C1). Of them, Soustelle, Lefebre-d'Ormesson, Métraux, Herodin, Hernández de Alba, Lesoure, and Besnerays were Americanists.

23. The volume of *Miscellanea* dedicated to Rivet in the year of his death cites a long list of "missions" or extended trips made by Rivet as an official delegate, eight of them between 1927 and 1939 to Argentina and Paraguay, Brazil, Mexico (three times), Guatemala, and El Salvador; Colombia and the Antilles; and again to Argentina, Brazil, Peru, and Bolivia (*Biographie de Paul Rivet* liv–lv).

24. Laurière has done much research to demonstrate the enduring impact of Rivet especially in Mexico, Colombia, and Brazil. See, for example, her article "México en los años treinta" and, on Colombia, "Los vínculos científicos de Gerardo Reichel-Dolmatoff." On the Institut français des hautes études brésiliennes, see Paulo Duarte (37–52)

25. "Je regrette que la nécessité impérieuse de rassembler le plus grand nombre d'objets possible m'empêche de faire des séjours prolongés parmi les Indiens et me prive ainsi de la possibilité de faire de l'ethnographie intensive, mais je suis talonné par le souvenir de ma salle vide qu'il me faut remplir dans le plus bref délai et le mieux que je puis. J'espère ainsi gagner le droit d'aller un jour vivre avec mes amis du Chaco" (Correspondance, Rivet Archive, 2AP1C METR).

26. The exportation of objects to Europe, however, would cause Métraux problems later on. As he writes in his journal, he was told in 1939 that he was being watched and that no artifacts were supposed to leave the country (*Itinéraires 1* 49).

27. Métraux Archive, Laboratoire d'anthropologie sociale, Fr/cdf/las/FAM. AS.P.01.03.

28. Santiago Bilbao indeed opens his extensively documented study *Alfred Métraux en la Argentina* by saying that in the 1960s, knowledge of Métraux's anthropological work in Argentina was almost nonexistent (7).

29. See Métraux's *Myths and Tales of the Matako Indians (the Gran Chaco, Argentina)* (1939) and *Myths of the Toba and Pilagá Indians of the Gran Chaco* (1946), as well as his article "Ethnography of the Gran Chaco," published in the *Handbook of South American Indians* (1946).

30. "Esta ciencia se ha impuesto en todos los dominios que interesan a lo humano, y gracias a la ampliación de nuestra sensibilidad artística se ha incorporado a la cultura de todo hombre realmente civilizado. Hay sin embargo una región mal conocida, mal explorada y de la que podemos esperar nuevos enriquecimientos, tanto para la ciencia como para la literatura. Esta materia inexplorada es la de las representaciones primitivas. Me refiero al mundo de ideas que los pueblos no civilizados se forman del universo" (Metraux, "El universo y la naturaleza").

31. This is clear from a short text published by Ocampo after Métraux's death in 1963, where she remembers her encounters and discussions with him in Buenos Aires and comments in particular on his article for *SUR* "Un mundo perdido."

32. "El drama de la inadaptación se representa sin cesar ante nosotros. Nuestra sociedad es una de las más cambiantes que ha habido. Las modalidades y las actitudes se transforman rápidamente y provocan conflictos diarios entre los que se atrasan y los que se anticipan al tiempo. A despecho de este movimiento ininterrumpido, nos obstinamos en considerar la tendencia del momento como eterna y como necesaria a la vida misma. Nuestra civilización no ha incorporado todavía la noción de cambio al número de sus ideas-fuerzas y en su negativa de reconocer la evidencia se encarniza en acumular los sufrimientos humanos perfectamente inútiles" (Metraux, "El problema de la civilización" 24).

33. The Colombian archaeologist Augusto Oyuela-Caycedo recently revealed that Reichel-Dolmatoff, before emigrating to Colombia in 1939, had been a member of Hitler's National Socialist Party and also of the SS, its elite group, where he participated in the infamous Night of the Long Knives, a purge of Nazi members that took place in 1934. Claudio Lomnitz, in an article written for the Mexican newspaper *La Jornada,* calls this an example of the dialectic animating Americanist anthropology throughout the twentieth century: "La mitología indígena fue espacio de curación para una Europa derrotada, y esa experiencia cultural e intelectual encontró aliado en el interés nacionalist por inventar los lenguajes simbólicos propios de cada país" (The indigenous mythology was a space of healing for a defeated Europe, and this cultural and intellectual experience found an ally in the nationalist interest for inventing the symbolic languages of each country) ("Expediente Reichel-Dolmatoff").

34. "Ce qui par contre n'est pas un rêve, c'est harmoniser dans chaque milieu américain les aspirations des deux races ou peuples actuels et de profiter des

qualités spécifiques à chacun pour le bien commun. Mais, me diront certains, que pouvons-nous espérer de la race indigène ? L'archéologue leur répondra qu'il ne faut pas la juger uniquement sur son état actuel mais aussi par ce qu'elle a pu réaliser par ses propres efforts, avant que la Conquête ne la paralyse momentanément. Le passé d'un peuple correspond à ses possibilités dans l'avenir. Pour cette raison, il est bon de se souvenir de ce que fut l'Indien américain et son tribut au progrès de l'humanité" (in: Laurière, *Paul Rivet* 594–95).

35. "Se trata de establecer zonas de coincidencia dentro de las cuales ningún país perdería los atributos de su soberanía. Entre los países que acabo de enumerar existe precisamente esta coincidencia marcada por la proximidad geográfica, el origen racial, la raíz idiomática y la semejanza de las costumbres. A esta unión latina podrían agregarse luego los pueblos hermanos de la América latina, aprovechando el excelente trampolín que nos ofrece el África occidental. También en la América latina, encontramos todos estos elementos de coincidencia que forman un vínculo tan estrecho, tan evidente entre los pueblos latinos de Europa" (Rivet, "Socialismo y unidad latina").

36. "Que no nos hablen de la ciencia por la ciencia ni del arte por el arte, sino del arte y de la ciencia al servicio del hombre. Que no nos hablen del progreso, de la cultura o de la civilización con alejamiento del interés concreto de la especie humana" (Silva Herzog 14–15).

37. "Al hablar del hombre pensamos en plural y no nos referimos al hombre económico, metafísico o biológico, porque esas son meras abstracciones; nos referimos al hombre en todos sus variados aspectos y contenido múltiple, al hombre en su total integridad. Y al bienestar, a la felicidad y a los destinos superiores de ese ser complejo y contradictorio precisa subordinar toda actividad creadora: la estructuración económica, los sistemas políticos y sociales, la investigación científica y la obra de arte. Hay que buscar en un nuevo humanismo los materiales para construir el mundo del mañana" (Silva Herzog 10).

38. In a farewell article written for the last issue of the Spanish exile journal *España Peregrina,* Juan Larrea writes that the new journal *Cuadernos Americanos* would be a "sisterly collaboration, open to the best writers of the continent, and opposed to the reactionary concept of Hispanidad" (in: González Neira 15). For the activities of the Instituto de Cultura Hispánica in Latin America, see Gustavo Guerrero's *Historia de un encargo.*

39. *Los orígenes del hombre americano* was published that same year of 1943 by Éditions de l'Arbre in Montreal in its original French version. A revised second edition with a new preface appeared in 1955 in French and in 1960 in Spanish.

40. Rivet had published his first article, on the origins of American Man, in 1925 in *L'Anthropologie* ("Les origines de l' homme américain").

41. See Spengler's only text dedicated to American cultures, "Das Alter der amerikanischen Kulturen," where Spengler concluded that it was paramount to determine the age of American cultures in order to be able to better assess their place in world history.

42. "En definitiva, el Pacífico no debe aparecérsenos ya como una inmensa extensión vacía, barrera infranqueable tendida entre el Antiguo y el Nuevo Mundo. Migraciones humanas lo atravesaron, a costa de cuántos esfuerzos y de qué dramas, para arribar a América y colonizarla; hubo después comerciantes audaces que lo cruzaron en forma más o menos regular hasta la época del descubrimiento, y estas travesías se efectuaron sin duda en ambos sentidos. Mucho antes que las naves de los grandes descubridores europeos, las sorprendentes piraguas melanésicas y polinésicas, y quizá también las primitivas balsas peruanas, habían *Sur*cado las rutas de este inmenso desierto marino. Una emocionante epopeya anónima precedió a la gran epopeya histórica. Es toda la historia de la Humanidad" (Rivet, *Los orígenes del hombre americano* 190).

43. "El sentido de la gran solidaridad humana debe ser, hoy más que nunca, exaltado y fortalecido. Todo hombre debe comprender y saber, que, en todas las latitudes, en todas las longitudes, otros seres, hermanos suyos sea cual fuere el color de su piel o la forma de sus cabellos, han contribuído a hacerle la vida más dulce o más fácil" (Rivet, *Los orígenes del hombre americano* 200).

44. In the later revised edition of *Los orígenes del hombre americano* I have not found updates to the bibliography used by Rivet for the first edition. Rivet did write a new preface where he expressed much greater optimism about the continuation of French Americanism since the end of World War II. His book enjoyed a good reception after the war, with translations into Portuguese (1960) and Italian (1973). It was not translated into English, however, and Rivet notes dryly in his concluding chapter of the third Spanish edition that a 1957 article by George F. Carter published in the *Johns Hopkins Magazine* had omitted reference to his publications, while speaking to the same questions of the earliest populations of the Americas (*Los orígenes del hombre americano* 194).

45. Cossío was alluding to the controversy in Cuba on the *homo cubensis* and also to another theory about the Argentinian Pampas: "Así algunos autores cubanos sostienen que fue en la Isla Mayor del Caribe donde estuvo el Paraíso Terrenal y nos hablan de un 'homo-cubanus'; otros, como Florentino Ameghino, reclaman para las pampas argentinas el privilegio de ser la cuna de la Humanidad" (201). For a discussion of the Cuban context of this nationalist pseudoscientific argument, see Rafael Rojas's essay ("Fernando Ortiz").

46. "Si esta unidad nacional, cultural y física no está aún realizada, ello no depende de una oposición sistemática contra el mestizaje, como la que encontramos en América del Norte con relación a los negros, sino más bien del obstáculo que la Naturaleza opone a la buena voluntad de los hombres" (Rivet, "Reflexiones sobre la América Latina").

47. Alberto zum Felde's "La tragedia del indio en *Sur*américa," for example, is a stylized account of the irrevocable tragedy of Inca descendents in Peru. For an updated comprehensive discussion of the essayistic and literary discourse of *mestizaje* in Mexico and the Andes, see Estelle Tarica's *The Inner Life of Mestizo Nationalism.*

48. Lévi-Strauss evokes his New York experience and his discovery of the volumes of the *Handbook of South American Indians* in his article "New York post- et préfiguratif," edited by the Smithsonian Institution.

49. For more information about the politics behind the decision to close the Musée de l'Homme, see Sally Price's book *Paris Primitive: Jacques Chirac's Museum on the Quai Branly.* She presents Jacques Chirac's decision to build a new museum instead of renovating the Musée de l'Homme as a result of Chirac's ambition to compete with the museums of former French presidents—the Centre Pompidou (Georges Pompidou), the Musée d'Orsay (Valéry Giscard d'Estaing), and the Grand Louvre (François Mitterand).

50. Ferdinand de Saussure's *Cours de linguistique générale* was published posthumously by his students in 1916. It became a seminal work for the study of language, giving rise to the structural linguistics of Roman Jakobson and other linguists and also contributing to Claude Lévi-Strauss's structural anthropology. De Saussure distinguished strictly between diachronic and synchronic approaches to language, claiming that the linguistic approach was properly synchronic, relying not so much on the history of language but on the formal study of language as a closed system of differential signs that each consisted of a signifier and a signified.

3. Jacques Roumain, Haiti, and the Margins of Latin America

1. See my article "Carpentier y el Bureau d'ethnologie haitienne" for more on Carpentier in Haiti.

2. The most discussed work of the time of the American occupation was William Seabrook's *The Magic Island* (1929). The Hollywood genre of "zombie" movies began its rise most notably with *White Zombie* (1932), starring Béla Lugosi.

3. The broader context of Métraux's work for UNESCO after 1946 has been studied by Harald Prins in his article "Toward a world without evil."

4. Against those who accuse Firmin of still acknowledging the idea of an inferior African civilization—even though not a race—Gérarde Magloire-Danton writes that he simply insisted on the lack of knowledge on Africa. She arrives at the conclusion that both Firmin and Price-Mars responded in their studies of Haitian culture and history to colonial representations of their country and stood in the tradition of a "scholarship of commitment" (151).

5. For Largey the three responded with their books to European ideas that challenged them. As he writes, "The three asserted Haitians' capability to appreciate and augment European culture. Yet, Firmin and Price did not dispute Africa's backwardness, nor did they consider the African influence on their culture as equal to European ideas. Instead, they complied with the European assessment of African culture as less advanced than Europe but capable of improvement and advancement according to European criteria" (35).

6. Nancy Parezo and Don Fowler write that "participation in the exhibition of Native peoples was a part of the campaign that anthropologists had been

waging for over two decades to gain public recognition of their professional identity" (8). Franz Boas represented Columbia University at the Louisiana Purchase Exposition, with a living exhibit of the Kwakiutl Indians.

7. For Price-Mars *anthropology* referred to "physical anthropology" and *ethnology* to archaeology, paleontology, prehistory, folklore, and linguistics (*Le bilan des études ethnologiques* 14).

8. See Shannon's account of Price-Mars's early years (14–33).

9. Price-Mars is interested in Frazer's famous distinction between imitative and sympathetic magic as forms of prescientific knowledge; he quotes Frazer and Sébillot, but not Boas, in his bibliography.

10. The programmatic anonymous declaration of the Sociedad del Folklore Cubano, in contrast to Price-Mars, mentions only at the very end "fantastic and supernatural beliefs" ("Actas de la *Sociedad del folklore cubano*. No. 1").

11. "Dans cette Amérique espagnole et anglaise nous avons la glorieuse destinée de maintenir avec le Canada et les Antilles françaises les traditions et la langue française, honneur funeste et périlleux car il nous valut un siècle d'isolement. . . . La République Dominicaine qui partage notre territoire ne participe pas de cette infortune, elle appartient à une Amérique Latine de 18 républiques. Des écrivains parlent à un public de 90 millions d'hommes, on reconnaît ses joies et ses peines. Nous devons connaître la littérature et l'âme de l'Amérique Latine. Les peuples ont vécu d'une vie aussi difficile que la nôtre, ont connu les mêmes tâtonnements, des vicissitudes semblables, l'ère des caudillos et des pronunciamientos, la période où s'affrontent les forces d'anarchie et les forces de cohésion et d'ordre, les temps pénibles de la puberté des jeunes nationalités" (N. Sylvain, "Chronique—Programme" 5).

12. Ugarte's political and literary essays really address the idea of a continent united by its Hispanic heritage, as can be gleaned from his major publications: *La evolución política y social de Hispanoamérica* (1910; The political and social evolution of Spanish America), *El porvenir de América Española* (1910; The future of Spanish America), *Mi campaña hispanoamericana* (1922; My Spanish American campaign), *La Patria Grande* (1922; The great fatherland), *El destino de un continente* (1923; The fate of a continent), and *Escritores Iberoamericanos del 1900* (1941; Iberoamerican writers of 1900).

13. "Et voici . . . à propos du 'nationalisme, dans la littérature sud-américaine' les conseils que donnait Manuel Ugarte, le penseur et critique urugayen [*sic*]. 'La critique européenne et le public qui suit l'évolution mondiale ne peuvent prendre en considération l'Amerique latine comme force nouvelle au point de vue artistique, que si elle apporte une nuance spéciale, et une originalité. . . . Ce que l'Amérique Latine attend—ce que l'on attend—c'est un art résultant de sa propre conscience, violente, inexpérimentée, naïve, avec des goûts romanesques d'aventure dotée d'une certaine finesse de perception, pleine de jeunesse et de confiance dans son avenir. Après avoir été spectateur, elle doit devenir acteur dans les ouvrages qui sortent de son esprit, se refléter dans les créations issues de son

milieu et se faire un art personnel, abandonnant tous les colonialismes, même les flatteurs. . . .' Voilà des conseils qui embrassent tout le problème de notre littérature autochtone et autonome, la vraie émancipation spirituelle" (N. Sylvain, "La jeune littérature haitienne" 47–48).

14. "Si nous écrivons en français, nous sommes, il ne faut pas l'oublier, des étrangers, peut-être même des barbares, nous n'avons pas à suivre les raffinements de sensibilité, essayer d'imiter, mais nous devons rendre nos sensations, exprimer nos sentiments. Nos poèmes sont traduits de l'Haitien, c'est à dire la traduction d'états d'âme qui nous sont propres. La grande règle n'est-elle pas de plaire, peu importe la formule mystérieuse suivant laquelle s'opère la transmutation, l'honnête homme respire le parfum, s'enchante de la musique si elle l'émeut. Le reste est littérature" (N. Sylvain, "La jeune littérature haitienne" 53).

15. For example, the subjects of the Apr.–Sept. issue of 1939 were: social economy, ethnography, history, history of science, medicine, social medicine, philology, scientific philosophy, politics and diplomacy, international politics, ethnology, social psychiatry, "psychogenia," ethnic and historical psychology, comparative religion, sociology, juridical sociology, juridico-religious sociology, religious sociology, technology, and urbanism. The literary and artistic subjects covered also ranged widely: stories, art criticism, folklore, criticism, music, novellas, Haitian pages, prose poems, poetry, prose, and communal life.

16. For a summary and comparison of the political thought of the Communists and the Griots in the 1930s, see Matthew Smith's excellent account (13–39).

17. "Aux splendeurs orientales de l'antique Saba, nous rêvions de mêler la raison latine, et que de ce mélange conforme au genie de notre race naquît une civilisation intégralement haitienne" (Brouard, "Doctrine de la nouvelle école").

18. For an informed description of the ideological divergences between Georges Montandon and Paul Rivet, and consequently between Roumain and the Griots, see André-Marcel d'Ans's article. Montandon became an anti-Semite in the 1930s, collaborated under the German occupation, and was assassinated in 1944 together with his wife (d'Ans 1383–85).

19. In a review published in *Le Mercure de France*, republished by Denis and Duvalier with a preface, the reviewer associated the authors, because of their pronouncements on race, with Italian and German Fascism (Denis and Duvalier, "Le *Mercure de France* et les Griots").

20. As we have seen in chapter 1, on Ortiz, the Afro-Cuban movement shaped by Ortiz defined itself as antiracist and included members of the white upper class, as well as middle-class mulatto poets. Similarly, in Puerto Rico, the white poet Luis Palés Matos, like Nicolás Guillén and Emilio Ballagas in Cuba, distanced himself from the "tyranny of racial ancestry" (Kutzinski 155).

21. See Martha Cobb's chapter "Roots, Patterns and the Word" (3–24). Cobb's study on the literary "New Negro" reconstructs the pan-African literary movements in the United States and the Caribbean and takes as its point of departure the identification of black writers with their African heritage.

22. As Ramsey explains, "Vodou is the name by which Afro-Haitian spiritual beliefs and ritual practices are today known in official Kreyòl orthography and most scholarly writing." In Haiti, it has traditionally referred to a particular mode of dancing and drumming, with a large number of regional variations (*Spirits and the Law* 6–7).

23. See the following essays authored by Denis and Duvalier under the rubric of ethnography: "Une céremonie du culte Péthro"; "Une céremonie en l'honneur de Damballah"; and "Une cérémonie d'initiation. Le laver-tête dans le culte vaudouesque."

24. This insider/outsider status was similar to that of Lydia Cabrera and Zora Neale Hurston, analyzed by Emily Maguire. Neither of the Haitian contributors to *Les Griots* had formal training in anthropology, of course, and therefore the distance they sought from their object of study was as much one of social class as of professional standing. Their narrative voices are similar, however, in that they all felt the need to legitimize themselves by referring to science and in particular to anthropology and to folklore as the fields within which they wished to be recognized (Maguire 148–58).

25. The differences in opinion became apparent when Roumain, in a letter to Kléber Jacob from the Griots group, insisted on his affiliation with the Institut d'ethnologie and other Parisian institutions associated with Paul Rivet and wrote that had he been a student of the Ecole d'anthropologie only, the Haitian president could not have entrusted him with the direction of the Bureau d'ethnologie (*Oeuvres complètes* 731). The Ecole d'anthropologie was a rival of the Institut d'ethnologie, oriented toward physical anthropology.

26. Ginetta Candelario has argued that the identification with an autochtonous past served in the case of the Museo del hombre dominicano as a way of distinguishing Dominicans from two historic threats to their sovereignty, Spain and Haiti (108–9).

27. See Ramsey for a detailed account of the Catholic Church's antisuperstition campaign, the governmental assistance it received, and its effects on the population (*Spirits and the Law*).

28. According to Alfred Métraux, it was during a trip to the island of La Tortue that Métraux and Roumain first discussed the merciless destruction by Catholic priests of religious objects of great value and consequently the "need to put on record the story of voodoo" before it was too late (*Voodoo in Haiti* 17). Lescot's motivations for supporting these institutes is not quite clear. For Charlier-Doucet the paradox of the creation of the Bureau d'ethnologie by the same president who supported the Catholic Church's antisuperstition campaign can be explained by the "petite histoire" of the good relations of Roumain's friend and colleague Kurt Fisher with Senator Fombrun, who convinced Lescot that Roumain, at the institute, was going to be distracted from other political activities (110–11). Ramsey in turn follows Lescot's memoirs, where he writes that he came to deplore the campaign and considered it as a ploy of the French-

dominated Catholic church against his plans to install American missionaries in Haiti (*Spirits and the Law* 194).

29. The historian Hénock Trouillot considers Roumain therefore as an essentially European Marxist who did not have the same interest as Brouard, for example, in studying vodou as part of Haiti's culture (viii, 10–23).

30. Another section, in planning at the time of the publication of Roumain's text but never realized, was on ethnography, which was going to display Haitian (secular) everyday life.

31. As one can see in Arnoux Charles's bibliographical index of 1964, a relative majority of articles and books published by the bureau were dedicated to archeology and ancient history. The authors were Catts Pressoir, Roumain himself, Kurt Fisher, Rémy Bastien, Louis Maximilien, Albert Mangonès, Irving Rouse (Yale University), and Michel Aubourg (Charles). This changed in the 1950s, when Haitian folklore, popular culture, and vodou became prominent.

32. In 1943, the antisuperstition campaign of the Catholic Church ceased and vodou-related objects stopped being confiscated. Bastien's annual report comments dryly that "fewer objects have been added to the catalogue" (*Rapport annuel* 8).

33. "Un musée est avant tout un organisme social et pédagogique. Il est essentiellement destiné à l'enseignement des couches les plus larges de la population. Il doit être semblable à un livre ouvert et expliqué. Sa mission n'est pas de séduire une curiosité désœuvrée mais d'instruire et de stimuler l'étude" (Roumain, *Oeuvres complètes* 1159).

34. Fonds Métraux, Laboratoire d'anthropologie sociale, HAÏTI, Journaux et carnets de terrain, Carnet A. Metraux no. 88 Sept.–Oct. 1944, entry dated Sept. 25, 1944.

35. For Roger Dorsinville, Roumain made a mistake in not excluding Lorimer and Duvalier from the Bureau d'ethnologie (54).

36. In 1952, Carpentier wrote in the Venezuelan paper *La Nación* an enthusiastic report on Haitian ethnology that is excerpted in Oriol, Viaud, and Aubourg's *Le mouvement folklorique en Haiti* (113).

37. At the end of volume 1 of *Afroamérica* there appears a balance for the institution's finances. According to this report, its revenues came from membership fees and donations from several governmental and nongovernmental institutions. These might have ceased after 1945.

38. "Resolución del primer congreso demográfico interamericano sobre la población negra," *Afroamérica* 1.1–2 (1945): 147–72. Paul Rivet was also a member of the institute, even though he was not on its advisory board (Correspondence Roumain-Rivet, Rivet Archive).

39. "La hipótesis que subraya el estudio de las supervivencias culturales africanas en el Nuevo Mundo deriva de aquella concepción de la civilización humana que sostiene que la conducta social es algo aprendido, y no heredado o instintivo. Lo cual significa que, aunque haya tantas culturas—esto es, modos aceptados de conducta, configuraciones de instituciones, y sistema de valores y metas—como

sociedades existan, cada cultura o cualquiera de sus elementos, puede ser aprendido por cualquier individuo, sin importar a qué raza pertenezca, o por cualquier grupo que tenga la voluntad y la oportunidad de aprender. Se sigue de nuestro concepto de cultura como algo aprendido que el préstamo de tradiciones que un pueblo toma de otro es asunto fácil; la investigación ha establecido, en efecto, que el préstamo cultural es universal en la experiencia social humana. . . . El concepto de cultura en el cual nuestra hipótesis está basada involucra así la operación del principio del cambio constante—pero al mismo tiempo supone un alto grado de estabilidad en cada cultura, la cual se asegura por la transmisión de una generación a la siguiente de hábitos, costumbres, creencias e instituciones" (Aguirre Beltrán, "Problema, método y teoría" 191).

40. Roumain does not mention Ortiz much in his study. He cites Ortiz's *Historia de la arqueología indocubana* (1922)—not his dictionaries and not the *Contrapunteo cubano*—in his bibliography. He also cites, to be sure, Paul Rivet and Monfort de Créqui's "La langue Uru ou Pukina" (1925).

41. Roumain received a letter of protest from a Frédéric Kébreau, the chief of the Department of Botanic and Phytopathology at the National School of Agriculture, claiming that corn actually derived from another plant, teosint, and that therefore Roumain's reconstruction was faulty. In the following *Bulletin* of the Bureau of Ethnology, Roumain defended himself energetically against this claim (*Oeuvres complètes* 1069–70).

42. The Ciboney are a lesser-known group of indigenous people who populated Santo Domingo before the arrival of the Taínos.

43. Renn describes Roumain's interest in archaeology and paleontology as immediately related to the necessity of filling his new museum with objects (77).

44. Métraux quotes Roumain extensively in his own study, published later on, *Voodoo in Haiti*. The subchapter "The Drum as a Sacred Object" is dedicated entirely to the assotor drum ceremony as described by Roumain (182–86).

45. As we know from Ramsey, the Assotor drum, which was the biggest of the vodou drums, had virtually disappeared from Haiti by 1943, because vodou had been declared an illegal practice and the Assotor drums were the easiest objects to find at an inspection. Vodou had become a "performance" arranged for anthropologists or visitors, where special "informants" acted as messengers between those willing to organize a vodou ceremony and those who wanted to observe them, and at times the potential observers themselves had to help by obtaining permission for a ritual (Ramsey, "Prohibition, Persecution, Performance"). Roumain mentions in a note preceding *Le sacrifice* the houngan M. S. Abraham as his "guide" (*Oeuvres complètes* 1075). Probably Métraux's double conditional is closer to the truth: Roumain wrote a text based on the "description of a ceremony which the houngan Abraham would have celebrated had he been able to" (*Voodoo in Haiti* 184).

46. "Le mot hébreu désignant la fête, hag, signifiait exactement la danse. C'est le même mot que l'arabe hadj, qui dans les temps préislamiques désignait la

ronde processionnelle autor de la Ka'aba; le terme fut appliqué par extension au pélerinage tout entier" (Roumain, *Le sacrifice* 8).

47. Roumain's narrative scenario of the return to Guinea might have inspired the mythic flight away from Haiti of the protagonist Ti Noel at the end of Alejo Carpentier's *El reino de este mundo* (1949). Carpentier cites Roumain's *Le sacrifice du tambour-Assôtô(r)* in his prologue to the novel (15).

48. "Le Houngan trace un dernier veve. Il plante au milieu une bougie allumée. La cérémonie d'expulsion est achevée. La divinité a été renvoyée pour toujours, en Afrique, dans cette Guinée ancestrale, qui survit encore, enveloppée d'une brume mythologique, avec une ténacité extraordinaire dans la mémoire fidèle de ces descendants d'esclaves. Tout le monde se retire en chantant sur le même ton désolé: La famille est finie/Assotor est parti/Il n'a rien laissé après lui/C'est triste/Amen" (Roumain, *Le sacrifice* 133).

49. On vodou, see the following, all published within three years after Roumain's work: Mars, *La crise de possession dans le vaudou;* Denis and Duvalier, *L'évolution stadiale du Vodou;* Maximilien.

50. Leyburn explains the *coumbite* as the collective work of clearing a field or preparing it for cultivation, organized by informal neighborhood groups or Société Congo. Leyburn suggests that the word was borrowed from the Spanish *convidar,* to convey (199–200).

51. Hénock Trouillot, in contrast, considers that anthropology furnishes the details of peasant life from an informed perspective, enhancing the novel's air of authenticity yet avoiding the trappings of the ethnographer's eye by describing all events from the point of view of Manuel, an insider (189).

52. For Gaillard, the scene has a dreamlike quality, typical of tragedies (21).

53. Edmund Wilson's verdict that this was "yet another Communist novel written on the orders of Kremlin" has been somewhat tamed by Stephen H. Arnold in his "Approches critiques," which finds that the novel uses socialist realist techniques creatively (Roumain, *Oeuvres complètes* 1576). For example, the water, Arnold says, represents a concrete goal to be achieved, not so much a symbol of life and hope. Paul Ricoeur, in his preface to Claude Souffrant's book, sees in Roumain's work a general "elan," a politically engaged spirit common to all writers of the Negritude movement at that time.

4. Gilberto Freyre and the Science of Culture

1. See Lucia Pallares-Burke's *Gilberto Freyre. Um vitoriano dos trópicos* for a comprehensive analysis of Freyre's readings and intellectual influences leading up to the writing of *Casa-grande & senzala.*

2. The impact of da Cunha on Freyre is also evident in the fact that Freyre first published a book in Spanish translation on Euclides da Cunha (*Actualidad de Euclydes da Cunha*), of which the Portuguese-language essay is an expansion.

3. As Lilia Moritz Schwarcz has shown, the two great nineteenth-century schools of medicine in Bahía and in Rio de Janeiro adopted both eugenicist

principles and declared race the most important factor for envisioning a newly unified nation (234–97). Fernando Ventura Santos's article in turn argues that physical anthropology was a key component in the networks and scientific narratives producing the Brazilian nation-building process.

4. Mark Anderson's discussion of race and racial mixing in Euclides da Cunha's *Os Sertões* also depicts da Cunha as a "humane analyst," but one who considered *mestiçagem* as a transitory and problematic state of Brazil's population (550–52). For more discussions of racial conflict and identity in Machado de Assis, see Flynn, Calvo-González, and Mendes de Sousa.

5. The Sociedade Higiénica de São Paulo was founded in 1918, the Liga de Higiene Mental of Rio de Janeiro in 1922, and the First Brazilian Congress of Eugenics was organized in 1929. For the eugenicist movement in Latin America, see Nancy Stepan's book *The Hour of Eugenics,* in particular her section on Brazil (46–54).

6. See Sergio Miceli's edited two-volume anthology on the history of the social sciences in Brazil. Also, the published proceedings of the Conference on Latin American Studies in Rio de Janeiro (1965) holds several articles specific to Brazil, written by Florestan Fernandes and José Honorio Rodrigues (Diégues Júnior and Wood). For a more recent comment on the social sciences in Brazil, see Renato Ortiz's chapter "Notas sobre as ciencias sociais no Brasil."

7. Brazil's relation with France became closer in the first decades of the twentieth century mainly because of the French psychologist George Dumas's influence on the first director of the Universidade de São Paulo (Lefebvre). Fernanda Massi's chapter "Franceses e norte-americanos nas ciências sociais brasileiras 1930–1960" (410–61) considers the presence of both French and North American social scientists in Brazil as sometimes more, sometimes less inspiring, but indicative of the asymmetrical relations between France and Brazil, which was always considered a country on the periphery. As Massi states, surprisingly, Claude Lévi-Strauss's stay in São Paulo left relatively little impact at the time on students and colleagues, whereas Roger Bastide, who replaced Lévi-Strauss, stayed on for two decades, taught a generation of sociologists, and became quite involved with writers and artists as well (Peixoto; Pereira de Queiróz).

8. Clifford Geertz argued in 1988 that the "author-function" set anthropology apart from other social sciences precisely because the tension between intimate insight and scientific assessment had to be made productive.

9. On the "morphology of history" see Spengler's introduction to *The Decline of the West* (3–50). Spengler was widely read in Latin America, especially for his notion that any culture may rise to become a "great civilization," once its time had come (Birkenmaier, "Scenarios").

10. As Alfredo Cesar Melo has pointed out, this plasticity of Brazilian culture is what can best be compared to Fernando Ortiz's transculturation, as a process akin to cultural appropriation, but where both sides give and take something ("A face de Janus no ensaísmo latino-americano").

11. In one of his most inspired comparisons, Freyre even argues that much of the sexual precocity found by travelers in Brazil can be found in travel accounts of Spain as well as in statistics of Eskimo puberty—which does not mean, inversely, that race prevails over climate (*Masters and the Slaves* 265).

12. For the following details of Ramos's biography I rely on Maria José Campos's excellent chapter "Trajetória de luz: uma carreira de sucesso" in her study *Arthur Ramos. Luz e sombra na antropologia brasileira* (35–41), as well as on Ramos's obituary published in *Phylon* in 1951 (de Souza Carneiro).

13. As Brad Lange has shown, Ramos refrained in these brochures from racializing poverty and recommended that better hygiene, a nuclear family, and sexual education would lead to the improvement of Brazilian society. But the illustrations for Ramos's recommendations spoke another language: model families were always depicted as white; syncretic religious practices and dance were associated with atavism and social deviance (Lange 28–31).

14. Following the university reform of 1965, the Universidade do Brasil was renamed the Universidade Federal do Rio de Janeiro.

15. De Souza Carneiro writes: "It was Arthur Ramos who had the distinction of reviving the original methods of Nina Rodrigues and bringing them into conformity with the most modern methods of anthropology, especially in the field of culture comparison and acculturation" (73).

16. For the details of Freyre's biography, I rely on the "Cronología" compiled by Darcy Ribeiro for the Spanish edition of *Casa-grande* (Freyre, *Casa-grande y senzala* 472–567).

17. For example, in a letter from Nov. 22, 1948, Ortiz writes to Freyre: "Siempre aprovecho sus enseñanzas y exposiciones que afirman una vez más lo relevante de su alta personalidad. En mi trabajo y en los capítulos sucesivos lo cito en repetidas ocasiones" (I often draw from your teachings and expositions, which affirm once and again how relevant you are as an eminent figure. I cite you on repeated occasions in my work and in the following chapters) (Ortiz Archive, folder 319). I have not found mention of Ramos in Ortiz's correspondence at the National Library.

18. See Luitgarde Barros's description and the excerpts gathered by her for a trustworthy account of Ramos's imprisonment and negotiations with Vargas's government (54–59).

19. "A busca de 'soluções de compromisso' parece ter perpassado todo o pensamento governista e da elite da época" (Campos 306).

20. Freyre himself preferred to speak of "social democracy" ("Preface to Second Edition" xxx). Guimarães traces the concept of "racial democracy" back to Roger Bastide's journalistic writings, and to the Brazilian Black Movement leading up to the 1970s, but does not mention Ramos. Thales de Azevedo's *Democracia racial: ideologia e realidade* in turn reads the concept in relation to Brazilian literary history, focusing on the representation of the black voice in literature.

21. Later on, of course, the U.S. American reception of Freyre's work became more critical, with Stuart Schwartz, in *Sugar Plantations in the Formation of Brazilian Society,* calling the idea of a somewhat benign form of colonialism under the Portuguese a "sweet version" of slavery in Brazil. Nascimento himself later shifted the discussion toward the absence of political or racial democracy in Brazil, culminating in his stinging denunciation of Brazilian racism in his *O genocídio do negro brasileiro: processo de um racismo mascarado* (1978; The genocide of the Brazilian blacks: process of a masked racism). For a critical analysis of Freyre's reception and in particular that of the idea of racial democracy, see Avelar.

22. Ramos's late publications with reference to racial democracy, cited by Barros, were: "A mestiçagem é favorável ao Brasil" (Mixing races is favorable for Brazil), *Revista Brasileira da Medicina Pública* 10 (Rio de Janeiro) (Nov.–Dec. 1946): 5–23; "La question raciale et le monde démocratique," *Bulletin Internationale des Sciences Sociales* (Paris) 1.3–4 (1949); and *Le métissage au Brésil* (Paris: Hermann et fils Editeurs, 1952).

23. "Uma coisa é certa. A Guerra está sendo conduzida sob o signo do Homem. Protegidos pelas lições da Antropologia—considerada no seu sentido largo de ciencia do Homem e da Cultura—vamos combater, no plano ideológico, as tentativas criminosas daqueles que construiram mitos de superioridade e inferioridade de raças que servissem aos seus propósitos de rapiña e conquista" (A. Ramos, *Guerra e relacões de raca* 9).

24. "E é nesse sentido que Clews Parsons aponta a Antropologia, no seu significado largo de 'ciência do homem' como oferecendo uma técnica científica, não de 'adivinhar' os acontecimentos, mas num certo sentido, de predizê-los, dentro das leis da observação empírica" (A. Ramos, *Guerra e relacões de raca* 27).

25. "Um humanismo científico mais interessado que o outro nos problemas de relações interhumanas e de contactos interregionais sem que desse interesse saia prejudicada a ciência ou sacrificada a dignidade intelectual dos novos humanistas" (Freyre, *Problemas Brasileiros de Antropologia* 180–98).

26. Antonio Sergio Guimarães, for example, begins his otherwise well-informed article "Democracia racial: el ideal, el pacto, el mito" (2002) by citing Roger Bastide. Similarly, George Reid Andrews, in his 1996 article "Brazilian Racial Democracy, 1900–1990: An American Counterpoint," does not mention Arthur Ramos. Also, Paulina Alberto, in her book *Terms of Inclusion: Black Intellectuals and the Politics of Belonging in Twentieth-Century Brazil* (2011), studies use of the term *racial democracy* between 1945 and 1950 without mentioning Arthur Ramos. Finally, Alexandra Isfahani-Hammond associates racial democracy with Freyre, critiquing him for she calls an ideology of "white negritude" (1–15).

27. Robert C. Young has argued in this line that the idea of postcolonial hybridity, as theorized by Néstor García Canclini, cannot be applied to Freyre (in: Lund and McNee). Analyzing recent contrasting rereadings of Freyre, Christopher Dunn has proposed that they conform to a general polarization between ideas of

race perceived as coming from the United States and ideas of race identified with a specifically Latin American or Brazilian tradition (in: Lund and McNee 35–51).

28. Freyre's debt to Boas is clearest in his preface to *The Masters and the Slaves*, where he writes: "The scholarly figure of Professor Boas is the one that to this day makes the deepest impression upon me" (xxvi). Pallares-Burke finds that Boas had a delayed impact on Freyre, less noticeable at the moment of his studies under Boas at Columbia University but decisive in Freyre's conversion, during the 1920s, to the idea of racial mixing as a solution and not a problem (297–327).

29. Wissler, in his book *Man and Culture*, had designed a "culture scheme" that according to him followed a universal pattern and whereby every culture consisted of nine traits: speech, material traits (food habits, shelter, transportation, dress, tools, weapons, occupations), art, mythology and science, religion, family, property, government, and war.

30. "Cultura não é apenas lingua. É algo mais, que transcende às simples injunções políticas de um dado momento. É um determinismo dos povos. Neste sentido, podemos falar de uma cultura do Novo Mundo, caracterizada pelo seu espírito diferente, pelo seu 'sentido' na expressão de Keyserling, ou pelo seu 'Paideuma,' para empregar um conceito caro a Frobenius" (Ramos, *Guerra e relacões de raca* 120).

Renée Sylvain has characterized Frobenius's theory of *paideuma* and culture areas as a false start, not untypical of the early history of any science. Interestingly, Frobenius played a role not only for Ramos but also for the Negritude poets. For an insightful analysis of Frobenius's lack of recognition in his home country of Germany, see Marchand.

31. Rego Monteiro also published, together with P. L. Duchartre, a book titled *Légendes, croyances et talismans des indiens de l'Amazone* (1923), where the Amazon tribes are presented to the general reader in a short preface that emphasizes the primitiveness of their daily life in contrast to the complexity of their folklore. It ends by comparing the hieroglyphs of the Marajo in Brazil to those found in "Mexico," China, and Egypt. Rego Monteiro evidently wanted to place Amazon indigenous peoples as part of the world map of cultures.

32. As Ribeiro wrote, Freyre's indigenous ethnology was not his strong suit, but it was better than that of many of his contemporaries ("Prólogo" xxxv).

33. See also note 23 to this chapter, where Freyre updates Frobenius's classification of African culture areas by pointing to texts by Melville Herskovits. He used the occasion to polemically reply to Arthur Ramos, who had criticized Freyre for not having used current scholarship, noting that he had introduced Ramos to Herskovits in the first place (236–38).

34. There are many more Modernist paintings featuring Afro-Brazilian women, or else groups of people of distinctly mixed features, such as Lasar Segall's *Cabeça de mulata* (1927), Tarsila's *Operários* (1933), and Vicente do Rego Monteiro's *Seated Figure* (1924). The paintings analyzed here represent no more than a sampling of the artwork of the time.

35. Cândido Rondon was the head of the SPI during its first five years of existence, and he designed the SPI's policies toward the indigenous peoples living in Brazil. As Diacon has shown, Rondon was a great believer in positivist philosophy, according to which every culture would find its way to humanity if left alone. Rondon's policies were controversial because while protecting indigenous peoples from land claims and exploitation, Rondon also promoted the ultimate conversion of the indigenous into Brazilian citizens and thus their assimilation (Diacon 101–31). Rondon received a tribute in 1943 during the First Interamerican Congress of Indigenism im Mexico (Davis and Menget). For one of his most outspoken later critics, see Antonio Carlos de Souza Lima's *Um grande cerco de paz,* where Lima criticizes Rondon heavily for building what he called an oppressive wall of peace, or "cerco de paz," around the indigenous.

36. The first to seriously study the relations between indigenous and white populations were Charles Wagley and Marvin Harris, in their book *Minorities in the New World* (1958), and later, in 1970, Darcy Ribeiro in his study *Os indios e a civilização.* There Ribeiro asserts that none of the indigenous groups he studied were properly assimilated into the national society but instead were exterminated or else remained indigenous, identifying themselves as different from Brazilians and victims of their aggressive expansion (*Os índios e a civilizacão* 7–17). More recently, Mércio P. Gomes has argued from a different perspective that the "paradigm of acculturation" never accounted for the many ways in which cultures met in Brazil. He sees the beginning of a different period from the 1970s on, when indigenous communities in Brazil and elsewhere began to grow again, organize themselves, and find ways of preserving an identity of their own (Gomes ix–xvi).

37. "Creio aliás, que diante dos conflitos de fronteiras e zonas de influência entre os estudos sociais, o melhor é o estudante fugir do excesso de especialização em determinada ciência social para adquirir, no contacto como as outras, maior riqueza de observações e maior variedade de pontos de vista. A organização universitária nos Estados Unidos, se por um lado favorece e anima a especialização, permite por outro ao estudante grande flexibilidade no seu programa de estudo. . . . Ao cientista em geral, e ao cientista social em particular, toca a responsabilidade de um mínimo de cultura generalizada indispensável ás suas especializações. Sem ese mínimo, compreende-se talvez um grande físico ou um grande químico; mas não se compreende um grande sociólogo ou um grande economista" (Freyre, *O estudo das ciencias sociais* 46).

38. "Se formos considerados *amador,* que nos console Havelock Ellis: o maior apologista dos *amadores* ingleses e do seu 'unsystematic method of thinking'" (Freyre, *Sociologia* 66).

39. Helen Delpar's history of Latin American scholarship in the United States, for example, mentions literary studies of Latin America only in passing. For an informed account of the rise of Latin American literature and literary criticism after World War II, see Rolena Adorno's essay "Havana and Macondo: The Humanities in U.S. Latin American Studies, 1940–2000."

40. There is a detailed account by Chor Maio of the UNESCO Brazil project ("Abrindo a 'caixa-preta'").

41. Charles Wagley, the author and supervisor of the first book published as a result of the UNESCO program on race relations in Brazil, wrote in his preface to the second edition of 1963: "Racial origin has not become a serious point of conflict in Brazilian society. Brazilians can still call their society a racial democracy. Thus the book preserves its original validity and much of what it says of particular parts of the country has been shown by more recent studies to be of wider application as well. Brazil remains as a lesson in racial democracy for the rest of the world" (2).

Epilogue

1. Jane Guyer has discussed the continuous engagement of anthropology as a discipline with the evolving definition and institutional anchorage of area studies. For a critical history of area studies see Vicente L. Rafael's "The Cultures of Area Studies in the U.S."

2. For a panorama of Hispanic studies and Latin American studies in the United States, see Anne J. Cruz's "American Hispanism(s)," as well as my article "El hispanismo en América" and, from a linguistic perspective, José del Valle's "El lugar de las lenguas en las *lenguas modernas.*" Rachel Donadio's article on the "culture wars" unleashed by Alan Bloom's 1987 book *The Closing of the American Mind* comments on the discussions about not only the inclusion of women and minorities into the literature curriculum taught at universities and colleges but also the creation of interdisciplinary ethnic studies programs as a factor contributing, in the view of some, to the "balkanization" of cultural knowledge. On glotopolitics see José del Valle's "Glotopolítica, ideología y discurso."

Bibliography

"Actas de la *Sociedad del folklore cubano*. No. 1." *Archivos del Folklore Cubano* 1.1 (1923): 77–79.

A. W. "Glosario de Afronegrismos by Fernando Ortiz." *Journal of the Royal African Society* 25.97 (1925): 103–4.

Abellán, José Luis. *La idea de América. Origen y evolución*. 1972. Madrid: Iberoamericana, Vervuert, 2009.

Adorno, Rolena. "Havana and Macondo: The Humanities in U.S. Latin American Studies, 1940–2000." *The Humanities and the Dynamics of Inclusion since World War II*. Ed. David A. Hollinger. Baltimore: Johns Hopkins UP, 2006. 372–405.

———. "Racial Scorn and Critical Contempt." *Diacritics* 4.4 (1974): 2–7.

Aguirre Beltrán, Gonzalo. "Problema, método y teoría en los estudios afroamericanos, según Melville J. Herskovits." *Afroamérica* 2.3 (1946): 187–96.

———. *El proceso de aculturación*. Mexico: Universidad Nacional Autónoma de México. Dirección general de publicaciones, 1957.

Alberto, Paulina. "Democracy: São Paulo and Rio de Janeiro, 1945–1950." *Terms of Inclusion: Black Intellectuals and the Politics of Belonging in Twentieth-Century Brazil*. Charlotte: U of North Carolina P, 2011. 151–95.

Altamira, Rafael. *Mi viaje a América (libro de documentos)*. Madrid: Librería general de Victoriano Suárez, 1911.

Andermann, Jens. *The Optic of the State: Visuality and Power in Argentina and Brazil*. Pittsburgh: U of Pittsburgh P, 2007.

Anderson, Benedict. *Imagined Communities: Reflections on the Origins and Spread of Nationalism*. 1983. Rev. ed. London and New York: Verso, 1991.

Anderson, Mark D. "From Natural to National Disasters: Drought and the Brazilian Subject in Euclides da Cunha's Os Sertões." *Hispania (USA)* 91.3 (2008): 547–57.

Andrews, George Reid. "Brazilian Racial Democracy, 1900–1990: An American Counterpoint." *Journal of Contemporary History* 31.3 (1996): 483–507.

Anonymous. "Revista de Libros. Lorimer Denis et Francois Duvalier, Evolution stadiale du vodou. Bulletin no. 3 du Bureau d' Ethnologie de la Republique d' Haïti. Port-au-Prince, 1944." *Afroamérica* 2.3 (1946): 150–51.

Antoine, Jacques Carmeleau. *Jean Price-Mars and Haiti.* Washington, D.C.: Three Continents, 1981.

Arroyo, Jossianna. *Travestismos culturales: literatura y etnografía en Cuba y en Brasil.* Pittsburgh: U of Pittsburgh, Instituto Internacional de Literatura Iberoamericana, 2003.

Avelar, Idelber. "Cenas dizíveis e indizíveis: Raça e sexualidade em Gilberto Freyre." *Luso-Brazilian Review* 49.1 (2012): 168–86.

Azevedo, Thales de. *Democracia racial. Ideologia e realidade.* Petrópolis: Editora Vozes, 1975.

Barfield, Thomas. *The Dictionary of Anthropology.* Malden and Oxford: Blackwell, 1997.

Barkan, Elazar. *The Retreat of Scientific Racism: Changing Concepts of Race in Britain and the U.S.* New York: Cambridge UP, 1992.

Barreal, Isaac. "Prólogo." *Etnia y sociedad. Fernando Ortiz.* Ed. Isaac Barreal. Havana: Editorial de Ciencias Sociales, 1993. vii–xxxiii.

Barros, Luitgarde Oliveira Cavalcanti. *Arthur Ramos e as dinâmicas sociais de seu tempo.* 2nd ed. Maceió: Universidade Federal de Alagoas, 2005.

Bastien, Rémy Auguste. *Anthologie du folklore haitien.* Acta Anthropologica. Mexico, 1946.

———. *Rapport annuel du Bureau d'ethnologie de la République d'Haiti.* Port-au-Prince: Bureau d'ethnologie, 1943.

Bataille, Georges. "Musée." *Documents* 2 (1930): 300. Paris: Jean-Michel Place, 1991.

Bataillon, Francoise. "L'IFAL de 1945 a 1964." *IFAL 1945–1985.* Ed. Claude Bataillon and Georges Couffignal. Mexico City: Instituto Francés de América Latina, 1986. 21–60.

Beaujour, Michel. "Anthropology and Ethnography." *The Columbia History of Twentieth-Century French Thought.* Ed. Lawrence D. Kritzman. New York: Columbia UP, 2006. 136–40.

Beaulieu, Christian. "Philologie. Pour écrire le créole." *Les Griots* 4 (1939): 589–99.

Beckett, Greg. "Thinking with Others: Savage Thoughts about Anthropology and the West." *Small Axe* 17.3 (2013): 166–81.

Benedict, Ruth. *Patterns of Culture.* 1934. Boston: Houghton Mifflin, 1989.

Bernand, Carmen. "Mestizos, mulatos y ladinos en Hispanoamérica: un enfoque antropológico de un proceso histórico." *Motivos de la antropología americanista. Indagaciones en la diferencia.* Ed. Miguel León-Portilla. Mexico: Fondo de cultura económica, 2001. 105–33.

Bethell, Leslie, and Ian Roxborough, eds. *Latin America between the Second World War and the Cold War, 1944–1948.* New York: Cambridge UP, 1992.

Bilbao, Santiago A. *Alfred Métraux en la Argentina. Infortunios de un antropólogo afortunado.* Caracas: Comala.com, EdiciónXdemanda, 2002.

Biographie de Paul Rivet, fondateur du Musée de l'homme. Miscellanea. Paul Rivet. Octogenario dicata. I. 1958. Universidad Nacional Autónoma de México.

Birkenmaier, Anke. "Carpentier y el Bureau d'Ethnologie Haitienne. Los cantos vodú de *El reino de este mundo.*" *Foro Hispánico* 25.1 (2004): 17–33.

———. "El hispanismo en Estados Unidos. Literatura, estudios culturales y lingüística en el panorama actual." *Nuevos hispanismos interdisciplinarios y trasatlánticos.* Ed. Julio Ortega. Madrid: Iberoamericana-Vervuert, 2010. 199–213.

———. "Scenarios of Colonialism and Culture: Oswald Spengler's Latin America." *Modern Language Notes* 28.2 (2013): 256–76.

Bloch, Marc. *The Historian's Craft.* 1954. Trans. Peter Putnam. Manchester: Manchester UP, 1992.

Bloch, R. Howard. "New Philology and Old French." *Speculum* 65.1 (1990): 38–58.

Boas, Franz. "Changes in the Bodily Form of Descendants o Immigrants." Washington, D.C.: GPO, 1911.

———. "Methode der Ethnologie by F. Graebner." *Science* ns 34.884 (1911): 804–10.

———. "El prejuicio racial." *Ultra* 4 (1938): 538–43.

———. "Some Philological Aspects of Anthropological Research." *A Franz Boas Reader. The Shaping of American Anthropology (1883–1901).* 1906. Ed. George W. Stocking Jr. Chicago: Chicago UP, 1989. 183–88.

———. "The Study of Geography." *Volksgeist as Method and Ethic: Essays on Boasian Ethnography and the German Anthropological Tradition.* 1887. Ed. George W. Stocking Jr. History of Anthropology. Madison: U of Wisconsin P, 1996. 9–17.

Borges, Jorge Luis. "Prólogo." *Obra Crítica.* Pedro Henríquez Ureña. Ed. Emma Susana Speratti Piñero. Mexico: Fondo de Cultura Económica, 1960. Vii–xiii.

Botero, Clara Isabel. "José de Recasens. La construcción de una tradición científica en Colombia." *Antípoda. Revista de Antropología y Arqueología* 11 (2010): 285–338.

Braudel, Fernand, Carmen Bassols Batalla, and Carlos Antonio Aguirre Rojas. "A través de un continente de historia: Brasil y la obra de Gilberto Freyre." *Revista Mexicana de Sociología* 61.2 (1999): 167–87.

Bronfman, Alejandra. *Measures of Equality: Social Science, Citizenship, and Race in Cuba, 1902–1940.* Envisioning Cuba. Ed. Louis A. Pérez. Chapel Hill and London: U of North Carolina P, 2004.

Brouard, Carl. "Déclaration no. 4: Que sont les Griots." *Les Griots* 4 (1939): 465–68.

———. "Doctrine de la nouvelle école." *Les Griots* 1 (1938): 2.

———. "Question à l'ordre du jour. Paganisme et vaudou." *Les Griots* 5 (1939–40): 617–20.

Brouard, Carl, et al. "Déclaration." *Les Griots* 1 (1938): 1.

Burguière, André. *The Annales School: An Intellectual History.* Ithaca and London: Cornell UP, 2006.

Burke, Peter. *The French Historical Revolution: The Annales School, 1929–1989.* Stanford: Stanford UP, 1990.

Burke, Peter, and Maria Lúcia Garcia Pallares-Burke. *Gilberto Freyre: Social Theory in the Tropics.* Oxford: Peter Lang, 2008.

Cabrera, Lydia. *Cuentos negros de Cuba.* 1936. Ed. Prólogo de Rosario Hiriart. Intro. Fernando Ortiz. Barcelona: ICARIA editorial, 1989.

Cairo Ballester, Ana. "Nicolás Guillén y las polémicas sobre la cultura mulata." *Revista de la Biblioteca Nacional José Martí* 93.1–2 (2002).

Camejo, Enrique. "L'espèce humaine." *Estudios Afrocubanos. Revista Trimestral* 1.1 (1937): 155.

Camp, Jean. "Editorial: Terres Latines appelle les terres latines/Tierras Latinas llama a las tierras latinas." *Terres latines/Tierras latinas* 5 (1946): 1–3.

Campos, Maria José. *Arthur Ramos. Luz e sombra na antropologia brasileira. Uma versão da democracia racial no Brasil nas décadas de 1930 e 1940.* Rio de Janeiro: Edicões Biblioteca Nacional, 2004.

Candelario, Ginetta E. B. *Black behind the Ears: Dominican Racial Identity from Museums to Beauty Shops.* Durham and London: Duke UP, 2007.

Carpentier, Alejo. "Paul Rivet, l'Amérique et le Musée de l'Homme." *Revue des Deux Mondes* 12 (1976): 52–56.

———. "Prólogo." *El reino de este mundo (relato).* Mexico: E.D.I.A.P.S.A., 1949. 7–17.

Castellanos, Israel. *Medicina legal y criminología afro-cubanas.* Havana: Molina y cia., Impresores, 1937.

Castellanos, Jorge. *Pioneros de la etnografía afrocubana. Fernando Ortiz, Rómulo Lachatañeré, Lydia Cabrera.* Miami: Ediciones Universal, 2003.

Cate-Arries, Francie, and Jonathan F. Arries. "Entre Cortés y Cuauhtémoc: El exilio español de 1939 en México." *Nueva Literatura Hispánica* 3 (1999): 105–25.

Chacón y Calvo, José María. "Ortiz, F. Glosario de afronegrismos. Con un prólogo de Juan M. Dihigo." *Revista de Filología Española* 12 (1925): 301–2.

Charles, Arnoux. "Index bibliographique des bulletins et publications du Bureau d'ethnologie de la République d'Haiti." *Bulletin du Bureau d'Ethnologie d'Haiti* 4th ser. 30 (1964): 47–56.

Charlier-Doucet, Rachelle. "Anthropologie, politique et engagement social. L'expérience du Bureau d'ethnologie d'Haiti." *Gradhiva* ns 1 (2005): 109–25.

Chor Maio, Marcos. "Abrindo a 'caixa-preta': o projeto UNESCO de relacões raciais." *Antropologias, histórias, experiências.* Ed. Fernanda Peixoto, Heloisa Pontes, and Lilia Schwarcz. Belo Horizonte: Editora UFMG, 2004. 143–69.

———. "UNESCO's Anti-Racist Agenda: Research on Race Relations in Brazil in the 1950s." Paris: UNESCO, 2005[?]. July 4, 2011. http://portal.unesco.org/fr/ev.php-URL_ID=30394&URL_DO=DO_TOPIC&URL_SECTION=201.html.

Chor Maio, Marcos, and Ricardo Ventura Santos. "Cientificismo e antirracismo no pós-2a Guerra Mundial: uma análise das primeiras Declaracões sobre Raça da Unesco." *Raça como questão. História, ciência e identidades no Brasil.* Ed. Marcos Chor Maio and Ricardo Ventura Santos. Rio de Janeiro: Editora Fiocruz, 2010. 145–71.

Clifford, James. "On Ethnographic Surrealism." *The Predicament of Culture: Twentieth-Century Ethnography, Literature, and Art.* Cambridge and London: Harvard UP, 1988. 117–52.

Cobb, Martha. *Harlem, Haiti and Havana: A Comparative Critical Study of Langston Hughes, Jacques Roumain, Nicolás Guillén.* Washington D.C.: Three Continents, 1979.

Cohn, Deborah. *The Latin American Literary Boom and U.S. Nationalism during the Cold War.* Nashville: Vanderbilt UP, 2012.

Comhaire-Sylvain, Suzanne. *Le Créole Haitien. Morphologie et syntaxe.* Weteren: Imprimerie De Meester; Port-au-Prince: L'Auteur, 1936.

Conklin, Alice L. *In the Museum of Man: Race, Anthropology, and Empire in France, 1850–1950.* Ithaca: Cornell UP, 2013.

Conn, Robert T. *The Politics of Philology: Alfonso Reyes and the Invention of the Latin American Literary Tradition.* Lewisburgh: Bucknell UP; London: Associated UP, 2002.

Corral, Rose, Arturo Souto Alabarce, and Valender James, eds. *Poesía y exilio. Los poetas del exilio español en México.* Mexico: El Colegio de México, 1995.

Cossío, José L. "Los orígenes del hombre americano." *Cuadernos Americanos* 13.1 (1944): 201–5.

Cruz, Anne J. "American Hispanism(s)." *South Atlantic Review* 73.4 (2008): 86–106.

d'Ans, André-Marcel. "Jacques Roumain et la fascination de l'ethnologie." *Jacques Roumain. Oeuvres complètes. Edition critique.* Ed. Léon-Francois Hoffmann. Paris: ALLCA, 2003. 1378–425.

Dash, J. Michael. *Haiti and the United States: National Stereotypes and the Literary Imagination.* 1988. 2nd ed. London and New York: Macmillan, St. Martin's, 1997.

———. *Literature and Ideology in Haiti, 1915–1961.* London and Basingstoke: Macmillan, 1981.

———. *The Other America: Caribbean Literature in a New World Context.* New World Studies. Ed. A. James Arnold. Charlottesville and London: UP of Virginia, 1998.

Davis, Shelton H., and Patrick Menget. "Pueblos primitivos e ideologías civilizadas en el Brasil." *Los indios y la antropología en América Latina.* Ed. Carmen

Junqueira, E. de Assis Carvalho, et al. Buenos Aires: Busqueda Yuchan, 1984. 87–125.

Dayan, Joan. *Haiti, History, and the Gods.* Berkeley: U of California P, 1995.

Debaene, Vincent. "'Etudier des états de conscience.' La réinvention du terrain par l'ethnologie, 1925–1939." *L'Homme. Revue francaise d'anthropologie* 179 (2006): 7–61.

Degiovanni, Fernando. *Los textos de la patria. Nacionalismo, políticas culturales y canon en Argentina.* Buenos Aires: Beatriz Viterbo, 2010.

DeGraff, Michel, and Molly Ruggles. "A Creole Solution for Haiti's Woes." *New York Times* Aug. 2, 2014, sec. Op-Ed: A17.

de la Campa, Román. *Latin Americanism.* Minneapolis: U of Minnesota P, 1999.

Deleporte, Sarah. "A Resolutely New Outlook?" Paper presented at France and Its Others: New Museums, New Identities. U of Chicago Center in Paris, June 1–2, 2007. Unpublished.

———. "The Trocadero Matrix: Politics and Practice in French Ethnographic Museums." PhD dissertation, University of Chicago, 2006. Unpublished.

de L'Estoile, Benoît. *Le goût des autres. De l'exposition coloniale aux arts premiers.* Paris: Flammarion, 2006.

———. "Rationalizing Colonial Domination: Anthropology and Native Policy in French-Ruled Africa." *Empires, Nations, and Natives: Anthropology and State Making.* Ed. Federico Neiburg Lygia Sigaud Benoit de L'Estoile. Durham and London: Duke UP, 2005.

Delpar, Helen. *Looking South: The Evolution of Latin Americanist Scholarship in the United States, 1850–1975.* Tuscaloosa: U of Alabama P, 2008.

Del Sarto, Ana, Alicia Ríos, and Abril Trigo, eds. *The Latin American Cultural Studies Reader.* Durham and London: Duke UP, 2004.

del Valle, José. "Glotopolítica, ideología y discurso: categorías para el estudio del estatus simbólico del español." *La lengua, patria común? Ideas e ideologías del español.* Ed. José del Valle. Lengua y Sociedad en el Mundo Hispánico. Madrid and Frankfurt: Iberoamericana/Vervuert, 2007. 13–31.

———. "El lugar de las lenguas en las *lenguas modernas:* hacia una nueva cartografía de la linguística hispánica en EE.UU." *Prácticas y políticas linguísticas. Nuevas variedades, normas, actitudes y perspectivas.* Ed. Klaus Zimmermann. Madrid: Iberoamericana-Vervuert, 2014. 81–104.

———. "Menéndez Pidal, la regeneración nacional y la utopía lingüística." Del Valle and Gabriel-Stheeman 109–37.

del Valle, José, and Luis Gabriel-Stheeman, eds. *La batalla del idioma. La intelectualidad hispánica ante la lengua.* Madrid: Iberoamericana Vervuert, 2004.

Denis, Hector. "De nos onomatopées." *Les Griots* 1.1 (1938): 137–39.

Denis, Lorimer, and François Duvalier. "Déclaration no. 2. L'essentiel de la doctrine des Griots." *Les Griots* 2 (1938): 151–53.

———. "Doctrine: Pour un humanisme totalitaire." *Les Griots* 4 (1939): 468–73.

———. *L'évolution stadiale du Vodou [Introduction à l'étude comparée des données historico-culturelles de la culture populaire et des origines ethniques du peuple haïtien]*. Publications du Bureau d'ethnologie de la Republique d'Haiti, no. 3. Port-au-Prince: Imprimerie de l'Etat, 1944.

———. "*Le Mercure de France* et les Griots." *Les Griots* 2 (1938): 222–25.

———. "Le noir d'Afrique et la civilisation européenne." *Les Griots* 1.1 (1938): 3–13.

———. "Sociologie. Le Noir d'Afrique et la civilisation européenne." *Les Griots* 1 (1938): 3–13.

Depestre, René. "La France et Haiti. Le mythe et la réalité." *Gradhiva* ns 1 (2005): 19–45.

de Souza Carneiro, Edison. "Arthur Ramos: Brazilian Anthropologist (1902–1949)." *Phylon* 12.1 (1951): 73–81.

Diacon, Todd A. *Stringing Together a Nation: Cândido Mariano da Silva Rondon and the Construction of a Modern Brazil, 1906–1930*. Durham and London: Duke UP, 2004.

Dias, Nélia. *Le Musée d'ethnographie du Trocadéro (1878–1908). Anthropologie et muséologie en France*. Paris: Editions du Centra National de la Recherche Scientifique, 1991.

Díaz, María del Rosario. "Ethnography at the University of Havana." Font and Quiroz 55–63.

Diégues Júnior, Manuel, and Bryce Wood, eds. *Social Science in Latin America*. New York and London: Columbia UP, 1967.

di Leo, Octavio. *El descubrimiento de África en Cuba y Brasil. 1889–1969*. Madrid: Editorial Colibrí, 2001.

Donadio, Rachel. "Revisiting the Canon Wars." *New York Times* Sept. 16, 2007, sec. Sunday Book Review.

Dorsinville, Roger. *Jacques Roumain*. Paris: Présence Africaine, 1981.

Duany, Jorge. *The Puerto Rican Nation on the Move: Identities on the Island and in the United States*. Chapel Hill: U of North Carolina P, 2002.

Duarte, Maria Horta. "Between the National and the Universal: Natural History Networks in Latin America in the Nineteenth and Twentieth Centuries." *ISIS* 104.4 (2013): 777–87.

Duarte, Paolo. *Paul Rivet por êle mesmo*. São Paulo: Editora Anhambi, 1960.

Duno Gottberg, Luis. *Solventando las diferencias. La ideología del mestizaje en Cuba*. Madrid: Iberoamericana Vervuert, 2003.

Escarpit, Robert G. "Premiers résultats/Primeros resultados." *Terres latines/Tierras latinas* 6 (1946): 1–4.

Espinosa, Aurelio M. "Archivos del Folklore Cubano." *Journal of American Folklore* 40.158 (1927): 416–19.

Evans, R. Tripp. *Romancing the Maya: Mexican Antiquity in the American Imagination, 1820–1915*. Austin: U of Texas P, 2004.

Faber, Sebastiaan. *Exile and Cultural Hegemony: Spanish Intellectuals in Mexico, 1939–1975*. Nashville: Vanderbilt UP, 2002.

Fanon, Frantz. *Black Skin, White Masks. Peau noire, masques blancs.* 1952. Trans. Richard Philcox. Rev. ed. New York: Grove, 2008.

Fluehr-Lobban, Carolyn. "Anténor Firmin and Haiti's Contribution to Anthropology." *Gradhiva* ns 1 (2005): 95–108.

Flynn, Alex, Elena Calvo-González, and Marcelo Mendes de Sousa. "Whiter Shades of Pale: 'Coloring In' Machado de Assis and Race in Contemporary Brazil." *Latin American Research Review* 48.3 (2013): 3–24.

Font, Mauricio A., and Alfonso W. Quiroz, eds. *Cuban Counterpoints: The Legacy of Fernando Ortiz*. Lanham: Lexington, 2005. 55–63.

Franco, Jean. *The Decline and Fall of the Lettered City: Latin America in the Cold War.* Convergences: Inventories of the Present. Ed. Edward Said. Cambridge and London: Harvard UP, 2002.

Frank, Waldo. "Los dos medios mundos americanos." *Cuadernos Americanos* 2.3 (1942): 29–42.

Frazer, James. *The Golden Bough: A Study in Magic and Religion.* 1922. London: Penguin, 1996.

Freyre, Gilberto. *Actualidad de Euclydes da Cunha.* Colección problemas americanos. Ed. Newton Freitas. Buenos Aires: Escritorio Comercial do Brasil, 1942.

———. *Casa-grande & senzala. Formacão da família brasileira sob o regime da economia patriarcal.* 48th ed. Recife: Global Editora, 2003.

———. *Casa-grande y senzala. Introducción a la historia de la sociedad patriarcal en el Brasil. Prólogo y cronología de Darcy Ribeiro.* Caracas: Ayacucho, 1977.

———. "Euclydes da Cunha." *Perfil de Euclydes e outros perfís.* Colecão Documentos Brasileiros. Rio de Janeiro: José Olympio, 1944. 19–63.

———. *The Mansions and the Shanties (Sobrados e mucambos).* New York: Knopf, 1963.

———. *The Masters and the Slaves (Casa-grande & senzala).* 2nd English-language ed. New York: Knopf, 1968.

———. *O estudo das ciencias sociais nas universidades americanas. Conferencia lida na Faculdade do Direito do Recife, em 24 de maio de 1934.* Recife: Edião de Momento, 1934.

———. "Preface to the Second English-Language Edition of *The Masters and the Slaves.*" Trans. Samuel Putnam. *The Masters and the Slaves: A Study in the Development of Brazilian Civilization.* 2nd rev. English-language ed. New York: Knopf, 1968. xviii–lxx.

———. *Problemas brasileiros de antropologia.* Rio de Janeiro: Edicao da Casa do Estudante do Brasil, 1943.

———. *Sociologia. 1. Introducão ao estudo dos seus princípios.* Rio de Janeiro: José Olympio, 1945.

Fuente, Alejandro de la. *A Nation for All: Race, Inequality, and Politics in Twentieth-Century Cuba*. Envisioning Cuba. Chapel Hill: U of North Carolina P, 2001.

Gaillard, Roger. *L'univers romanesque de Jacques Roumain*. Port-au-Prince: Henri Deschamps, 1965.

Galbis, Ricardo. "El vocablo 'congrí.'" *Archivos del Folklore Cubano* 4 (1927): 185–86.

Gálvez, Manuel. *El espíritu de aristocracia y otros ensayos*. Buenos Aires: Agencia general de librería y publicaciones, 1924.

———. *El solar de la raza*. Buenos Aires: Editorial Tor, 1936.

García-Carranza, Araceli, and Biblioteca Nacional José Martí. *Bio-bibliografía de Don Fernando Ortiz*. Havana: Instituto cubano del libro, 1970.

García-Carranza, Araceli, Norma Suárez Suárez, and Alberto Quesada Morales. *Cronología Fernando Ortiz*. Havana: Fundación Fernando Ortiz, 1996.

Geertz, Clifford. "Being There: Anthropology and the Scene of Writing." *Works and Lives: The Anthropologist as Author*. Stanford: Stanford UP, 1988. 1–25.

Georges-Jacob, Kléber. "Questions à l'ordre du jour. Notes sur la culture." *Les Griots* 2 (1938): 226–31.

Girard, René. *Violence and the Sacred*. Trans. Patrick Gregory. Baltimore: Johns Hopkins UP, 1977.

Gomes, Mércio P. *The Indians and Brazil*. 1988. Trans. John W. Moon. Gainesville and Tallahassee: UP of Florida, 2000.

González Echevarría, Roberto. *Myth and Archive: A Theory of Latin American Narrative*. Cambridge: Cambridge UP, 1990. Durham and London: Duke UP, 1998.

González Neira, Ana. "*Cuadernos Americanos* y el exilio español: nacimiento de una revista universal (1942–1949)." *Cuadernos Americanos* 127 (2009): 11–30.

Gotkowitz, Laura, ed. *Histories of Race and Racism: The Andes and Mesoamerica from Colonial Times to the Present*. Durham and London: Duke UP, 2011.

Graebner, Fritz. *Methode der Ethnologie*. Heidelberg: Carl Winter's Universitätsbuchhandlung, 1911.

Guerra, Lillian. *The Myth of José Martí: Conflicting Nationalisms in Early Twentieth-Century Cuba*. Envisioning Cuba. Chapel Hill: U of North Carolina P, 2005.

Guerrero, Gustavo. *Historia de un encargo: "La catira" de Camilo José Cela*. Colección Argumentos. Barcelona: Anagrama, 2008.

Guimarães, Antonio Sérgio Alfredo. "Democracia racial: el ideal, el pacto y el mito." *Estudios Sociológicos* 20.59 (2002): 305–33.

Guridy, Frank Andre. *Forging Diaspora: Afro-Cubans and African Americans in a World of Empire and Jim Crow*. Chapel Hill: U of North Carolina P, 2010.

Gutiérrez Vega, Zenaida. *Fernando Ortiz en sus cartas a José Ma. Chacón (1914–1936, 1956)*. Madrid: Fundación Universitaria Española, 1982.

Guyer, Jane I. "Anthropology in Area Studies." *Annual Review of Anthropology* 33 (2004): 499–523.

Hatzfeld, Helmut A. "Hispanic Philology in Latin America." *Americas* 3.3 (1947): 347–62.

Helg, Aline. "Race in Argentina and Cuba, 1880–1930: Theory, Policies, and Popular Reaction." *The Idea of Race in Latin America, 1870–1940*. Ed. Richard Graham. Austin: U of Texas P, 1990. 37–71.

Henrique Cardoso, Fernando. "Gilberto Freyre, perene." *Pensadores que inventaram o Brasil.* São Paulo: Companhia das Letras, 2013. 91–137.

Henríquez Ureña, Pedro. *Historia de la cultura en la América hispánica.* Mexico: Fondo de cultura económica, 1947.

———. *Obra Crítica.* Biblioteca Americana. Ed. Emma Susana Speratti Piñero. Mexico: Fondo de Cultura Económica, 1960.

——— "Raza y cultura hispánica." *Pedro Henríquez Ureña. Ensayos.* Repertorio Americano, Jan. 6, 1934. Ed. José Luis Abellán and Ana María Barrenechea. Madrid and Paris: ALLCA XX, 1998. 319–26.

Herder, Johann Gottfried, "Essay on the Origin of Language." Johann Gottfried Herder and Jean-Jacques Rousseau. *On the Origin of Language.* Trans. John H. Moran and Alexander Gode. Reprint. Chicago: U of Chicago P, 1986.

Herskovits, Melville J. *Life in a Haitian Valley.* New York and London: Knopf, 1937.

———. "Problem, Method and Theory in Afroamerican Studies." *Afroamérica* 1.1 (1945): 5–24.

Humboldt, Alexander von. *Political Essay on the Island of Cuba: A Critical Edition.* Alexander von Humboldt in English. Ed. Vera M. Kutzinski and Ottmar Ette. Chicago: U of Chicago P, 2011.

———. *Views of the Cordilleras and Monuments of the Indigenous Peoples of the Americas.* Alexander von Humboldt in English. Ed. Vera M. Kutzinski and Ottmar Ette. Chicago: U of Chicago P, 2011.

Hyppolite, Michelson Paul. *A Study of Haitian Folklore.* Trans. Edgar Laforest and Pansy Hart. Port-au-Prince: Imprimerie de l'Etat, 1954.

Isfahani-Hammond, Alexandra. *White Negritude: Race, Writing, and Brazilian Cultural Identity.* New York: Palgrave Macmillan, 2008.

Kuklick, Henrika. *The Savage Within: The Social History of British Anthropology, 1885–1945.* New York: Cambridge UP, 1991.

Kutzinski, Vera M. *Sugar's Secrets: Race and the Erotics of Cuban Nationalism.* New World Studies. Ed. A. James Arnold. Charlottesville and London: UP of Virginia, 1993.

Lachatañeré, Rómulo. *Manual de santería. El sistema de cultos "Lucumís."* Estudios afro-cubanos. Havana: Editorial Caribe, 1942.

———. *!!Oh, mío Yemayá!!* Intro. Fernando Ortiz. Manzanillo: Editorial "El Arte," 1938.

Lagemann, Ellen. *The Politics of Knowledge: The Carnegie Corporation, Philanthropy, and Public Policy.* 1989. Chicago: U of Chicago P, 1992.

Lange, Brad. "Importing Freud and Lamarck to the Tropics: Arthur Ramos and the Transformation of Brazilian Racial Thought, 1926–1939." *Americas* 65.1 (2008): 9–34.

Largey, Michael. "The Politics of Musical Ethnography: Jean Price-Mars and the Ethnological Movement." *Vodou Nation: Haitian Art, Music, and Cultural Nationalism.* Chicago and London: U of Chicago P, 2006. 23–61.

Larson, Carolyne Ryan. "'The Ashes of Our Ancestors': Creating Argentina's Indigenous Heritage in the Museo Etnográfico, 1904–1930." *Americas* 69.4 (2013): 467–92.

Laurière, Christine. "Jacques Roumain, ethnologue haitien." *L'Homme. Revue francaise d'anthropologie,* no. 173 (2005): 187–98.

———. "México en los años treinta y el desarrollo de las ciencias humanas. Un caso ejemplar, Paul Rivet." *Una concepción atlántica del americanismo. En los pasos de Francois Chevalier.* Ed. Véronique Hébrard. Paris: Éditions des archives contemporaines, 2013. 19–35.

———. *Paul Rivet. Le savant et le politique.* Paris: Publications Scientifiques du Muséum national d'Histoire naturelle, 2008.

———. "Los vínculos científicos de Gerardo Reichel-Dolmatoff con los antropólogos americanistas franceses (Paul Rivet, Claude Lévi-Strauss)." *Antípoda. Revista de Antropología y Arqueología* 11 (2010): 101–24.

Lebovics, Herman. *True France: The Wars over Cultural Identity, 1900–1945.* The Wilder House Series in Politics, History, and Culture. Ithaca and London: Cornell UP, 1999.

Lefebvre, Jean-Paul. "Les professeurs français des missions universitaires au Brésil (1934–1944)." *Cahiers du Brésil* Contemporain 12 (1990). May 31, 2011. http://www.revues.msh-paris.fr/vernumpub/8-J.P%20Lefebvre.pdf.

Leiris, Michel. "Le Musée de l'Homme." *Le Musée Vivant* 708 (1937).

Lévi-Strauss, Claude. *Anthropologie structurale.* 1958. Paris: Plon, 1974.

———. "Le dédoublement de la représentation dans les arts de l'Asie et de l'Amerique." *Renaissance* 3 (1945): 33–53.

———. "New York post- et préfiguratif." *Le regard éloigné.* Paris: Plon, 1983. 345–56.

———. *Les structures élémentaires de la parenté.* Paris: Presses Universitaires de France, 1949.

Leyburn, James G. *The Haitian People.* Yale UP, 1941. Caribbean Series, 9. Ed. Sidney W. Mintz. New Haven and London: Yale UP, 1966.

Lomnitz, Claudio. "Bordering on Anthropology: Dialectics of a National Tradition." *Deep Mexico, Silent Mexico: An Anthropology of Nationalism.* Minneapolis: U of Minnesota P, 2001. 228–63.

———. "Expediente Reichel-Dolmatoff." *La Jornada* 2012, sec. Opinión.

———. "On the Origin of the 'Mexican Race.'" *Histories of Race and Racism: The Andes and Mesoamerica from Colonial Times to the Present.* Ed. Laura Gotkowitz. Durham and London: Duke UP, 2011. 204–21.

López, Antonio. *Unbecoming Blackness: The Diaspora Cultures of Afro-Cuban America.* New York and London: New York UP, 2012.

López-Baralt, Mercedes. *Para decir al Otro. Literatura y antropología en nuestra América.* Madrid: Iberoamericana-Vervuert, 2005.

Lowie, Robert H. *The History of Ethnological Theory.* New York: Rinehart, 1937.

Lund, Joshua, and Malcolm McNee, eds. *Gilberto Freyre e os estudos latino-americanos.* Pittsburgh: U of Pittsburgh, Instituto Internacional de Literatura Iberoamericana, 2006.

Mabille, Pierre. "Souvenirs d'Haiti." *Messages de l'étranger. Revue* 84.17, 1951. Paris: Plasma, 1981.

Magloire-Danton, Gérarde. "Anténor Firmin and Jean Price-Mars: Revolution, Memory, Humanism." *Small Axe* 18 (2005): 150–70.

Maguire, Emily A. *Racial Experiments in Cuban Literature and Ethnography.* Gainesville and Tallahassee: UP of Florida, 2011.

Mangonès, Edmond, and Louis Maximilien. *L'art précolombien d'Haiti. Catalogue de l'Exposition précolombienne organisée a l'occasion du III Congrès des Caraibes sous le haut patronage de son Excellence Mr. Sténio Vincent.* Port-au-Prince: Imprimerie de l'Etat, 1941.

Marcelin, Emile. "Essai sur le langage créole." *La Revue Indigène. Les arts et la vie* 2 (1927): 65–68. Nendeln: Kraus Reprint, 1971.

Marcelin, Milo. *Mythologie vodou (rite arada).* 2 vols. Port-au-Prince: Les Editions Haitiennes, 1954.

Marchand, Suzanne L. "Leo Frobenius and the Revolt against the West." *Journal of Contemporary History* 32.2 (1997): 153–70.

Mariátegui, José Carlos. *Seven Interpretive Essays on Peruvian Reality.* 1928. Trans. Marjory Urquidi. Austin: U of Texas P, 1993.

Marinello, Juan. "Un guacalito de cubanismos." *Archivos del Folklore Cubano* 2.3 (1924): 363–69.

———. "Un guacalito de cubanismos." *Archivos del Folklore Cubano* 3 (1925).

Mars, Louis. *La crise de possession dans le vaudou. Essais de psychiatrie comparée.* Bibliothèque de l'Institut d'Ethnologie de Port-au-Prince. Port-au-Prince: Imprimerie de l'Etat, 1946.

———. "La mentalité haitienne et la psychiatrie." *Les Griots* 1 (1938): 100–110.

Martí, José. *Selected Writings.* Trans. Esther Allen. Ed. Esther Allen. New York: Penguin, 2002.

Maximilien, Louis. *Le vodou haitien. Rite radas—canzo. Preface du Dr. Pierre Mabille.* Port-au-Prince: Imprimerie de l'état, 1945.

Mejías-López, Alejandro. *The Inverted Conquest: The Myth of Modernity and the Transatlantic Onset of Modernism.* Nashville: Vanderbilt UP, 2009.

Melo, Alfredo Cesar. "A face de Janus no ensaísmo latino-americano." *Chasqui: revista de literatura latinoamericana* 36.1 (2007): 121–32.

———. "Hibridismos (in)domáveis. Possíveis contribucões da obra de Gilberto Freyre para uma teoria pós-colonial lusófona." *Luso-Brazilian Review* 51.1 (2014): 68–92.

Métraux, Alfred. "Le Bureau d'ethnologie de la République d'Haiti." *Afro-américa* 1.1–2 (1945): 81–84.

———. "El Instituto de Etnología de la Universidad de Tucumán." *La Nación* July 9, 1932.

———. *Itinéraires 1 (1935–1953)*. Bibliotheque scientifique. Ed. André-Marcel d'Ans. Paris: Payot, 1978.

———. "Jacques Roumain, archéologue et ethnographe." *Jacques Roumain. Oeuvres complètes. Cahiers d'Haiti* 4 (Nov. 1944): 25. Ed. Léon-Francois Hoffmann. Paris: ALLCA, 2003. 1633–36.

———. "Un mundo perdido. La tribu de los chipayas de Carangas." *SUR (Buenos Aires)* 3 (1931): 98–131.

———. "El museo del indio sudamericano en Gotemburgo (Suecia)." *Diario de la prensa* Jan. 1, 1930.

———. *Myths and Tales of the Matako Indians (the Gran Chaco, Argentina)*. Gothenburg: Göteborgs Etnografiska Museum, 1939.

———. *Myths of the Toba and Pilagá Indians of the Gran Chaco*. Philadelphia: American Folklore Society, 1946.

———. "El problema de la civilización. La noción del cambio en el dominio moral e intelectual de las sociedades." *SUR (Buenos Aires)* 30 (1937): 7–27. SUR Digital Edition.

———. "El universo y la naturaleza a través de las representaciones míticas de dos tribus salvajes de la Argentina." *SUR (Buenos Aires)* 10 (1935): 54–69.

———. "Victoria Ocampo y la etnología." *SUR (Buenos Aires)* 346 (1980): 73–75.

———. *Voodoo in Haiti*. Oxford UP, 1959. Trans. Hugo Charteris. Ed. and intro. Sidney W. Mintz. New York: Schocken, 1972.

Miceli, Sergio, ed. *História das ciências sociais no Brasil*. Vol. 1. 2 vols. São Paulo: Vértice, Editora Revista dos Tribunais, 1989.

Miller, Christopher L. *Nationalists and Nomads: Essays on Francophone African Literature and Culture*. Chicago and London: U of Chicago P, 1998.

Monnier, Alain, ed. *Nostalgie du néolithique. De Lausanne a Las Lomitas. Documents sur Alfred Métraux ethnologue*. Geneva: Société d'Etudes Alfred Métraux & Labor et Fides, 2003.

Moré, Belford. "La construcción ideológica de una base empirica: selección y elaboración en la gramática de Andrés Bello." Del Valle and Gabriel-Stheeman 67–93.

Moritz Schwarcz, Lilia. *The Spectacle of the Races: Scientists, Institutions, and the Race Question in Brazil, 1870–1930*. 1999. Trans. Leland Guyer. New York: Hill and Wang, 1999.

Motorola, Patricia, and Marialys Perdomo. "La Academia Cubana de la Lengua." *Opus Habana* 12.3 (2009–10): 4–16.

Naranjo Orovio, Consuelo. "Las redes de un exilio errante: republicanos españoles en Santo Domingo, Puerto Rico y Cuba." *El exilio republicano español en la sociedad dominicana.* Ed. Reina C. Rosario Fernández. Santo Domingo: Comisión Permanente de Efemérides Patrias, Archivo General de la Nación, Academia Dominicana de la Historia, 2010. 131–61.

Naranjo Orovio, Consuelo, and Miguel Angel Puig-Samper Mulero. "Spanish Intellectuals and Fernando Ortiz (1900–1941)." Font and Quiroz 9–39.

Nascentes, Antenor. "Glosario de afronegrismos." *Archivos del Folklore Cubano* 4 (1926): 157–61.

Nicholls, David. *From Dessalines to Duvalier: Race, Colour, and National Independence in Haiti.* 1979. Rev. ed. New Brunswick: Rutgers UP, 1996.

Nouzeilles, Gabriela. "The Transcultural Mirror of Science: Race and Self-Representation in Latin America." *Literary Cultures of Latin America.* Ed. Mario J. Valdés and Djelal Kadir. Vol. 3. 3 vols. New York: Oxford UP, 2004. 284–99.

Nutini, Hugo C. "Aportaciones del americanismo a la teoría y la práctica de la antropología moderna." *Motivos de la antropología americanista.* Ed. Miguel León-Portilla. Mexico: Fondo de cultura económica, 2001. 13–73.

Ocampo, Victoria. "Carta a Alfred Métraux." *Alfred Métraux en la Argentina. Infortunios de un antropólogo afortunado. Cuadernos* (Paris) 74 (1963): 7–8. Ed. Santiago A. Bilbao. Caracas: Comala.com, EdiciónXdemanda, 1963. 221–22.

Oriol, Jacques, Leonce Viaud, and Michel Aubourg. *Le mouvement folklorique en Haiti* ser. 2, no. 9. Ed. Bureau d'ethnologie de la République d'Haiti. Port-au-Prince: Imprimerie de l'état, 1952.

Ortiz, Fernando. *Un catauro de cubanismos. Apuntes lexicográficos.* Colección de libros y documentos inéditos o raros. Ed. Fernando Ortiz. Vol. 4. Havana, 1923.

———. *Contrapunteo cubano del tabaco y el azúcar. (Advertencia de sus contrastes agrarios, económicos, históricos y sociales, su etnografía y su transculturación).* 1940. Ed. María Fernanda Ortiz Herrer. Madrid: EditoCubaEspaña, 1999.

———. "Cuba, Martí and the Race Problem." *Phylon* 3.3 (1942): 253–76.

———. *Cuban Counterpoint: Tobacco and Sugar.* Trans. Harriet de Onís. Intro. Fernando Coronil. Durham and London: Duke UP, 1995.

———. *El engaño de las razas.* Havana: Páginas, 1946.

———. *Glosario de afronegrismos.* Havana: Imprenta "El siglo XX," 1924. Pensamiento cubano. Havana: Editorial de Ciencias Sociales, 1990.

———. "El lenguaje vernáculo de Cuba." *Archivos del Folklore Cubano* 2.1 (1924): 68–72.

———. “Martí y las razas.” *Etnia y sociedad. Fernando Ortiz.* Conferencia leída en La Habana el 9 de junio de 1934. Ed. Isaac Barreal. Havana: Editorial de Ciencias Sociales, 1993. 110–35. *Revista Bimestre Cubana* 48.2 (1941): 203–33.

———. “Martí y las razas de librería.” *Cuadernos Americanos* 15.3 (1945): 185–98.

———. “El mutuo descubrimiento de dos mundos.” *Etnia y sociedad. Fernando Ortiz.* Ed. Isaac Barreal. Havana: Editorial de Ciencias Sociales, 1993. 21–27.

———. “Ni racismos, ni xenofobias.” *Revista Bimestre Cubana* 70 (1955).

———. *La reconquista de América. Reflexiones sobre el panhispanismo.* Sociedad de Ediciones Literarias y Artísticas. París: Librería Paul Ollendorff, 1910.

———. “La sinrazón de los racismos.” *Revista Bimestre Cubana* 70 (1955): 161–83.

Ortiz, Renato. “Notas sobre as Ciencias Sociais no Brasil.” *Ciencias sociais e trabalho intelectual.* São Paulo: Olho d’Água, 2002. 175–97.

Pallares-Burke, Maria Lúcia Garcia. *Gilberto Freyre. Um vitoriano dos trópicos.* São Paulo: Editora UNESP, 2005.

Parezo, Nancy J., and Don D. Fowler. *Anthropology Goes to the Fair: The 1904 Louisiana Purchase Exposition.* Lincoln and London: U of Nebraska P, 2007.

Paul Rivet. Fondateur du Musée de l’Homme (1876–1958). Paris: Imprimerie Nationale, 1976.

Peixoto, Fernanda. “Lévi-Strauss no Brasil: a formacão du etnólogo.” *Mana* 4.1 (1998). Apr. 13, 2011. www.scielo.br/scielo.php?script=sci_arttext&pid=S0104-93131998000100004.

Penny, H. Glenn. *Objects of Culture: Ethnology and Ethnographic Museums in Imperial Germany.* Chapel Hill: U of North Carolina P, 2007.

Pereira de Queiróz, Maria Isaura. “Roger Bastide, professor da Universidade de São Paulo.” *Estudos Avancados* 8.22 (1994): 215–20.

Pérez Firmat, Gustavo. “The Philological Fictions of Fernando Ortiz.” *Notebooks in Cultural Analysis: An Annual Review.* Ed. Norman F. Cantor and Nathalia King. Vol. 2. 2 vols. Durham: Duke UP, 1985. 190–207.

Picón-Salas, Mariano. *De la conquista a la independencia.* 1944. Mexico: Fondo de cultura económica, 1994.

Poole, Deborah. “Introduction.” *A Companion to Latin American Anthropology.* Ed. Deborah Poole. Malden and Oxford: Blackwell, 2008. 1–9.

Price, Sally. *Paris Primitive: Jacques Chirac’s Museum on the Quai Branly.* Chicago and London: U of Chicago P, 2007.

Price-Mars, Jean. *Le bilan des études ethnologiques en Haiti et le cycle du nègre.* Port-au-Prince: Imprimerie de l’etat, 1954.

———. “Préface.” *La critique. Les tendances d’une génération.* Ed. Lorimer Denis, François Duvalier, and Arthur Bonhomme. Port-au-Prince: Impr. du Collège Vertières, 1934. i–xiii.

———. *So Spoke the Uncle.* Ainsi parla l'oncle. 1928. Trans. Magdaline W. Shannon. Washington, D.C.: Three Continents, 1983.

Prins, Harald E. L. "Toward a World without Evil: Alfred Métraux as UNESCO Anthropologist (1946–1962)." Paris, 2007. Abstract. UNESCO. Aug. 19, 2011. http://portal.unesco.org/en/ev.php-URL_ID=30431&URL_DO=DO_TOPIC&URL_SECTION=201.html.

Quesada, Ernesto. *El día de la raza y su significado en Hispano-América. Verbum* 12.46. Buenos Aires: Talleres Gráficos de Araujo Hnos., 1918.

———. *Nuestra raza. Discurso pronunciado en el teatro Odeón el 12 de octubre de 1900.* Buenos Aires: Librería Bredahl, 1900.

Rachum, Ilan. "Origins and Historical Significance of Día de la Raza." *Revista Europea de Estudios Latinoamericanos y del Caribe* 76 (2004): 61–81.

Radcliffe, Kendahl, Jennifer Scott, and Anja Werner, eds. *Anywhere but Here: Black Intellectuals in the Atlantic World and Beyond.* Jackson: UP of Mississippi, 2015.

Rafael, Vicente L. "The Cultures of Area Studies in the U.S." *Social Text* 41 (1994): 91–111.

Ramos, Arthur. *Las culturas negras en el Nuevo Mundo.* 1937. Trans. Ernestina de Champourcin. Mexico: Fondo de Cultura Económica, 1943.

———. *Guerra e relações de raça.* Rio de Janeiro: Departamento editorial da União Nacional dos Estudantes, 1943.

Ramos, Julio. *Divergent Modernities: Culture and Politics in Nineteenth-Century Latin America.* Trans. John D. Blanco. Durham and London: Duke UP, 2001.

Ramsey, Kate. "Prohibition, Persecution, Performance: Anthropology and the Penalization of Vodou in Mid-20th-Century." *Gradhiva* ns 1 (2005): 165–79.

———. *The Spirits and the Law: Vodou and Power in Haiti.* Chicago: U of Chicago P, 2011.

Redfield, Robert. *The Folk Culture of Yucatán.* Chicago: U of Chicago P, 1941.

Redfield, Robert, Ralph Linton, and Melville J. Herskovits. "Memorandum for the Study of Acculturation." *American Anthropologist* 38.1 (1936): 149–52.

Rego Monteiro, Vicente de. *Quelques visages de Paris / Algumas vistas de Paris.* 1925. Trans. Regina Salgado Campos. Ed. Jorge Schwartz. São Paulo: EDUSP, Imprensaoficial, 2005.

Renn, Ludwig. "La vida." *Afroamérica* 1.1–2 (1945): 75–78.

Reyes, Alfonso. "América y los 'Cuadernos Americanos.'" *Cuadernos Americanos* 2.2 (1942): 7–11.

———. "Posición de América." *Cuadernos Americanos* 8.2 (1943): 7–23.

Ribeiro, Darcy. *Os índios e a civilizacão. A integracao das populacões indígenas no Brasil moderno.* Rio de Janeiro: Editora Civilizacão Brasileira, 1970.

———. "Prólogo." Trans. Juan García Gayo. *Casa-grande y senzala. Introducción a la historia de la sociedad patriarcal en el Brasil.* Ed. Gilberto Freyre. Caracas: Biblioteca Ayacucho, 1977. ix–xli.

Ricard, Robert. *La conquête spirituelle du Mexique*. Travaux et Mémoires de l'Institut d'Ethnologie de Paris. Vol. 20. Paris: Institut d'Ethnologie, 1933.

Rivarola, Rodolfo. *La Raza como ideal*. Buenos Aires: Imprenta de José Tragant, 1918.

Rivet, Paul. *L'espèce humaine*. Encyclopédie Française. Ed. Comité de l' Encyclopédie Française. Vol. 7. 20 vols. Paris: Larousse, 1936.

———. "L'ethnologie." *La science française*. Ed. J. Cavalier. Paris: Librairie Larousse, 1938. 5–12.

———. "Institut d'ethnologie. *Mélanges et nouvelles américanistes.*" *Journal de la Société des Américanistes* 17 (1925): 379–80.

———. *Los orígenes del hombre americano*. Trans. José Recasens. Ediciones Cuadernos Americanos 5. Mexico: Cuadernos Americanos, 1943.

———. "Les origines de l'homme américain." *L'Anthropologie* 35 (1925): 293–319.

———. "Proceedings of the XXIX International Congress of Americanists." *Acculturation in the Americas: Proceedings and Selected Papers of the XXIX International Congress of Americanists*. Ed. Sol Tax. Chicago: U of Chicago P, 1951. 1–7.

———. "Reflexiones sobre la América Latina." *Cuadernos Americanos* 6 (1943): 129–38.

———. "Socialismo y unidad latina. Conferencia desarrollada por el profesor Paul Rivet el dia 31 de agosto de 1944." *Adelante (Mexico)* (1944): 2.

Rivet, Paul, and Georges de Créqui-Montfort. *Bibliographie des langues aymará et kičua*. Université de Paris. Travaux et mémoires de l'Institut d'ethnologie. 4 vols. Paris: Institut d'Ethnologie, 1951–56.

Riviale, Pascal. "L'américanisme francais à la veille de la fondation de la Société des Américanistes." *Journal de la Société des Américanistes* 81 (1995): 207–31.

Rodríguez, Miguel. *Celebración de "la raza": una historia comparativa del 12 de octubre*. Mexico: Universidad Iberoamericana, Departamento de Historia, 2004.

Rojas, Rafael. "Fernando Ortiz: contra el *homo cubensis*." *Motivos de Anteo. Patria y nación en la historia intelectual de Cuba*. Madrid: Colibrí, 2008. 249–77.

———. "The Moral Frontier." *Essays in Cuban Intellectual History*. New York: Palgrave Macmillan, 2008. 25–43.

Romero, Sílvio. *Ensayos literarios*. Ed. Antonio Candido. Caracas: Biblioteca Ayacucho, 1982.

Ronze, Raymond. *Paul Rivet (1876–1958)*. Paris: Groupement des universités et grandes écoles de France pour les relations avec l'Amérique Latine, 1958.

Rosenberg, Fernando J. *The Avant-Garde and Geopolitics in Latin America*. Pittsburgh: U of Pittsburgh P, 2006.

Roth Pierpont, Claudia. "The Measure of America: How a Rebel Anthropologist Waged War on Racism." *New Yorker* Mar. 8, 2004: 48–63.

Roumain, Jacques. *Contribution à l'Etude de l'Ethnobotanique Précolombienne des Grandes Antilles. Suivi de L'Outillage Lithique des Ciboney d'Haiti.* 1942–43. Collection Mémoire Vivante. Port-au-Prince: Presses Nationales d'Haiti, 2007.

———. *Masters of the Dew.* 1944. Trans. Langston Hughes and Mercer Cook. Oxford: Heinemann, 1978.

———. *Oeuvres complètes.* Collection Archivos. Madrid: ALLCA XX, 2003.

———. *Le sacrifice du tambour-Assôtô(r).* 1943. Port-au-Prince: Presses Nationales d'Haiti, 2007.

Rutsch, Mechthild. *Entre el campo y el gabinete. Nacionales y extranjeros en la profesionalización de la antropología mexicana (1877–1920).* Mexico City: Instituto Nacional de antropología e historia, UNAM, 2007.

Sá, Lúcia. *Rain Forest Literatures: Amazonian Texts and Latin American Culture.* Minneapolis and London: U of Minnesota P, 2004.

Saldaña, Juan José, ed. *Science in Latin America: A History.* Historia social de las ciencias en América Latina. 1996. Austin: U of Texas P, 2006.

Salomon, Noel. "José Martí y la toma de conciencia latinoamericana." *Cuatro Estudios Martianos.* Havana: Casa de las Américas, 1980. 19–44.

Santí, Enrico Mario. *Fernando Ortiz: Contrapunteo y transculturación.* Madrid: Colibrí, 2002.

Shannon, Magdaline W. *Jean Price-Mars, the Haitian Elite and the American Occupation, 1915–1935.* Basingstoke: Macmillan, St. Martin's, 1996.

Silva Herzog, Jesús. "Lo Humano, Problema Esencial." *Cuadernos Americanos* 1.1 (1942): 9–17.

Skidmore, Thomas E. *Black into White: Race and Nationality in Brazilian Thought.* Durham and London: Duke UP, 1993.

———. "Raízes de Gilberto Freyre." *Journal of Latin American Studies* 34.1 (2002): 1–20.

Smith, Matthew J. *Red and Black in Haiti: Radicalism, Conflict, and Political Change, 1934–1957.* Chapel Hill: U of North Carolina P, 2009.

Souffrant, Claude. *Une négritude socialiste. Religion et développement chez J. Roumain, J. S. Alexis, L. Hughes.* Paris: L'Harmattan, 1978.

Soustelle, Jacques. *La famille Otomi-Pame du Mexique central.* Travaux et mémoires de l'Institut d'ethnologie. Ed. Université de Paris. Vol. 26. Paris: Institut d'ethnologie, 1937.

———. "Pour une culture populaire." *Le Musée Vivant* 1 (1937): 1.

Souza Lima, Antonio Carlos de. *Um grande cerco de paz. Poder tutelar, indianidade e formacão do Estado no Brasil.* Petrópolis: Vozes, 1995.

Spengler, Oswald. "Das Alter der amerikanischen Kulturen." *Ibero-Amerikanisches Archiv* 7 (1933): 95–102.

———. *The Decline of the West. Complete in One Volume.* 1918–22. Trans. Charles Francis Atkinson. New York: Knopf, 1939.

Stepan, Nancy Leys. *The Hour of Eugenics: Race, Gender and Nation in Latin America.* London and Ithaca: Cornell UP, 1991.

Stocking, George W., Jr. "Franz Boas and the Culture Concept in Historical Perspective." *Race, Culture, and Evolution: Essays in the History of Anthropology.* New York and London: Free P, Collier-Macmillan, 1968. 195–233.

———, ed. *A Franz Boas Reader: The Shaping of American Anthropology, 1883–1911.* 1974. Chicago and London: U of Chicago P, 1989.

———. *Race, Culture, and Evolution: Essays in the History of Anthropology. With a new Preface.* 1968. Chicago and London: U of Chicago P, 1982.

Stoczkowski, Wiktor. "Racisme, antiracisme et cosmologie lévi-straussienne. Un essai d'anthropologie réflexive." *L'Homme. Revue francaise d'anthropologie* 182 (2007): 7–53.

Sylvain, Normil. "Chronique—Programme." *La Revue Indigène. Les arts et la vie* 1 (1927): 1–10. Nendeln: Kraus Reprint: 1971.

———. "La jeune littérature haitienne." *Revue Indiène. Les arts et la vie* 2 (1927): 42–53. Nendeln: Kraus Reprint, 1971.

Sylvain, Renée. "Leo Frobenius. From 'Kulturkreis to Kulturmorphologie.'" *Anthropos* 91.4–6(1996): 483–94.

Szurmuk, Mónica, and Robert McKee Irwin. "Presentación." *Diccionario de estudios culturales.* Szurmuk and Irwin 9–42.

———, eds. *Diccionario de estudios culturales.* Mexico: Siglo XXI, 2009.

Tarica, Estelle. *The Inner Life of Mestizo Nationalism.* Minneapolis and London: U of Minnesota P, 2008.

Tax, Sol, ed. *Acculturation in the Americas. Proceedings and Selected Papers of the XXIXth International Congress of Americanists.* Chicago: U of Chicago P, 1949.

Toby-Marcelin, Philippe. *Contes et légendes d'Haiti.* Paris: Nathan, 1967.

———. "Problèmes à l'ordre du jour. Créole ou Francais." *Les Griots* 3 (1939): 381–83.

Trouillot, Hénock. *Dimension et limites de Jacques Roumain.* 2nd ed. Port-au-Prince: Editions Fardin, 1981.

Trouillot, Michel-Rolph. *Silencing the Past: Power and the Production of History.* Boston: Beacon, 1995.

Uribe, Carlos Alberto. "La antropología en Colombia." *América Indígena (México)* 40.2 (1980): 282–308.

Valdés Bernal, Sergio. *Lengua nacional e identidad cultural del cubano.* Havana: Editorial Félix Varela, 2006.

———. "Por qué Catauro?" *Catauro. Una revista cubana de antropología* (1999): 114–15.

Valdez, Juan R. *Tracing Dominican Identity: The Writings of Pedro Henríquez Ureña.* New York: Palgrave Macmillan, 2011.

Vasconcelos, José. *The Cosmic Race: La raza cósmica.* 1925. Ed. Didier T. Jaén. Baltimore and London: Johns Hopkins UP, 1997.

———. “Discurso en la Universidad el Día de la Raza.” *José Vasconcelos y el espíritu de la Universidad*. Ed. Javier Sicilia. Mexico: Universidad Nacional Autónoma de México, 2001. 107–11.

Ventura Santos, Ricardo. “Guardian Angel on a Nation’s Path: Contexts and Trajectories of Physical Anthropology in Brazil in the Late 19th and Early 20th Centuries.” *Current Anthropology* 53.S5 (2012): S17–S32.

Wagley, Charles, ed. *Race and Class in Rural Brazil*. 1952. 2nd ed. New York: UNESCO International Documents Service, Columbia UP, 1963.

Wagley, Charles, and Marvin Harris. *Minorities in the New World: Six Case Studies*. New York: Columbia UP, 1958.

Wauchope, Robert. *Lost Tribes and Sunken Continents: Myth and Method in the Study of American Indians*. Chicago and London: U of Chicago P, 1962.

———. “Los orígenes del hombre americano, by Paul Rivet.” *Hispanic American Historical Review* 24.3 (1944): 497–500.

Weinberg, Liliana. “Transculturación.” *Diccionario de estudios culturales latinoamericanos*. Szurmuk and Irwin 277–83.

Wissler, Clark. *Man and Culture*. New York: Thomas Y. Crowell, 1923.

Yankelevich, Pablo, ed. *México, país refugio. La experiencia de los exilios en el siglo XX*. Mexico: Plaza y Valdés, 2002.

Young, Robert J. C. *Colonial Desire: Hybridity in Theory, Culture and Race*. London and New York: Routledge, 1995.

Zea, Leopoldo. *En torno a una filosofía americana*. Jornadas. México D.F.: El Colegio de México, 1945.

Zéphir, Flore. “The Languages of Haitians and the History of Creole: Haiti and Its Diaspora.” *The Haitian Creole Language: History, Structure, Use, and Education*. Ed. Arthur K. Spears and Carole M. Berotte Joseph. Lanham and Boulder: Lexington, 2010. 55–83.

zum Felde, Alberto. “La tragedia del indio en Suramérica.” *Cuadernos Americanos* 9.3 (1943): 129–41.

Züñiga Montúfar, Tobías. “El Día de la Raza.” *Selecciones de La Tribuna y de La Prensa*. San José and Costa Rica: El Apolo, 1935. 91–101.

Index

Italicized page numbers refer to illustrations.

AAA. *See* American Anthropological Association (AAA)
Academia Cubana de la Lengua (Cuban Academy of Language), 29–30, 37
acculturation: Amerindians, 176n36; Bastien on, 96; coining of term, 9; debate, 40–41; Herskovits on, 9, 40, 73; interwar focus, 144; Malinowski on, 40; "Memorandum for the Study of Acculturation" (Redfield et al.), 40; postwar studies, 73; Rivet on, 73
Adorno, Rolena, 143, 160n18, 176n39
Afroamérica (periodical), 98–101, 124
Afro-American studies, 98–101
Afro-Brazilian movement, 140
Afro-Cuban anthropology, 167n20; culture, 22, 34, 36–37, 156n37; poetry, 43–44; and transcultural African diaspora, 149n9
Agassiz, Louis, 112
Aguirre Beltrán, Gonzalo, 9, 37, 40, 99–101; *La población negra de México,* 101
Alonso, Amado, 16
Altamira, Rafael, 22, 26, 152n8
Altieri, Radamés, 59
American Anthropological Association (AAA), 3, 38, 40
Americanism, 5–6, 162n33; Borges on, 145; de la Campa on, 11; Frank on, 67; International Congress of Americanists, 73; Rivet on, 3, 47, 49; Société des Américanistes, 7, 47–48, 50, 71; Spanish, Ortiz on, 23. *See also* Latin Americanist anthropology
—French, 49, 53, 128–29; and Amerindians, 48–51, 54–55, 57–64, 68, 147n1, 158n1; and ethnology, 52, 160n12; Freyre and, 139; history of, 48, 52–53; interaction with Latin America, 9–10; Lévi-Strauss on, 73; and museum practice, 47, 50. *See also* Rivet, Paul
Amerindians, 59, 61, 136; and acculturation, 176n36; and Brazilian anthropology, 116, 120, 122–23, 125, 128–33, 137, 140, 147n1, 147n3, 158n1; Comhaire-Sylvain on, 95–96; French Americanism and, 48–51, 54–55, 57–64, 68; Freyre on, 116, 130–31, 175n32; Guaman Poma as, 160n18; and Haitian anthropology, 89, 95–96, 102–3; Martí on, 45, 158n52; *mestizaje* and, 149n13; Métraux's Chaco research (Argentina), 57–60; in Mexico, 71; mythology, and postwar Europe, 162n33; preservation of languages, 38–39, 54, 58; and rescue anthropology, 47–48; Rivet's network on, 54–56; Serviço de Proteção aos Índios, 137, 176n35
Anderson, Benedict, 150–51n25
Anderson, Mark, 172n4
Anderson Imbert, Enrique, 73–74
Andrade, Jonathas de, 1–2, 18, 147n1; *Cartazes para o Museu do Homem do Nordeste,* 2
Andrade, Mario de, 133
Andrade, Oswald de, 133
Annales school, 52, 56, 116, 160–61n19, 161n21

antiracism: Afro-Cuban anthropology, 167n20; Freyre on, 125; interwar focus on, 5–6; Rivet on, 7
Arce, Manuel Maples, 88
Archivos del Folklore Cubano (periodical), 23–24, 38, 152n9
area studies, 17; critique, 143–45; Freyre on, 139–40; and literary studies, 140; Rivet and, 7. *See also* culture areas
Ariel (Rodó), 14, 20
Arnold, Stephen H., 171n53
Arroyo, Jossianna, 1, 112
Asociación Nacional contra las Discriminaciones Racistas, 38
"Association populaire des amis des musées," 51
Ateneo group, 14
Aubourg, Michel, 98
Avelar, Idelber, 124, 174n21
Azevedo, Thales de, 141, 173n20

Bachiller y Morales, Antonio, 26, 39
Barkan, Elazar, 41, 157n48
Bastide, Roger, 38, 113, 124, 141, 172n7, 173n20
Bastien, Rémy, 96, 98, 169n32
Bataille, Georges, 51
Baudin, Louis, 55
Beaujour, Michel, 160n15
Beaulieu, Christina, 92
Beckett, Greg, 15–16
Bello, Andrés, 13, 150n22
Benedict, Ruth, 9, 35, 60–61, 125, 138
Bethell, Jonathan, 9–10
Bilbao, Santiago, 59
Bilden, Rüdiger, 131
Blanco, Tomás, 37
Bloch, Marc, 56, 160–61n19
Bloch, R. Howard, 150n24
Bloom, Alan, 177n2
Boas, Franz: approach to language, 38–39, 156n43; Boas school of anthropology, 6, 126–27; and comparative anthropology, 52–53; and cultural anthropology, 12; Freyre and, 8, 111, 121, 126, 138, 175n28; on Graebner, 126–27; in Latin America, 8, 148n10; on linguistics, 57; at Louisiana Purchase Exhibition (1904), 166n6; on natural and human sciences, 56–57; Ortiz and, 21, 38–39; on philology, 57; on racial prejudice, 8, 38; and Rivet, 8; scientific/intellectual network of, 8–9; students, 8–9, 60
Bola de Nieve (Ignacio Jacinto Villa Fernández), 32, 37
Bonilla y San Martín, Adolfo, 24–25, 30
Borges, Jorge Luis, 145
Bosch, Juan, 38
Bosch Gimpera, Juan, 38, 65, 69
Botero, Clara Isabel, 62–63
Braudel, Fernand, 114, 121–22
Brazil: as culture of compromise, 124; French and U.S. social scientists in, 113, 172n7; government policy on indigenous peoples, 137, 176n35; and *mestiçagem,* 113–14, 125; racial policies, 112–13, 118, 171–72n3, 172n5; and racial whitening, 112; social sciences in, 111, 113; and sugar plantation economy, 15–16; UNESCO Project on Race Relations in, 123, 140–41
Brazilian anthropology, 112–14; anthropological museums, 112–13; colonialism, 128–29; in Northeast, 15; studies on indigenous peoples, 137, 176n36. *See also* Freyre, Gilberto; Ramos, Arthur
Breton, André, 76
British school of social anthropology, 39–40
Bronfman, Alejandra, 34–37
Brouard, Carl, 89–90, 92
Bulletin du Bureau d'ethnologie haitienne (periodical), 95–97, 103
Bulnes, Faustino, 20
Bunge, Carlos Octavio, 4, 20
Bureau d'ethnologie (Haiti): creation of, 93–94, 168n28; decline of, 97–98; mission of, 94–96, 98; publications by, 95, 169n31; staff of, 95, 97–98; and vodou, 94
Bureau d'ethnologie (Paris), 7
Burke, Peter, 112, 117, 124, 139, 161n21

Cabrera, Lydia, 35–37, 81, 156nn37–38, 168n24
Caillois, Roger, 9
Camp, Jean, 65
Campos, Lucia, 124
Candelario, Ginetta, 168n26
Cardoso, Fernando Henrique, 115
Caribbean, 11, 15–16, 151n28

Carpentier, Alejo, 37, 47, 76, 171n47
Carrión, Miguel de, 37
Casa-grande & senzala (Freyre). See *Masters and the Slaves, The* (Freyre)
Caso, Alfonso, 71, 99
Castellanos, Israel, 34–35, 37, 46
Castellanos, Jorge, 36
Catholic Church, 131–32; Haitian antisuperstition campaign, 94, 106, 168–69n28, 169n32, 170n45
Cavalcanti, Emiliano di, 133; *Mulata, 134*
Césaire, Aimé, 76, 91, 97
Césaire, Suzanne, 76, 97
Chacón y Calvo, José María, 23–25, 27, 30, 37, 154n23
Charlier-Doucet, Rachelle, 95, 168n28
Cieza de León, Pedro, 55
Clifford, James, 53, 160n15
Cobb, Martha, 167n21
Cohen, Marcel, 49
Cohn, Deborah, 144
Coll y Toste, Cayetano, 13, 26, 29
Colombia: anthropology, 62–63; European wartime exiles, 62–63
colonialism, 16, 49, 53, 139
Columbus Day, 19–20
Comhaire-Sylvain, Suzanne, 37, 95, 97
Congreso Demográfico Interamericano, 31–32
Conklin, Alice, 50, 160n17
Conn, Robert, 151n27
Coronil, Fernando, 157n45
Cossío, José L., 69–70, 164n45
Costa Pinto, L. A., 141
Courlander, Harold, 76
Covarrubias, Miguel, 99
Creole language: Griots group, 92; Haitian indigenists, 88–89; Haitian literature, 84; linguistic studies, 95; Roumain on, 102, 106–7; status in Haiti, 11, 77, 81–86; as term, 18
Cuadernos Americanos (periodical), 65–67, 69–71, 163n38
Cuba: Día de la raza, 19, 21; race in, 21, 34–35, 41; struggle for control of culture, 36–37, 156n37. See also Ortiz, Fernando, *and entries under* Afro-Cuban anthropology
Cuban Alliance for a Free World, 32, 154n25
Cuervo, Rufino José, 13
Cullen, Countee, 88
cultural anthropology, 3
cultural contact: Aguirre Beltrán on, 100; Boas school, 126–27; diffusionist school, 126–27; Freyre on, 61, 125; Herskovits on, 99–100; interwar focus, 144; as issue, 10; Malinowski on, 40; Métraux on, 61; Ortiz on, 61; Price-Mars on, 85
cultural politics: d'Harcourt on, 53; French anthropology and, 53–56; Freyre on, 125; Ortiz on, 22; U.S., regarding Latin America, 143–44
cultural studies, 11–12, 144
culture: as anthropological spectacle, 5; Benedict on, 60; Latin American, 2–5, 18; modern concept, 8; postwar conception, 65–67, 71; versus *raza,* 20, 23; relation to language, 10–11. *See also* acculturation; transculturation
culture areas: Boas school, 126–27; diffusionist school, 126–27; Freyre on, 127, 131–32; Rivet on, 7, 52, 54, 57

da Cunha, Euclides, 112
Darío, Rubén, 14
Dash, Michael, 76, 84, 86, 91, 107
Debaene, Vincent, 114
"Declaration against racisms" (AAA), 38
de Gaulle, Charles, 64
Degiovanni, Fernando, 151n29
de la Campa, Román, 11
Deleporte, Sarah F., 50, 159n8
de l'Estoile, Benoît, 49–51, 72
Delpar, Helen, 149n17, 176n39
Del Valle, José, 14, 22, 150n23, 177n2
"Democracia racial" (Nascimento), 124
Denis, Lorimer: and conservative anthropology, 53; and Griots, 89–93; and Haitian anthropology, 95–98; and International Institute of Afro-American Studies, 98; "Pour un humanisme totalitaire," 92–93; works on vodou, 96, 101, 168n23
Depestre, René, 76, 86
d'Harcourt, Raoul, 53
Día de la raza, 19–20; Ortiz's opposition to, 31–34
Diaquoi, Louis, 89
Dias, Nélia, 158n2, 159n4
Diccionario de la Lengua Castellana, Real Academia Española, 24–29

diffusionism, 126–27; on cultural evolution, 126–27; Lévi-Strauss on, 72–73; Lowie on, 160n13; Rivet on, 52–53
diglossia of Haiti, 77, 106
Dihigo, Juan M., 25–26, 37
di Leo, Octavio, 112
Dominican Republic, 86, 94, 151n28
Dorsainvil, J. C., 78
Duchartre, P. L., 175n31
Duhamel, Georges, 88
Dumas, George, 172n7
Dunham, Katherine, 76
Dunn, Christopher, 174–75n27
Duno Gottberg, Luis, 22, 149n13
Durkheim, Émile, 53, 78, 158n3
Duvalier, François: and conservative anthropology, 53; factors in rise of, 77; and Griots, 89–93; Haitian anthropology, 95–98; "Pour un humanisme totalitaire," 92–93; on Roumain, 105–6; works on vodou, 96, 101, 168n23

Ecole d'Anthropologie (Paris), 53
Ecuador, 19, 48
El Salvador, Día de la raza in, 19
Emmanuel, Paul, 96
Encyclopédie Française, 52, 160–61n19
Equality of the Human Races, The (Firmin), 77
Escola livre de sociología e política (Brazil), 113
Espinosa, Aurelio, 152n9
essays: on Hispanic race, 6; in interwar anthropology, 144–45; Latin American tradition of, 149n16; racial, Ortiz analysis of, 33; Roumain, 101–6; and visibility of ancient cultures, 13
ethnography: ethnographic surrealism, 53, 160n15; Haitian, 78–80, 89, 93–98, 104; interwar anthropology and, 6, 41; Musée d'Ethnographie (Paris), 47, 50; Ortiz and, 42; as personal experience, 114; of Price-Mars, 79–81, 93; Rivet network and, 47–50, 52, 58, 69, 73
ethnology: Boas on, 126, 148n10; *Bulletin du Bureau d'ethnologie haitienne* (periodical), 95–97, 103; Bureau d'ethnologie (Paris), 7; in Colombia, 62–63; English anthropology and, 72; and French Americanism, 52, 160n12; Freyre on, 125; Graebner on, 126–27; Haitian, 40, 75–77, 79–80, 86, 93–98; Institut d'ethnologie (Haiti), 75–76, 86, 93–98; Institut d'ethnologie (Paris), 7, 47, 49–50, 55, 76, 161n22; Lévi-Strauss on, 72–73; Musée d'Ethnologie (Haiti), 75, 93–98; Museums of ethnology, Tucumán, 57–59; Rivet network and, 49–50, 52–53, 55–59, 62–63; as term, 52, 160n12; "Travaux et mémoires de l'Institut d'ethnologie," 55. *See also* Bureau d'ethnologie (Haiti)
eugenics movement, 4, 113, 120–21, 147–48n4
exile, World War II and, 9–10, 62–65

Fanon, Frantz, 79
Febvre, Lucien, 52, 160–61n19
Felipe, León, 66
Fernandes, Florestan, 125, 141
Firmin, Anténor, 77–78
Fisher, Kurt, 168n28
folklore: *Archivos del Folklore Cubano* (periodical), 23–24, 38, 152n9; Cuban folklore studies, 23–24; Griots group on, 81, 92–93; Haitian folklore movement, 75, 77, 81, 97; Haitian folklore studies, 83, 95–96, 98; Hyppolite on, 83; Ortiz on, 22–24; Price-Mars on, 79–81, 83; Sociedad del Folklore Cubano, 22–24, 37–38, 166n10; vodou and, 81
Fowler, Don, 165–66n6
Franco, Jean, 151n30
Frank, Waldo, 67
Frazer, James, 80, 166n9
Freud, Sigmund, 78, 117, 122
Freyre, Gilberto: on anthropology, 14, 115–16, 125, 127, 138; on area studies, 139–40; Boas and, 8, 111, 121, 126, 138, 175n28; career, 111, 123–24, 137–39; and cultural contact debate, 61, 125; on culture areas, 127; and development of Latin American anthropology, 2–3; and eugenicist theories, 120–21; exile, 9, 123; interdisciplinary approach, 111, 117, 137–40; Luso-Tropicalism, 125–26, 139; method of, 114–16, 118–19, 121–23, 128, 139; and Museum of the Man of the Northeast, 1, 147n1; Ortiz and, 38, 124, 173n17; publication of source documents, 54–55;

racial democracy concept, 10, 124, 140, 173n20; Ramos and, 122, 175n33; reputation as intellectual, 111–12; on slavery, 127; on social sciences, 137–40; and Vargas regime, 123–24; writing style, 114
—on Brazilian culture, 2, 118, 124; *plasticidade* in, 10, 118; Portuguese influence, 118–20, 125–26, 131, 139, 174n21
—on culture: evolutionism, 131; hybridity, 120, 125
—on race: antiracism, 125; contradictions within, 3, 131–32; tensions between U.S. and Latin American paradigms of, 174–75n27
—works by: *Dona Sinhá e o Filho Padre,* 112; "O estudo das ciencias sociais nas universidades americanas," 137–38; *The Mansions and the Shanties,* 123; *O Outro Amor de D. Paulo,* 112; *Perfil de Euclydes e outros perfis,* 112; *Problemas brasileiros de antropologia,* 127, 138; *Sociologia,* 138–39. See also *Masters and the Slaves, The* (Freyre)
Frobenius, Leo, 126, 131, 175n30
Fuente, Alejandro de la, 147n3

Galbis, Francisco, 24
Gálvez, Manuel, 19–20, 152n5
Gamio, Manuel, 8
Gaos, José, 9
García Bárcena, Rafael, 88
García Calderón, Ventura, 87
García Canclini, Néstor, 10, 174n27
García-Carranza, Araceli, 154n25, 155n27
Garcilaso de la Vega, 12–13, 55
Georges-Jacob, Kléber, 90
Giner de los Ríos, Francisco, 21–22
Giorgi, Bruno, 133; *Mulata, 136*
Gobineau, Arthur, Count of, 4, 23, 77, 112
Gomes, Mércio P., 176n36
González Echevarría, Roberto, 12, 116
González Neira, Ana, 67
Gotkowitz, Laura, 20
Graebner, Fritz, 52, 126–27
Granger, Gilles Gaston, 113
Grant, Madison, 4
Griaule, Marcel, 114
Griots, Les (periodical), 77, 81, 89–93, 167n15
Griots group, 89–93; and anthropology as contested ground, 93, 168n25; as both insiders and outsiders, 92, 168n24; Creole and, 84, 92; emphasis on African heritage, 90; on folklore, 81, 92–93; and Haitian anthropology, 96; on Haitian racial inferiority complex, 89; racialist views, 86, 89–91; as term, 92; on vodou, 92–93
Grupo Minorista, 37
Guaman Poma de Ayala, Felipe, 12–13, 55, 160n18; *First Chronicle and Good Government,* 55, 160n18; *Nueva corónica y buen gobierno,* 55, 160n18
Guerra, Lillian, 21
Guerra, Ramiro, 37
Guerrero, Gustavo, 163n38
Guillén, Nicolás, 37, 43
Guimarães, Antonio S., 173n20, 174n26
Guridy, Frank Andre, 148n9
Gurvitch, Georges, 113

Haiti: antisuperstition campaign, 94, 106, 168–69n28, 169n32, 170n45; conflict over national language, 77, 81–86; folklore movement, 75, 77, 97; Price-Mars on, 79, 90–91; U.S. occupation, 75, 79, 81, 86, 89; wartime U.S. and European visitors, 75–76
Haitian anthropology: anthropological institutions, 93–98; excavations, 96; exhibitions of indigenous culture, 95–96; folklore studies, 83, 95–96, 98; and vodou, 94–96, 101, 168n28. *See also* Denis, Lorimer; Price-Mars, Jean; Roumain, Jacques; vodou
Haitian culture: Herskovits on, 8–9, 40; Price-Mars on, 85; Roumain on, 106–10
Haitian folklore movement, 75, 77, 97; popularity after U.S. withdrawal, 81
Haitian indigenism and Creole versus French language, 86–89; *Les Griots,* 91; and Latin America, 86–87, 89–90; *Revue Indigène* and, 84, 86–89
Haitian literature, 84, 86. See also *Griots, Les* (periodical); *Revue Indigène* (periodical)
Hanke, Lewis, 73–74
Hatzfeld, Helmut, 150n23, 151n29
Haya de la Torre, Raúl, 63–64

Helg, Aline, 4, 147n3
Henríquez Ureña, Pedro, 6, 19–20, 151n27, 152n6, 158n1
Herder, Johann G. von, 13–14, 89
Hernández Catá, Alfonso, 37
Hernández de Alba, Gregorio, 62–63
Herskovits, Melville: on acculturation, 9, 40, 73; on Afro-American studies, 99–100; and cultural contact debate, 61; dialogue with Ortiz, 21; Freyre and, 175n33; in Haiti, 76; and International Institute of Afro-American Studies, 99–100; study of Haitian rural life, 8–9, 40, 76, 109
Hispanic race concept, 6, 14–15, 22; Ortiz's rejection of, 22–29, 31–34
Hispanism, 67; responses to, 67, 163n38
historical morphology, 117
history, 13; Lévi-Strauss on, 72–73; Rivet on, 56–57
Honorat, Lamartinière, 98
humanism, 14–15, 150–51n25; Silva Herzog on, 66
humanist anthropology: Freyre on, 14, 115–16, 125, 138; postwar, 65–67, 71; Rivet on, 15, 52–53
Humboldt, Alexander von, 13, 39, 56
Hurston, Zora Neale, 76, 168n24
Huxley, Julien, 123
hybridity: in African–Afro-American transnational networks, 148n9; Freyre on, 118–20, 125–26, 130; Latin Americanist anthropology and, 11. See also *plasticidade* (plasticity)
Hyppolite, Michelson Paul, 83

inadaptation: Métraux on, 48, 61, 137; Rivet on, 48
indigenismo, 63–64
indigenous populations. *See* Amerindians
Inquiry into the Nature of Race Relations in Africa, An (Malinowski), 40
Institución Hispano-Cubana de Cultura (IHCC), 30–31, 38
Institut d'ethnologie (Haiti), 75–76, 86, 93–98
Institut d'ethnologie (Paris), 7, 47, 49–50, 55, 76, 161n22
Institut francais d'anthropologie (IFA), 48
institutionalization of anthropology: in Colombia, 62–63; division of Latin American culture studies, 145; Freyre and, 139–40; Griots and, 93; Herskovits and, 100; museum matrix at Trocadero, 50, 71–72, 128–29, *129,* 159n8; museum matrix in Latin America, 57, 62–63, 93–97
institutionalization of racial orders, 147n3
Instituto de Antropología (Argentina), 58–59
Instituto de Cultura Hispánica, 67
Instituto Francés de América Latina (IFAL), 64–65
Instituto Indigenista (Colombia), 63
Instituto Nacional de Etnología (INE) (Colombia), 62–63
Instituto Panamericano de Geografía e Historia, 31
International Congress of Americanists, 73
International Institute of Afro-American Studies (IIAAS), 98–101
interwar period: and Americanist years, 5–6; anthropology in, 18, 144–45; and antiracism, focus on, 5–6; and cultural anthropology, 3, 5, 144; cultural histories of Latin America, 47; internationalist humanism and, 98, 144; scientific/intellectual networks of, 7–9; shifting alliances in, 15

Jaén, Didier T., 151–52n2
Janvier, Louis, 77–78, 165n5
Johnson, Charles S., 99
Journal de la Société des Américanistes (*JSA*), 7, 47, 57–58

Kirchhoff, Paul, 9
Klineberg, Otto, 99, 123, 141
Krause, Fritz, 137
Kroeber, Alfred, 52, 131
Kutzinski, Vera, 4, 149n13, 157n50

Lachatañeré, Rómulo, 35–37, 46, 81, 156n40
Lam, Wifredo, 76
language: Boas approach, 38–39, 156n43; conflict over Haitian Creole, 77, 81–84; Latin Americanism, 10–11; and national identity, 13–14; Ortiz's dictionaries, 24–29. *See also* Spanish language in America
Larbaud, Valéry, 88

Largey, Michael, 165n5
Larrea, Juan, 66
Larson, Carolyne Ryan, 59
Latin American anthropology, 54; and Americanism, 5–6; early, 1–5, 18; history of, 12–15, 143–44, 149n18, 149–50n19; and International Institute of Afro-American Studies, 98–101; networks, 9–10; publication of source documents, 54–55. *See also* Latin Americanist anthropology
Latin American history, 73–74
Latin Americanist anthropology: anti-racism, 5–6; focus on material culture in, 48; interwar years as methodological threshold, 17–18; Ortiz's network and, 38; on relation of language and culture, 10–11; role of texts, 11–12; scientific/intellectual networks, 7–9
Latin American studies: Cold War interest in, 143–44; shifting disciplinary boundaries in, 143–45
Laurière Christine, 48–49, 54, 62, 97, 158n2, 159n6, 161n24
Le Bon, Gustave, 78
Lebovics, Herman, 160n16
Légitime, F. D., 78
Lehmann, Henri, 62
Lehmann-Nitsche, Roberto, 59
Leiris, Michel, 51, 114
Lenz, Rodolfo, 13
Lescot, Élie, 76, 94, 168–69n28
Lévi-Strauss, Claude: and Annales school, 161n21; in Brazil, 113, 172n7; career of, 71–72; and participant-observer approach, 114; review of Rivet's *Orígenes del hombre Americano,* 70; structuralist anthropology, 72–74; and UNESCO, 141
Lévy-Bruhl, Lucien, 36, 48–49, 80, 92, 132, 158n3
linguistics: Boas on, 57; Rivet on, 54, 57, 160n17. *See also* philology
Linton, Ralph, 40
literature: and Amerindian culture, 60; and area studies, 140, 143; and Brazilian anthropology, 14, 113, 115–16, 133, 138–39; and Cuban anthropology, 22, 30–32, 36–38, 41–44, 100–101; and folklore, 79, 81; and French Americanists, 51, 60, 64; Freyre and, 111–12, 115–16, 123–24, 138–40; growth of interest in, 143–44; and Haitian anthropology, 11, 76–77, 79–80, 83–84, 86–90, 95–96, 105–10; Indigenist poets, 84, 86–90, 98; and Latin American anthropology, 10–12, 14–17, 20, 28, 73–74, 143–45; and Mexican anthropology, 65–67, 71; and negotiation of identity, 7; organic notion of culture including, 65–67; postwar separation from anthropology, 73; and transculturation, 10; of transnational black intellectuals, 7; and visibility of ancient cultures, 13. *See also* folklore
Locke, Alain, 37, 99
Lombroso, Cesar, 21–22
Lomnitz, Claudio, 19, 151n29, 152n3, 162n33
López, Antonio, 156n36, 156n40
López-Baralt, Mercedes, 149n18
Louisiana Purchase Exhibition (1904), 78–79, 165–66n6
Loveira, Carlos, 37
Lowie, Robert, 138, 160n13

Mabille, Pierre, 76, 96–97
Macunaíma (Andrade), 133
Magloire-Danton, Gérarde, 165n4
Maguire, Emily, 36, 156nn37–38, 168n24
Malinowski, Bronislaw: Herskovits critique, 40; Ortiz and, 9, 21, 39–40, 42; and participant-observer approach, 114; on transculturation, 40–41
mambís, 26–27
Mañach, Jorge, 37
Mangonès, Edmond, 37, 95, 97
Maran, René, 84
Marcelin, Emile, 88–89
Marcelin, Milo, 83
Mariátegui, José Carlos, 88
Marin, Louis, 53
Marinello, Juan, 24, 37
Maritain, Jacques, 97
Mars, Louis, 91–92
Martí, José, 20–21, 39, 44–46, 64, 152n7
Martínez del Río, Pablo, 69
"Martí y las razas" (Ortiz), 44–46, 157–58n51
Massi, Fernanda, 172n7

Masters and the Slaves, The (Freyre), 114–22; audience, 117–18; "balance of antagonisms," 119; and debate on cultural change, 10; and eugenics, 120–21; Freyre's methods, 114–16, 119–22; on indigenous cultures, 129–33; influence on discussion of Brazilian race and culture, 141; on *plasticidade* in Brazilian culture, 10, 118; on race, past versus present, 130, 140; and racial democracy, 10, 124, 140; structure, 116–17
Mauss, Marcel, 49–50, 71, 158n3
Maximilien, Louis, 83, 95–97
Meillet, Antoine, 49
Mejías-López, Alejandro, 15
Melo, Alfredo Cesar, 116, 126, 172n10
Menéndez Pidal, Ramón: Cuban Academy of Language, 29–30; on Hispanic race, 22; and IHCC, 30; Ortiz and, 22, 24–25, 154n23; on philology, 39
Menéndez y Pelayo, Marcelino, 25
Mensajes (periodical), 30
Mestiça (Portinari), 133, *135*
mestiçagem, 113–14, 125
mestizaje: in Cuba, 149n13; Ortiz's rejection of, 33–34; Rivet on, 71
Métraux, Alfred, 57–62; and antisuperstition campaign, 168n28; in Argentina, 57–61; articles in *SUR,* 59–61; career, 61–62, 140; Chaco research (Argentina), 57–60; on cultural contact, 61; in Haiti, 76, 96–98; on inadaptation, 48, 61, 137; Rivet's network, 8, 57–58; on Benedict, 61; social activism by, 61; in Tucumán (Argentina), 57–59; on vodou, 8
Miller, Christopher, 91
Miller, Marilyn, 149n13
Mintz, Sidney, 16, 38
Miomandre, Francis de, 65, 88
miscegenation: Freyre on, 123, 147n1; Price-Mars on, 80. *See also* scientific racism
Montagu, Ashley, 141
Montandon, George, 53, 90, 93
Montessori, Maria, 123
Moré, Belfored, 150n22
Morse, Richard, 38
mulata, erotic lure acquired by, 4
Mulata (Cavalcanti), 133, *134*
Mulata (Giorgi), 133, *136*
mulatto poetry, Ortiz on, 43
Muñoz Marín, Luis, 38
Murra, John, 73–74
Musée de l'Homme (Paris): closing, 72, 165n49; mission of, 51; modernist aesthetic of, 50–51; resistance network, 62; Rivet and, 7, 47, 49–51, 55, 71–72
Musée Vivant, Le (Musée de l'Homme bulletin), 51
museum(s): Brazilian anthropological museums, 112–13; French Americanism and, 47, 50; Musée des Arts et Traditions Populaires (France), 51; Musée d'Ethnographie (Paris), 47, 50; Musée d'Ethnologie (Haiti), 75, 93–98; Musée du Quai Branly (Paris), 72, 165n49; Museo del hombre dominicano (Dominican Republic), 94; Museo Paraense (Museu Paraense Emílio Goeldi) (Brazil), 112; museum matrix at Trocadero, 50, 71–72, 128–29, *129,* 159n8; museum matrix in Latin America, 57, 62–63, 93–97; Museum of Anthropology (Rio de Janeiro), 113; Museum of the Man of the Northeast, 1–2, *2,* 147n1; Museums of ethnology, Tucumán, 57–59; Museu Nacional do Rio de Janeiro, 112; Museu Paulista (Brazil), 112; National Museum of Natural History (Paris), 48, 50. *See also* Musée de l'Homme (Paris)
Myrdal, Gunnar, 99

Naranjo Orovio, Consuelo, 154n25
Nascentes, Anténor, 24
Nascimento, Abdias do, 124, 140, 174n21
nationalism: Americanist anthropology, 162n33; Colombia, 52; d'Harcourt on, 53; Germany, 150n25; Haitian, 77, 81, 87, 91; Martí on, 44; Mexico, 149n13; and pan-Hispanism, 23, 150–51n25; Rivet against, 69–70; South American literature and, 87
National Museum of Natural History (Paris), 48, 50
Négritude movement, 91
networks, scientific/intellectual: and Americanist years, 6; of Boas, 8–9; in Brazilian museums, 112; European migrants to Latin America and, 62; of Freyre, 7; of Herskovits, 9; and Institución Hispano-Cubana de Cultura

(IHCC), 30–31; and International Institute of Afro-American Studies, 98–101; interwar period, 7–9; Latin Americanist anthropologist-writers, 7; of Ortiz, 7, 30, 34–41, 46; of Rivet, 7–9, 57–58; of Roumain, 7; U.S. network interaction with Latin America group, 10, 62
Nimuendaju, Curt, 137
noirisme (Haiti), 77
Nordenskjöld, Erland, 8
Nouzeilles, Gabriella, 147n2

Ocampo, Victoria, 59–60, 161n32
Oliveira Lima, Manuel de, 111–12
Onis, Federico de, 9
Oriol, Jacques, 98
Ortega y Gasset, José, 66
Ortiz, Fernando: and acculturation, 40–41; and *Afroamérica*, 99–101, 124; Boas and, 21, 38–39; and "Colección de libros cubanos," 39; and cultural contact, 61; and Día de la raza, 21, 31–34; Freyre and, 38, 124, 173n17; and Hispanic race concept, 31–34; on Iberoamerican philological tradition, 31; and International Institute of Afro-American Studies, 98–101; international visibility, 31, 41, 157n45; Lachatañeré's critique, 36; on *mestizaje*, 33–34; on mulatto poetry, 43; organizations founded and memberships, 22, 29–32, 155n27; publication of source documents, 54–55; Roumain and, 93; scientific/intellectual network of, 7, 30, 34–41, 46; and Sociedad del Folklore Cubano, 22–24; and transculturation, 9–10, 29, 41
—and anthropology: Cuban folklore studies, 23–24; focus on everyday life, 116; transition from race to cultural anthropology, 45–46
—as philologist, 22–30; dictionaries, 24–29; on etymologies, 28–29; Martí's views on race, 45–46; organizations founded, 29–30; reception, 27, 29; rejection of pan-Hispanism, 22–29
—on race: in *Cuban Counterpoint,* 43; early work, 21–22; efforts to reform, 34–35, 41; in "Martí y las razas," 34–35; as mediator, 34; rejection of concept, 21, 31–34, 44–46, 99, 125; specter of race, 5, 18, 33–34; U.S. problems of, 33
—works by: *Catauro de cubanismos,* 24–25, 31; "Colección de libros cubanos," 39; *Contrapunteo cubano del tabaco y el azúcar* (*Cuban Counterpoint: Tobacco and Sugar*), 9, 29, 40–44, 157n45; *El engaño de las razas,* 5, 21, 32–33, 125; *Glosario de afro-negrismos,* 24–28; "Martí y las razas" ("Cuba, Martí, and the Race Problem"), 34–35, 44–46, 157–58n51; *Los negros brujos,* 22, 36; *La reconquista de América,* 22–23
Ortiz de Montellano, Bernardo, 66
Oyuela-Caycedo, Augusto, 162n33

paideuma (*Frobenius*), 127–28, 175n30
Paiget, Jean, 123
Palavecino, Enrique, 58–59
Palés Matos, Luis, 38
Pallares-Burke, Maria L. G., 112, 117, 124, 139, 175n28
pan-African movement, 91, 167n21
Pané, Fray Ramón, 12
pan-Hispanism. *See* Hispanism
Parezo, Nancy, 165–66n6
participant-observer approach, in Freyre, 114
Paul, Emmanuel, 98
Pellicer, Carlos, 88
Pérez Firmat, Gustavo, 24–25
Peters, Dewitt, 76
philology: Boas on, 57; Latin American anthropologists and, 11; Lévi-Strauss on, 73; and nationalism, 13–14; postwar humanism in, 66–67; Rivet on, 57. *See also* Ortiz, Fernando: as philologist
physical anthropology: Boas on, 8, 56; and Brazilian anthropology, 112; decline, 5, 18; in French anthropology, 48, 50, 52–53; Institut d'ethnologie (Haiti), 97; Ortiz on, 32, 34; Ramos on, 122–23, 126; Rivet on, 56, 63
Pichardo, Estéban, 13, 29
Pichardo, Manuel S., 37
Pierson, Donald, 113, 139
Pietschmann, Richard, 55
Pitt-Rivers, Augustus, 131–32
plasticidade (plasticity), 10, 61, 118, 149n14, 172n10

Poole, Deborah, 149n13
Portinari, Cândido, 133; *Mestiça, 135*
Portuguese heritage in Brazil, Freyre on, 118–20, 125–26, 131, 139, 174n21
positivism: and European philology, 150n24; in Latin America, 4; positivist criminology, 21–22, 36; reaction against, 14
Pratt, Mary Louise, 10
Price, Hannibal, 77, 165n5
Price, Sally, 165n49
Price-Mars, Jean: on assimilation in Haiti, 85; on colonialism, 79, 83, 165n4; and Creole, 77, 81–84; on cultural contact, 85; as director of Institut d'ethnologie, 94; on folklore, 79–81, 83; and Griots group, 89, 91; on Haitian anthropological institutions, 95, 97–98; and International Institute of Afro-American Studies, 98–99; on race and racism, 78–79, 90–91; and vodou, 78–80, 85
—ethnography of, 79–80, 93; comparative method, 79–80; focus on folklore, 79–81
Primer Congreso Demográfico Interamericano (First Interamerican Congress of Demography), 31–32, 99

Quatrefages, Armand de, 52
Quesada, Ernesto, 19–20, 148n6, 152n5
Quesada, Gonzalo de, 45

race(s): activism against scientific theories, 61; in early Latin American anthropology, 2–5; equality of, Haitian works on, 77–78; and evolution in Brazil, 112–13, 118, 121, 171–72n3, 172n5; meaning in Spanish versus U.S., 15; Montandon on, 90; ongoing usage of concept, 2–4; Ortiz's rejection of concept, 21, 31–34, 44–46, 99; Price-Mars on, 80; Reyes on, 67; as specter, 5, 18, 33–34, 141; turn away from, 21, 32, 140; UNESCO projects on, 123, 140–41. *See also* Freyre, Gilberto: on race; Hispanic race concept; Ortiz, Fernando: on race; *raza*
Races of Mankind, The (Benedict and Weltfish), 61
racial democracy: Brazil, 10; "Democracia racial" (Nascimento), 124; Freyre on, 10, 124, 140, 173n20; Ramos on, 124–25; Wagley on, 177
racial politics: Benedict on, 61; Césaire on, 76; Cuban anthropology, 37; Freyre on, 118, 124–25, 132–33; Haitian anthropology, 76, 85, 89–90; interwar anthropology, 144–45; La Raza on, 19; Métraux on, 61; Ortiz on, 5, 32; Ramos on, 124–25; Rivet on, 69–70; Spain, 23; UNESCO, 140–41. *See also* eugenics movement; scientific racism
racism: Boas against, 8; Métraux on, 61
Radiguet, Raymond, 88
Rama, Angel, 10
Ramos, Arthur: on Brazilian culture, 124–25, 127–28; career, 122–24, 140; and Cuban anthropology, 37, 101; on *paideuma,* 127–28; on race, 124–25, 128; and racialization of poverty, 173n13; on slavery, 127; and Vargas regime, 124; on World War II as war of racial ideology, 125
—as anthropologist: and diffusionist school, 126; Freyre and, 122, 175n33; and International Institute of Afro-American Studies, 99; method, 122–23, 173n15
—on anthropology: branches, 127; goals, 125
—works by: *A aculturação negra no Brasil,* 123; *Las culturas negras en el Nuevo Mundo,* 127; *O folclore negro do Brasil,* 126; *Guerra e relações de raça,* 123, 124–25; *Introdução à antropologia brasileira,* 122–23; *O negro Brasileiro,* (*The Negro in Brazil*), 122
Ramos, Julio, 14, 44, 158n52
Ramsey, Kate, 81, 97, 168n22, 168–69n28, 170n45
raza: versus *cultura,* 20, 23; La Raza (political party), 19; meanings, 19–21. *See also* race(s)
Real Academia Española, 24–30
Recasens, José de, 62
Redfield, Robert, 40, 73
Regionalist Congress (1926), 123
Rego Monteiro, Vincente de, 128–29, 175n31, 175n34; "Trocadero," *129*
Reichel-Dolmatoff, Gerardo, 62, 162n33
rescue anthropology, Rivet and, 47–48

Revista de Estudios Afrocubanos (periodical), 32, 37–38
Revista del Instituto de Antropología (periodical), 58–59
Revista del Instituto de Etnología (periodical), 57–59
Revista del Instituto Etnológico Nacional (periodical), 63
Revista de Occidente (periodical), 66
Revista Unión Ibero-Americana (periodical), 23
Revue Indigène (periodical), 77, 86–89, 93
Reyes, Alfonso, 6, 9, 66–67, 71, 151n27
Ribeiro, Darcy, 114, 116, 176n36
Ricard, Robert, 55
Ricoeur, Paul, 171n53
Rilke, Rainer María, 88
Rivet, Paul: and acculturation, 73; on Americanist years, 5; and antiracism, 7; career, 48, 50, 64–65, 140; in Colombia, 62–64; conservative opposition to, 53; and diffusionist school, 7, 126; exile in Americas, 9, 62–64; on humankind, 67; and inadaptation, 48; on *indigenismo*, 63–64; and Institut francais d'anthropologie, 48; and *Journal de la Société des Américanistes*, 47; Lévi-Strauss and, 73; and linguistics, 54, 57, 160n17; on *mestizaje*, 71; Métraux and, 58; and Musée de l'Homme, 7, 47, 49–51, 55, 71–72; on philology, 57; publication of source documents, 54–55; Roumain and, 7–8, 53; scientific/intellectual network, 7–8, 57–58; as socialist, 8; and Société des Américanistes, 47, 71; and specter of race, 18; travels in Americas, 57, 161n23; and *Ursprache* theory, 54
—as anthropologist: and cultural anthropology as discipline, 12; as pioneer of Americanism, 47; reception in Americas, 47, 71, 74, 93, 95, 158n1; and rescue anthropology, 47–48; students in Latin America, 57, 93; and unification of French anthropological research, 48–51
—on anthropology: as comparative, 52–53; focus on everyday life, 56; focus on human origins, 54; focus on texts, 54–55, 57; historical approach, 53–54, 56, 61; history, 56–57; humanism, 15, 52–53; interdisciplinary approach, 56, 63; and popular culture, 51
—works by: *Bibliographie des langues aymará et Kičua*, 54; *La métallurgie en Amérique précolombienne*, 55; *Los orígenes del hombre americano*, 10, 67–71, 164n44; "Reflexiones sobre la América Latina," 70–71; "Socialismo y unidad latina," 64
Rodó, José Enrique, 14, 20, 64, 87, 151n26
Rodrigues, Nina, 112, 118, 123, 125–26, 173n15
Roig de Leuchsenring, Emilio, 37
Rojas, Rafael, 20, 164n45
Romero, Sílvio, 112
Romero, Simón, 14
Rondon, Cândido, 176n35
Roquette-Pinto, Edgard, 113, 118, 137
Rosenberg, Fernando, 133
Roumain, Jacques: and antisuperstition campaign, 168n28; as communist, 75, 93, 169n29; on Creole language in Haiti, 11, 77; Haitian anthropological institutions and, 93–97; on Haitian culture, 10; and Haitian indigenism, 86, 91; and Institute and Museum of Ethnology, 75; and International Institute of Afro-American Studies, 98–99; novels, 75, 93, 105–10; Ortiz and, 170n40; poetry, 84; and *Revue Indigène*, 93; Rivet and, 7–8, 53; scientific essays by, 101–6; scientific/intellectual network of, 7; and specter of race, 18
—as anthropologist, 12, 17–19, 168n25; and cultural anthropology, 12; and Haitian anthropology, 93; and humanism, 15; method, 101–6; on vodou, 75, 94, 104–10, 169n29
—works by: *Contribution à l'Etude de l'Ethnobotanique Précolombienne des Grandes Antilles*, 101–3; *Les fantoches*, 105; *Gouverneurs de la rosée* (*Masters of the Dew*), 75, 93, 106–10, 171n53; "L'outillage lithique des ciboney d'Haiti," 98, 103–4; *Le sacrifice du tambour-Assotô(r)* 104–8
Roumer, Emile, 84
Roxborough, Ian, 10

Rubín de la Borbolla, Daniel F., 69–70
Ruche, La (periodical), 76
Russell, Bertrand, 123

Sá, Lúcia, 133
Sahagún, Bernardino de, 12
Said, Edward, 4–5, 157n45
Salomon, Noel, 152n7
Santí, Enrico Mario, 156n44
Santos, Eduardo, 62
Sarmiento, Domingo Faustino, 4
Saussure, Ferdinand de, 72, 165n50
Schmidt, Max, 137
Schottelius, Justus Wolfram, 62
Schwarcz, Lilia Moritz, 171–72n3
Schwartz, Stuart, 174n21
science française, La (periodical), 53
scientific racism, 3, 21, 32, 61, 140, 145, 147n2, 157n48. *See also* miscegenation
Sébillot, Paul, 80
Senghor, Léopold, 91
Serviço de Proteção aos Índios (SPI), 137, 176n35
Silva Herzog, Jesús, 66–67
Skidmore, Thomas, 112, 141, 147n3
slavery, 127
social Darwinism, influence in Latin America, 4–5
Sociedad de Estudios Afrocubanos, 32, 35, 37
Sociedad del Folklore Cubano, 22–24, 37–38, 166n10
Sociedade Brasileira de Antropologia e Etnologia (SBAE), 122
Société d'anthropologie (France), 48, 77
Société des Américanistes, 7, 47–48, 50, 71
Sommer, Doris, 42
Soustelle, Jacques, 51, 55
Spain: civil war refugees in Americas, 9–10, 32; cultural presence, 6–7; limpieza de sangre, 4. *See also* Hispanic race concept
Spanish language in America, 20; Ortiz on, 22–31
Spencer, Herbert, 4, 152n7
Spengler, Oswald, 5, 66–67, 117, 148n6, 163n41
Stepan, Nancy, 147n4
Sterner, Richard, 99
Suárez, Constantino, 24
SUR (periodical), 59–61
Surco (periodical), 30
Sylvain, Georges, 84
Sylvain, Normil, 86–88
Sylvain, Renée, 175n30

Tannenbaum, Frank, 37, 116
Tarica, Estelle, 149n13, 164n47
Tarsila, 175n34
Tax, Sol, 73
Teatro Experimental Nacional (TEN), 124
Teixeira, Anísio, 113
terminology, 18
Tierras Latinas/Terres Latines (periodical), 64–65
Toby-Marcelin, Philippe, 83–84, 92
Torres, Alberto, 113
transculturation: coining of term, 9, 41; de la Campa on, 11; Malinowski on, 40–41; Ortiz on, 9–10, 29, 41
"Travaux et mémoires de l'Institut d'ethnologie" (TMIE), 55
Trigo, Abril, 11
Trouillot, Duverneau, 78
Trouillot, Hénock, 169n29
Trouillot, Michel-Rolph, 151n1, 152n4
Tylor, Edward B., 131

Ugarte, Manuel, 87, 166n12
Ultra (periodical), 30, 38
Unamuno, Miguel de, 22, 31–32
UNESCO (United Nations Educational, Scientific and Cultural Organization): conferences on race, 141; Hylean Amazon project, 62, 140; Marbial Valley (Haiti) study, 62, 76; Métraux at, 61–62, 76, 140; postwar projects on race and racism, 140–41; Project on Race Relations in Brazil, 123, 140–41, 177n41; Ramos at, 123, 140; Rivet at, 65; Social Sciences Department, 61–62, 123, 140
Unión Ibero-Americana, 23, 31
United States: Freyre on social sciences revolution in, 137–40; and Latin American studies, 149n17, 177n2; Ortiz on race problems in, 33
Universidade de São Paulo (University of São Paulo), 113, 172n7
Universidade do Brasil, 113
Uribe, Carlos, 63
Ursprache theory, Rivet and, 54

Valdés Bernal, Sergio, 24, 154n22
Valdés Pereira, Ildefonso, 101
Valdéz, Juan, 20, 151n27
Vargas, Getulio, 123–24, 140
Varona, Enrique José, 30, 37
Vasconcelos, José, 19–20, 33, 64, 87, 151–52n2, 152n5
Ventura Santos, Fernando, 113, 141, 172n3
Vila, Pablo, 62
vodou, 94–96, 101, 168n28; and cultural contact, 85; as folk practice, 92; *Les Griots* on, 91–93; Haitian antisuperstition campaign, 94, 106, 168–69n28, 170n45; Haitian folklore movement, 81; Haitian works on, 78–81, 83; interest generated by studies of, 76; Métraux's work on, 8; regulation, 91; as religion, 75, 78–80; Roumain on, 75, 94, 104–10, 169n29; as term, 18
von den Steinen, Karl, 137

Wagley, Charles, 141, 176n36, 177n41
Wallace, Henry A., 32–33
Weltfish, Gene, 61
Wiener, Leo, 28
Wilson, Edmund, 171n53
Wissler, Clark, 52, 126–27, 131, 175n29
World War II, migrations and exiles, 9–10, 62–65

Zambrano, María, 41
Zea, Leopoldo, 6
Zumeta, Cesar, 20

Recent Books in the New World Studies Series

Supriya M. Nair, *Pathologies of Paradise: Caribbean Detours*

Colleen C. O'Brien, *Race, Romance, and Rebellion: Literatures of the Americas in the Nineteenth Century*

Kelly Baker Josephs, *Disturbers of the Peace: Representations of Madness in Anglophone Caribbean Literature*

Christina Kullberg, *The Poetics of Ethnography in Martinican Narratives: Exploring the Self and the Environment*

Maria Cristina Fumagalli, Bénédicte Ledent, and Roberto del Valle Alcalá, editors, *The Cross-Dressed Caribbean: Writing, Politics, Sexualities*

Philip Kaisary, *The Haitian Revolution in the Literary Imagination: Radical Horizons, Conservative Constraints*

Jason Frydman, *Sounding the Break: African American and Caribbean Routes of World Literature*

Tanya L. Shields, *Bodies and Bones: Feminist Rehearsal and Imagining Caribbean Belonging*

Stanka Radovic, *Locating the Destitute: Space and Identity in Caribbean Fiction*

Nicole N. Aljoe and Ian Finseth, editors, *Journeys of the Slave Narrative in the Early Americas*

Stephen M. Park, *The Pan American Imagination: Contested Visions of the Hemisphere in Twentieth-Century Literature*

Maurice St. Pierre, *Eric Williams and the Anticolonial Tradition: The Making of a Diasporan Intellectual*

Elena Machado Sáez, *Market Aesthetics: The Purchase of the Past in Caribbean Diasporic Fiction*

Martin Munro, *Tropical Apocalypse: Haiti and the Caribbean End Times*

Jeannine Murray-Román, *Performance and Personhood in Caribbean Literature: From Alexis to the Digital Age*

Anke Birkenmaier, *The Specter of Races: Latin American Anthropology and Literature between the Wars*